Crime and Punishment in America

ALMANAC

Crime and Punishment in America

ALMANAC

VOLUME 2

Richard C. Hanes and Sharon M. Hanes
Sarah Hermsen, Project Editor

U·X·L
An imprint of Thomson Gale,
a part of The Thomson Corporation

THOMSON

GALE

Detroit • New York • San Francisco • San Diego • New Haven, Conn. • Waterville, Maine • London • Munich

Crime and Punishment in America: Almanac

Richard C. Hanes and Sharon M. Hanes

Project Editor
Sarah Hermsen

Rights Acquisitions and Management
Ann Taylor

Imaging and Multimedia
Dean Dauphinais, Lezlie Light, Dan Newell

Product Design
Michelle Dimercurio

Composition
Evi Seoud

Manufacturing
Rita Wimberley

Library of Congress Cataloging-in-Publication Data

Hanes, Richard Clay, 1946–Crime and punishment in America. Almanac / Richard C. Hanes and Sharon M. Hanes ; Sarah Hermsen, project editor.
    p. cm. — (Crime and punishment in America reference library)
    Includes bibliographical references and index.
    ISBN 0-7876-9163-1 (set hardcover : alk. paper) — ISBN 0- 7876-9164-X (v. 1) — ISBN 0-7876-9165-8 (v. 2)
1. Criminal justice, Administration of—United States—History. 2. Crime—United States—History. 3. Punishment—United States—History. I. Hanes, Sharon M. II. Hermsen, Sarah. III. Title. IV. Series.
HV9950.H39 2005
364.973'09—dc22
                                                                        2004017067

Contents

Volume 1

Volume 2

Reader's Guide

Crimes are forbidden acts considered harmful or dangerous. They fall outside society's rules of proper behavior. Some acts—such as murder, robbery, and rape—violate the behavioral codes of almost every society. Other acts may be considered crimes in one culture but not in another. In criminal law both society and the individual victim, when there is one, are considered harmed by crimes. Each crime threatens some aspect of society; for example, white-collar crime—business-related crimes such as fraud or embezzlement—threatens the economy, and the illegal dumping of waste threatens the quality of the environment. For this reason, a victim's approval is not necessary for the government to prosecute a crime and punish the offender.

Over the past four centuries, crime and punishment in America have steadily changed as society has changed. Some types of behavior considered criminal in colonial times, such as idleness and heresy, have ceased to be treated as crimes, while other behaviors, such as computer hacking and toxic-waste dumping, have since been added to the list of prohibited acts. Technological advances have improved the abilities of criminals to commit crimes and avoid detection, but such advances have also aided law enforcement officials in their work. The rise of the automobile in the early twentieth century resulted in an increase in interstate crime and faster getaways for the criminals, but with their new patrol cars police were able to respond more readily to calls for help. At the end of the twentieth century, advances in telecommunications introduced new methods of breaking the law but also gave law enforcement officials many new ways to catch criminals and expanded crime-fighting to an international stage.

In a democratic society, the rules of behavior that maintain social order come from citizens, not from a church or from a royal head of state such as a king. These rules are set through judicial decisions, legal history, and cultural tradition. Rules are also established by legislatures, or law-making bodies, acting through democratic principles by passing laws of government based on the beliefs, opinions, and desires of the citizens. The rules and consequent punishments for violations are organized in sets and written down. Those who break the codes of criminal law in the United States are subject to the U.S. criminal justice system—arrest by law enforcement authorities, court trial, and punishment.

As English colonists established settlements in the New World beginning in the early seventeenth century, they brought English common law with them. This law included the well-known process of accusation, arrest, decision to prosecute or to dismiss, trial, judgment, and punishment. However, in colonial America rigid social order had to be maintained for survival of the first settlements and the colonists had to modify the English legal system to accommodate their unique situation in the New World. For example, there were often too few people residing in a given area for jury trials to be practical. In addition, many areas lacked a person with the proper law training to serve as a judge. Often an officer of the colony or a respected member of the community made legal decisions. Another difference between English courts and the developing American legal system involved the death penalty—the punishment of death to those convicted of serious crimes. American criminal courts applied the death penalty to fewer crimes than English courts. Colonists were also more respectful of individual civil liberties, believing the accused had a legal right to fairness.

With independence from England following the American Revolution (1775–83), a new American criminal justice system came into being. The common-law crime system gradually gave way to statutory criminal law. In contrast to common law, in statutory law acts are deemed criminal when the legislative body responds to a changing society's needs and passes a law prohibiting some activity or behavior. During the nineteenth century other basic changes in criminal justice arrived, such as professional policing and penitentiaries, or prisons.

Although fairness in the criminal justice system is a trait traditionally valued by American citizens, it has not always been evident. Throughout much of American history political power was held by one segment of society—white Protestant males. As a result black Americans, immigrant minorities, women, and other segments of society felt the full weight of law for much of American history. For example in the early twentieth century women could be arrested for voting and blacks could be convicted and executed simply because they were accused of a crime, regardless of the evidence available. The march for equality before the law and fairness in criminal justice procedures as guaranteed by the U.S. Constitution made steady progress through the late twentieth century.

The criminal justice system today is composed of many parts and numerous players. Legislatures, usually under pressure from society, make laws defining crime. Police and detectives apprehend offenders. Courts, prosecutors, defense lawyers, and judges determine the offenders' guilt. Prison wardens and guards, probation officers, and parole board members carry out the sentences. Criminal justice can be found in many varied settings, ranging from street community policing on bicycles to high-tech forensic laboratories; from isolation cells in a maximum-security prison to the historic chamber of the U.S. Supreme Court.

For an action to be considered a crime, not only does a loss or injury have to occur, but there must typically be a proven willful "intent" to commit the act. A harmful action that is an accident and did not occur from irresponsible behavior is not usually considered a crime. Crimes defined in the codes of law are either felonies or misdemeanors. Felonies are major crimes resulting in prison sentences of longer than one year. For certain felonies, namely murder cases, and in certain states, the punishment might be the death penalty, also known as capital punishment. Other felonies include robbery and rape. Misdemeanors are minor crimes punishable by fines or short periods of time, up to one year, in a local jail. Misdemeanors are sometimes called "petty" crimes, including such acts of petty theft as stealing a lawnmower from a shed or a compact disc player from a car.

Academics search for reasons why social deviance grew during the twentieth century. Criminologists and other professionals attempted to find the causes of crime in the hope of finding a cure for crime. Even though crime can be highly predictable—despite a seeming randomness at times—progress has been slow in isolating the causes.

Even less clear than the root cause of crime is the effect of the justice system on criminal activity. Crime seems to increase even as efforts to combat crime are intensified. Crime impacts millions of people, and the prevention, control, prosecution, rehabilitation, and punishment of criminals result in extraordinary expenses—not to mention the losses resulting from the crimes themselves. By the end of the twentieth century, operation of the criminal justice system at federal, state, and local levels cost $130 billion a year in addition to the $20 billion a year in losses to crime. On the other hand, industries related to crime and punishment create thousands of jobs, and the various forms of crime-related entertainment bring in many millions of dollars.

Features

Crime and Punishment in America: Almanac presents a comprehensive overview of the development of the American justice system. The two-volume set covers in twenty-five chapters various topics including violent crime, crimes against property, cyber crime, terrorism, environmental crime, organized crime, public order crime, school violence, and white-collar crime, from the first European settlements of the seventeenth century to the early twenty-first century. The *Almanac* also describes elements of the criminal justice system including courts, policing, forensic science, corrections, military justice, American Indian criminal justice systems, and juvenile justice. Additional chapters address the influences of moral and religious values as well as the media on crime and punishment. Each chapter contains sidebars highlighting people and events of special interest as well as a list of additional sources students can go to for more information. More than 160 black-and-white photographs illustrate the material. Each volume begins with a timeline of important events in the history of crime and punishment; a "Words to Know" section that introduces students to difficult or unfamiliar terms, and a "Research and Activity Ideas" section. The two volumes conclude with a general bibliography and a subject index so students can easily find the people, places, and events discussed throughout *Crime and Punishment in America: Almanac.*

Crime and Punishment in America Reference Library

Crime and Punishment in America: Almanac is only one component of the three-part Crime and Punishment in America Reference Library. The set includes two other titles:

Crime and Punishment in America: Biographies (one volume) presents the life stories of twenty-six individuals who have played key roles in the history of crime and punishment. People from all walks of life are included. Some held prominent national roles in developing or influencing the U.S. criminal justice system; others were defendants in key court trials that contributed significantly to the field. Profiled are well-known figures such as former Federal Bureau of Investigation (FBI) director J. Edgar Hoover, authors Charles Dickens and Truman Capote, Supreme Court justice Felix Frankfurter, domestic terrorists Ted Kaczynski and Timothy McVeigh, and social reformer Jane Addams. A number of lesser-known individuals are included as well, such as early female lawyers Belva Ann Lockwood and Arabella Mansfield, criminal defendants Daniel McNaughtan and Ernest Miranda, New York City police chief George Washington Walling, and political radical Emma Goldman.

Crime and Punishment in America: Primary Sources (one volume) tells the story of the criminal justice system in the words of the people who shaped the field and the laws that contributed to its development. Eighteen excerpted documents touch on a wide range of topics related to crime and punishment. Included are excerpts from colonial and federal laws, such as the Harrison Narcotic Drug Act of 1914; the Magna Carta; trial transcripts; newspaper accounts; government documents; various publications, including "The Al

Qaeda Training Manual" and Charles Dickens's *American Notes*; and notable speeches.

A cumulative index of all three titles in the Crime and Punishment in America Reference Library is also available.

Comments and Suggestions

We welcome your comments on *Crime and Punishment in America: Almanac* and suggestions for other topics to consider. Please write to: Editor, *Crime and Punishment in America: Almanac*, U•X•L, 27500 Drake Road, Farmington Hills, Michigan 48331-3535; call toll-free: 1-800-877-4253; fax to 248-699-8097; or send e-mail via http://www.gale.com.

Timeline of Events

1215   King John signs the Magna Carta in England, recognizing certain fundamental liberties and rights of landowners.

1609   English and other European colonists begin settling the East Coast of North America, adapting the English common-law criminal justice system to the New World. One such adaptation is establishing the position of sheriff.

1611   The colony of Virginia issues "Lawes Divine, Morall and Martiall" to maintain a strict control over the settlement's residents during its infancy.

1692   A series of witchcraft trials occurs in Massachusetts, leading to the conviction and execution of several supposed witches.

1740s   Slave patrols are established in the southern colonies to monitor slave activities. Such patrols are considered a forerunner of policing.

1775   The American Revolution (1775–83) erupts, driven partly by the colonists' desire to increase fairness and obtain legal protections in the criminal justice system.

1787 The U.S. Constitution is adopted, establishing a new national governmental system that includes a Supreme Court and gives Congress authority to make laws and establish other federal courts as needed.

1787 The first prison reform organization is established in Philadelphia, the Philadelphia Society for Alleviating the Miseries of Public Prisons, promoting rehabilitation over punishment.

1789 Congress passes the Judiciary Act, establishing the Supreme Court and various levels of federal courts, such as district and appellate (where district court decisions are appealed or reviewed) courts, and identifies their jurisdictions (the geographic area over which a court has legal authority). The act also created the U.S. attorney, attorney general, and marshal offices.

1790 Congress passes the Crimes Act, outlining seventeen federal crimes.

1790 Philadelphia opens the Walnut Street Jail, introducing a four-tier prisoner system based on type of offender. The system includes isolation for some prisoners.

1791 The first ten amendments to the U.S. Constitution, known collectively as the Bill of Rights, are adopted. The amendments contain several sections concerning crime and punishment, including freedom from unreasonable search and seizure, freedom from self-incrimination, the right to legal counsel, and freedom from cruel and unusual punishment.

1794 The Pennsylvania legislature becomes the first in the United States to define the crime of first-degree murder and eliminates the death penalty for all crimes other than first-degree murder.

1819 The state of New York opens the Auburn maximum security prison for men, an institution that becomes the model for prison-industry programs.

1829 Sir Robert Peele establishes a professional police force in London, England, becoming a model for future policing developments in U.S. cities.

1829 Pennsylvania opens the Eastern State Penitentiary, also known as Cherry Hill, which becomes the model for the Separate System, in which inmates are placed in solitary confinement around the clock.

1835   New York becomes the first state to stop public executions.

1844   New York City establishes the first city police force to address the rising crime rate.

1846   Michigan becomes the first state to abolish the death penalty.

1850   Allan Pinkerton establishes a private detective agency, known as the Pinkerton National Detective Agency, to provide security services for railroads and others.

1865   Congress creates the Secret Service in the U.S. Treasury Department to combat counterfeiting of U.S. currency.

1890   Congress passes the Sherman Antitrust Act to stop price fixing and to break up business monopolies.

August 6, 1890 William Kemmler becomes the first prisoner executed by the electric chair at the Auburn Prison in New York.

1899   Illinois creates the nation's first juvenile court system.

1905   Pennsylvania creates the nation's first state police force.

1906   Congress passes the Pure Food and Drug Act, requiring companies to label the contents of foods, particularly addictive ingredients. Congress also bans the importation of opium.

1908   The Bureau of Investigation is created in the U.S. Department of Justice to conduct investigations. It becomes the Federal Bureau of Investigation (FBI) in 1935.

1910   Congress passes the Mann Act, which prohibits taking women across state lines to engage in prostitution.

1914   The U.S. Supreme Court in *Weeks v. United States* rules that evidence illegally obtained by a federal law enforcement officer cannot be used in a federal criminal trial.

1914 Congress passes the Harrison Act requiring anyone who produces, sells, or distributes opium, morphine, heroin, or cocaine to register with the Treasury Department and pay taxes. The Harrison Act becomes the model for future drug legislation.

1915 Alice Stebbins Wells establishes the International Association of Policewomen, which later becomes the International Association of Women Police.

1920s Adoption of the police car revolutionizes policing, increasing responsiveness but reducing contact between police and citizens.

1920 The Eighteenth Amendment to the U.S. Constitution goes into effect prohibiting the production, sale, and transportation of alcoholic beverages.

1923 August Vollmer establishes the nation's first modern crime laboratory in Los Angeles.

1924 J. Edgar Hoover becomes head of the Bureau of Investigation and builds it into a model professional police organization.

1925 Congress passes the Federal Probation Act, giving federal courts the legal authority to use probation in sentencing.

1927 The first women's federal prison is established in West Virginia.

1929 President Herbert Hoover becomes the first U.S. president to identify crime as a key national issue in his inaugural address. Hoover appoints George Wickersham as head of the National Commission on Law Observance and Enforcement to examine all aspects of the U.S. criminal justice system. The commission issues fourteen reports by 1931.

1930 The Bureau of Investigation begins the Uniform Crime Reporting (UCR) program, the first national crime statistics system.

1932 Congress responds to the kidnapping and murder of the infant son of famous aviator Charles Lindbergh by passing the Lindbergh Act, making it a federal crime to transport kidnap victims across state lines.

1932 The U.S. Supreme Court rules in one of the Scottsboro cases, *Powell v. Alabama,* that states must provide defense lawyers for those defendants who are charged with capital crimes and who are too poor to afford lawyers. In 1938 the Court extends this requirement to all defendants facing possible incarceration. In 1963 the Court rules that all indigent defendants are entitled to free legal counsel.

December 1933 Prohibition ends with the adoption of the Twenty-first Amendment to the Constitution, which repeals the Eighteenth Amendment.

1935 Congress passes the Ashurst-Summers Act, prohibiting the interstate transportation of goods produced in prisons. This act essentially ends prison industries, a key part of prison life since the early nineteenth century.

1937 The American Bar Association recommends that all motion picture and still cameras be banned from courtrooms. Congress adopts the recommendation in 1944, banning radio broadcasting, cameras, and, in 1962, television from federal courtrooms.

1939 Indiana passes the first law prohibiting driving while intoxicated.

1939 Criminologist Edwin Sutherland introduces the concept of white-collar crime.

1941 The American Society of Criminology, originally called the National Association of College Police Officials, is founded.

1941 Hervey Cleckley publishes *The Mask of Sanity,* which introduces the idea of psychopathic behavioral disorders contributing to criminal activity.

1946 The United Nations identifies genocide as a war crime under international law.

1950s The rise in popularity of television introduces law enforcement shows such as *Dragnet.*

1950 The congressional Kefauver Commission begins a two-year investigation of organized crime.

1951 Congress enacts the Uniform Code of Military Justice (UCMJ) for military services.

1961 The U.S. Supreme Court in its *Mapp v. Ohio* ruling establishes the criteria for preventing illegal searches and seizures.

1962 A federal court rules that prisons cannot restrict inmates from practicing the Islamic religion.

1966 The U.S. Supreme Court rules in *Miranda v. Arizona* that criminal suspects must be advised of their legal rights before interrogation. This rule becomes known as the Miranda warning.

1966 Author Truman Capote introduces the first true-crime book when *In Cold Blood* is published. The book later becomes a popular Hollywood movie.

1968 As part of President Lyndon B. Johnson's war on crime, Congress establishes the Law Enforcement Assistance Administration (LEAA) to provide funding assistance to states for fighting crime.

1970 Congress passes the Racketeer Influenced and Corrupt Organizations (RICO) Act, giving law enforcement greater legal power to combat organized crime.

1972 The FBI opens its new academy in Quantico, Virginia, and adds the Behavioral Science Unit.

1972 The Bureau of Justice Statistics begins the National Crime Victimization Survey (NCVS), collecting data on both attempted and successful crimes.

1972 Congress passes the Juvenile Delinquency Prevention Act, establishing general rules for state juvenile justice systems, including the separation of juveniles from adults during custody and incarceration.

1972 The U.S. Supreme Court in *Furman v. Georgia* declares that the manner in which most states apply death penalty sentencing decisions violates the Constitution's protection from cruel and unusual punishment. In 1976, with *Gregg v. Georgia,* the Supreme Court upholds a new process for deciding on the death penalty using a separate sentencing trial.

1975 The National Organization for Victim Assistance (NOVA) is established to coordinate the victims' rights movement.

1976   Congress passes the Resource Conservation and Recovery Act (RCRA), making it a crime to dispose of waste in a way that could cause harm to public health and the environment.

1978   Congress passes the Foreign Intelligence Surveillance Act to increase law enforcement's counterterrorism capabilities, including greater surveillance authority.

1978   Ted Kaczynski, known as the Unabomber, begins an eighteen-year period of domestic terrorism by mailing bombs to various targeted individuals. He is arrested in 1996 after killing three people and injuring twenty-three others with his explosive devices.

1980s   White-collar crime captures headlines as scandal erupts around a number of savings and loans corporations.

1980   The victims' rights group Mothers against Drunk Driving (MADD) is formed to lobby Congress and states for tougher laws.

1980   Wisconsin is the first state to pass a crime victims' bill of rights.

1982   The Broken Windows theory is introduced, emphasizing that community disorder breeds criminal activity. This theory leads to a reorientation of policing, focusing on petty crimes in order to curb major crimes. Foot patrols take the place of car patrols as community policing techniques are adopted around the nation.

1982   Texas becomes the first in the nation to execute a prisoner by lethal injection, which becomes the primary method of execution in the United States.

1982   Congress passes the Victim and Witness Protection Act to provide protection for victims involved in the criminal justice system as well as for witnesses and informants of federal crimes.

1984   Congress passes the first law addressing computer-related crime, the Computer Fraud and Abuse Act, which prohibits interference with computer systems involved in interstate communications and economic trade.

1986 The War on Drugs begins with passage of the Anti-Drug Abuse Act that leads to a major increase in arrests, court cases, and prison population. The act also makes money laundering a federal crime.

1988 Gang violence continues to escalate in the nation's cities as Los Angeles County reports 452 gang-related deaths for the year.

1989 The U.S. Supreme Court rules that execution of offenders as young as sixteen years of age does not violate the Constitution's Eighth Amendment barring cruel and unusual punishment.

1990 Congress passes the Victims' Rights and Restitution Act, confirming that victims had a right to compensation and use of federal services offering help to crime victims.

1990 California passes the first law criminalizing stalking. Other states soon follow.

1992 The acquittal of Los Angeles police officers who had been videotaped beating black motorist Rodney King triggers extensive rioting for several days in the city, leaving some sixty people dead, twenty-three hundred injured, and six thousand arrested.

1993 Islamic terrorists set off a car bomb in the underground parking garage of New York's World Trade Center, killing six people and injuring one thousand.

1994 In its "get tough on crime" push, Congress passes the Violent Crime Control and Law Enforcement Act, which increases the number of federal capital crimes from two to fifty-eight, provides $4 billion for new prison construction, adds 100,000 new police officers in police departments across the nation, and adopts a "three-strikes" sentencing guideline for repeat offenders committing federal crimes.

1994 Congress passes the Violence against Women Act, providing funding for assistance to women who are the victims of crime.

1995 The murder trial of former football star O. J. Simpson is televised around the world, drawing attention to the U.S. criminal justice system, particularly forensic science.

June 1995 In a domestic terrorist attack, Timothy McVeigh bombs the federal building in Oklahoma City, Oklahoma, killing 168 people. McVeigh is executed by lethal injection in 2001, the first person convicted of a federal crime to be executed in thirty-eight years.

1996 Congress passes the Communication Decency Act to regulate obscene material on the Internet. Courts rule it unconstitutional, a violation of free speech protections.

1996 Congress passes the Antiterrorism and Effective Death Penalty Act, enhancing law enforcement capabilities in terrorism cases and banning U.S. citizens and companies from doing business with or supporting organizations designated as foreign terrorist organizations by the U.S. State Department.

1998 Congress passes the Identity Theft and Assumption Deterrence Act, making identity theft a federal crime.

1998 Congress passes the Digital Millennium Copyright Act, protecting video and computer game manufacturers from Internet sales of pirated software.

May 1998 Having murdered his parents the day before, high school student Kip Kinkel, enters the cafeteria of Thurston High School in Springfield, Oregon, and opens fire, killing two students and wounding twenty-six others. He is convicted in 1999 of the four murders and of twenty-six counts of attempted murder.

October 1998 Ecoterrorists set fire to a Vail, Colorado, resort, causing extensive damage. The perpetrators allege that the resort damaged wildlife habitats.

2000 Congress passes the Religious Land Use and Institutionalized Persons Act, recognizing a prisoner's right to practice religion while incarcerated.

September 11, 2001 Terrorists of Middle Eastern origin crash three hijacked airliners into New York's World Trade Center and the Pentagon in Washington, D.C. A fourth hijacked airliner crashes in rural Pennsylvania on its way to a target. Almost 3,000 people are killed in the attacks.

October 2001 Congress passes the USA Patriot Act, giving law enforcement officials more power to combat the threat of terrorism.

2002 Criminal investigation of the bankruptcy of Enron, one of the nation's largest corporations, begins, leading to several convictions over the next few years on securities fraud violations.

March 2003 The U.S. Department of Homeland Security begins operation to combat terrorist threats.

Words to Know

A

Adjudication: The process of resolving an issue through a court decision.

Aggravated assault: An attack by one person upon another with intent to inflict severe bodily injury, usually by using a weapon.

AMBER Alert: (America's Missing: Broadcast Emergency Response) A national communications network for alerting the public immediately after the abduction of a youth under eighteen years of age has been reported and when the child is considered in danger. The alerts bring in the assistance of the local public in spotting the missing child or his or her abductor.

Appellate: Courts that do not hear original cases but review lower trial court decisions to determine if proper legal procedures were followed. Appeals are heard in front of a panel of judges without a jury.

Arraignment: A part of the criminal justice process during which the formal charges are read to the defendant. The defendant is advised of his or her rights, enters a plea of guilty or not guilty, and has bail and a trial date set.

Arson: Any intentional or malicious burning or attempt to burn a house, public building, motor vehicle or aircraft, or some other personal property of another person.

Assault: An attack that may or may not involve physical contact. Intentionally frightening a person or shouting threats could be considered assault.

B

Bail: Money paid for the temporary release of an arrested person and to guarantee that the accused will appear for trial.

Beyond reasonable doubt: A phrase referring to the need to determine a defendant's guilt with certainty. This level of certainty is required for criminal convictions.

Bill of Rights: The first ten amendments to the U.S. Constitution, adopted in 1791. The Bill of Rights includes various protections of civil liberties in the criminal justice system, including protection from cruel punishment, unreasonable search, and self-incrimination.

Biohazard: Any biological material that has the potential to cause harm to human beings or to the environment.

Black market: The illegal sale of goods in violation of government regulations, such as selling illegal liquor at very high prices.

Blasphemy: A colonial-era crime of showing a lack of reverence toward God.

Bootlegger: A person who illegally transports liquor.

Bullying: Behavior such as teasing and threats, exclusion from social activities, and more physical intimidation; a common form of behavior among juveniles.

Burglary: Forcefully entering a home to commit a crime.

C

Capital punishment: The execution of a criminal offender; also known as the death penalty.

Capitalism: An economic system in which private business and markets determine the prices, distribution, and production of goods largely without government intervention.

Child abuse: Causing physical or emotional harm to a child.

Child labor laws: Laws restricting the type of work children can do and the number of hours they can work. These laws are designed to protect children from dangerous, unsanitary factory and farm conditions and from long hours of work at low pay. Such laws also enable them to pursue an education.

Child neglect: A failure to provide a child's basic needs, including adequate food or shelter.

Child pornography: A felony criminal offense often involving photographing and videotaping nude children or children being sexually abused.

Chop shop: A place where stolen cars are taken apart and the parts individually sold.

Civil disobedience: Challenging rules of public behavior in a nonviolent manner.

Civil law: Laws regulating ordinary private matters, in contrast to criminal law.

Civil liberties: Certain basic protections from government interference offered by the U.S. Constitution, such as freedom from self-incrimination and freedom from unreasonable searches.

Common law: A legal system in use for several centuries in England that provides a set of judicial rules "commonly" applied to resolve similar disputes. Common law is built on a history of judge's decisions rather than relying on codes, or laws, passed by a legislature. The decisions are written down and compiled annually in legal volumes available for judges to refer to.

Communism: A political and economic system where a single party controls all aspects of citizens' lives and private ownership of property is banned.

Community-based corrections: Facilities, often located in neighborhoods, that allow convicted offenders to maintain normal family relationships and friendships while receiving rehabilitation services such as counseling, work training, and job placement.

Constable: A colonial policing figure who delivered warrants, supervised the volunteer night watchmen, and carried out the routine local government functions of the community.

Copyright: The legal right of an author, publisher, composer, or other person who creates a work to exclusively print, publish, distribute, or perform the work in public.

Coroner: A public official who investigates deaths that have not clearly resulted from natural causes.

Counterterrorism: A coordinated effort among many government agencies to fight and stop terrorism.

Court-martial: A court consisting of military personnel trying a case of another military person accused of violating military law.

Crime: A socially harmful act that is prohibited and punishable by criminal law.

Crime syndicate: A group of people who work together in an illegal business activity.

Criminal justice system: The loose collection of public agencies including the police, courts, and prison officials responsible for catching and arresting suspected criminals, determining their guilt, and imposing the sentence.

Criminology: The scientific study of criminal behavior to aid in preventing and solving crimes.

Cycle of violence: The tendency of people abused during childhood to commit abuse or other crimes as adults.

D

Defendant: A person accused of a crime.

Defense attorney: A lawyer who represents a defendant to provide him or her the best possible defense from the time of arrest through sentencing and, later, appeals of the case. The defense attorney is responsible for seeing that the constitutional rights of the defendant are protected.

Delinquents: Juveniles who commit acts considered adult crimes.

Democracy: A system of government that allows multiple political parties, the members of which are elected to various government offices by popular vote of the people.

Desertion: The military crime of abandoning a military post or assignment without approval.

Disposition: The legal term for a sentence in the criminal justice system; sentences may range from fines to imprisonment in a large, tightly guarded correctional facility.

Dissident: A person with opposing political views to those in power or the government.

DNA: DNA is deoxyribonucleic acid, the substance that chromosomes are made of. Chromosomes, long connected double strands of DNA that have a structure resembling a twisted ladder, contain an individual's genetic code, which is unique to every person (except identical twins, who share the same genetic code).

Double jeopardy: A rule stating that a person cannot be tried for the same offense twice.

Drug cartel: An organized crime group that grows and sells narcotics.

Drug trafficking: The buying or selling of illegal drugs.

E

Ecoterrorism: Terrorist activities that target businesses or other organizations that are thought to be damaging the environment. The term can also refer to terrorist actions designed to harm the environment of a political enemy.

Embezzlement: The stealing of money or property by a trusted employee or other person.

Encryption: The use of secret codes that can be translated into meaningful communications only by authorized persons who have knowledge of the code.

Environmental crime: To commit an act with intent to harm ecological or biological systems for the purpose of personal or corporate gain; actions that violate environmental protection laws.

Espionage: Spies acquiring information about the activities of another country.

Exclusionary rule: Evidence obtained illegally by the police cannot be used—will be excluded from consideration—in a court of law.

Extortion: Threats to commit violence or other types of harm with the intent of obtaining money or property from another person or group.

F

Felony: A serious crime that can lead to imprisonment or execution.

First-degree murder: A deliberate and planned killing; or, a murder in connection with the commission of another felony crime such as robbery or rape.

Forensic science: The application of a wide range of scientific knowledge within a court of law. Forensic science is used to analyze a crime scene, including weapon identification, fingerprinting, document analysis, chemical identification, and trace analysis of hair and fibers.

Forgery: The signing of a false name on a legal document such as a check, and the cashing of such a check at a store or bank using false identification.

Fraud: Intentionally deceiving another for personal economic benefit.

G

Grand jury: A group of citizens chosen from the community who determine in a hearing closed to the public if there is sufficient evidence to justify indictment of the accused and a trial. Only prosecutors present evidence in grand jury hearings, not attorneys representing the defendant.

Grand larceny: Theft of money or property of great value.

H

Habitual offender: A criminal who repeatedly commits crimes, often of various types.

Hacker: Someone who gains unauthorized access to a specific computer network system and reads or copies secret or private information.

Halfway house: Rigidly controlled rehabilitation homes for offenders who have been released early from prison or are on parole. Halfway houses were created to relieve prison overcrowding. Services can include counseling, treatment, and education programs, or halfway houses can simply be a place to live under supervision.

Hate crime: A violent attack against a person or group because of race, ethnicity, religion, or gender.

Hazardous waste: Any solid or liquid substance that because of its quantity, concentration, or physical or chemical properties may cause serious harm to humans or the environment when it is improperly transported, treated, stored, or disposed of.

Heresy: Holding a belief that conflicts with church doctrine. In some societies, during certain eras—such as colonial America—heresy has been prosecuted as a crime.

Hung jury: A circumstance wherein a jury cannot agree on a verdict; in such cases the defendant may face a retrial.

I

Identity theft: The theft of an individual's identifying information—including credit card numbers, social security number, or driver's license number—to allow a criminal to use another person's identity in making purchases or for other unauthorized activities.

Impartial jury: The notion that the members of jury will regard all evidence presented with an open mind.

Incarceration: Confining a person in jail or prison.

Indictment: A written accusation of criminal charges against a person.

Insider trading: Buying and selling securities based on reliable business information not available to the general public.

Insubordination: A military crime involving the disobeying of an authority, such as a military commander.

Intake worker: A person trained to work with youthful offenders, such as a probation officer.

Intellectual property (IP) theft: The theft of material that is copyrighted, the theft of trade secrets, and violations of trademarks.

Involuntary manslaughter: A homicide resulting from negligence or lack of regard for safety.

J

Jail: A facility operated by a city or county for short-term detention of defendants awaiting trial or those convicted of misdemeanors.

Jim Crow: State and local laws in the United States that enforced legal segregation in the first half of the twentieth century, keeping races separated in every aspect of life from schools to restrooms and water fountains. Such laws were particularly common in the South.

Jurisdiction: The geographic area or type of crime over which certain branches of law enforcement or courts have legal authority.

Juvenile courts: A special court system that has jurisdiction over children accused of criminal conduct, over youthful victims of abuse or neglect, and over young people who violate rules that apply only to juveniles.

L

Labor racketeering: The existence of a criminal organization that works its way into a position of power in a labor union in order to steal from the union's retirement and health funds.

Landmark decision: A ruling by the U.S. Supreme Court that sets an important precedent for future cases and can influence daily operating procedures of police, courts, and corrections.

Larceny: Theft of property, either with or without the use of force.

Loan sharking: Charging very high interest rates on loans.

M

Mafia: A crime organization originating in Sicily, Italy, that is thought to control racketeering in the United States.

Magistrate: In colonial times the magistrate was the key judicial official in local courts, often a key member of the community. In modern times, a magistrate is an official with limited judicial authority who issues arrest and search warrants, sets bail, conducts pretrial hearings, and hears misdemeanor cases.

Mail fraud: Using the mail system to make false offers to or otherwise defraud recipients.

Malice: The intent to inflict serious bodily harm.

Mandatory sentence: A specific penalty required by law upon conviction for a specific offense.

Manslaughter: A homicide not involving malice, or the intent to inflict serious harm.

Martial law: A legal system through which the military exerts police power in place of civilian rule in politically unstable areas to protect safety and property.

Mass murderer: A person who kills many people in a single crime episode.

Mediation: A process for resolving disputes in which both the victim and offender must agree to meet and attempt to settle their dispute in a face-to-face manner, under the guidance of a neutral party.

Midnight dumping: The illegal disposal of hazardous wastes under cover of darkness in a remote area.

Miranda rights: The rights of a defendant to obtain legal counsel and refrain from self-incrimination.

Misdemeanor: A minor crime usually punishable by brief jail time or a fine.

Mistrial: A circumstance whereby a trial is discontinued because of a serious mistake or misconduct on the part of attorneys, court officials, or jury members.

Money laundering: To make the tracking of crime profits very difficult by placing money gained from crime into legitimate financial institutions, often banks outside the United States; placing such money into accounts of bogus companies; or mixing such funds with legally obtained money in the bank accounts of legitimate companies owned or operated by organized crime groups.

Moral values: The commonly accepted standards of what is right and wrong.

Multiple homicide: A crime in which a person kills more than one person on a single occasion.

Murder: Killing another person with malicious intent.

N

Narcotic: Habit-forming drugs that relieve pain or cause sleep, including heroin and opium.

Neighborhood watch: A crime prevention program in which residents watch out for suspicious activity in their neighborhoods and notify the police if they spot criminal activity.

O

Obscene: Material that has no socially redeeming value and is considered offensive according to community standards of decency.

Organized crime: People or groups joined together to profit from illegal businesses.

Organized labor: A collective effort by workers and labor organizations in general to seek better working conditions.

P

Page-jacking: A fake Web site using the same key words or Web site descriptions as a legitimate site with the intention of misdirecting Internet traffic to another site such as a pornography site.

Paraphilia: Sexual behavior considered bizarre or abnormal, such as voyeurism (spying on others for sexual pleasure) or pedophilia (sexual desire involving children).

Parens patriae: The concept that the government has the right to become the parent of children in need—to save them from terrible living conditions or protect them from criminal influences.

Parole: The release of an inmate before the end of his or her sentence.

Pedophilia: Receiving sexual pleasure from activities that focus on children as sex objects.

Penitentiary or prison: A state or federal facility for holding inmates convicted of a felony.

Perjury: Intentionally making a false statement or lying while under oath during a court appearance.

Petition: Requesting to be heard by the courts on some dispute.

Petty larceny: Theft of small amounts of money.

Pillory: A form of colonial-period punishment consisting of a wooden frame that has holes for heads and hands.

Plea bargain: A guilty plea offered by the defendant in return for reduced charges, a lighter sentence, or some other consideration.

Pollutant: A man-made waste that contaminates the environment.

Pornography: Materials such as magazines, books, pictures, and videos that show nudity and sexual acts.

Prejudice: A judgment or opinion formed without sufficient information.

Preponderance of evidence: A sufficient amount of evidence to indicate the guilt of the accused. The term also refers to the level of evidence used in civil cases and juvenile courts.

Price-fixing: Governments or companies artificially setting the price for particular goods rather than letting the market determine pricing.

Probable cause: Sufficient evidence to support an arrest.

Probation: A criminal sentence other than jail or prison time for persons convicted of less serious crimes; those sentenced with probation are usually placed under court supervision for a specific period of time.

Prohibition: Prohibiting the production, sale, transport, and possession of alcoholic beverages resulting from the adoption of the Eighteenth Amendment to the U.S. Constitution in 1919 and the resulting Volstead Act of 1920; this amendment was repealed by the Twenty-first Amendment to the Constitution in December in 1933.

Property crimes: Theft where no force or threat of force is directed toward an individual; such crimes are usually driven by the prospect of financial gain.

Prosecutor: Public officials who represent the government in criminal cases. Prosecutors are often known as district attorneys or prosecuting attorneys in federal courts and are commonly elected or appointed to their positions.

Prostitution: A person offering sexual acts in return for payments, generally payments of money.

Public defender: A state-employed attorney who provides free legal counsel to defendants too poor to hire a lawyer.

Public order crime: Behavior that is banned because it threatens the general well-being of a community or society.

R

Racism: To be prejudiced against people of a different race.

Racketeering: The act of participating in a continuing pattern of criminal behavior.

Rape: Having sexual relations by force or the threat of force.

Rehabilitation: Providing treatment to an offender to prevent further criminal behavior.

Restitution: Compensation or payment by an offender to a victim; restitution may involve community service work rather than incarceration or payments.

Restraining trade: An effort to inhibit business competition through illegal means, such as fixing prices of goods and services artificially low.

Robbery: Taking money or property by force or the threat of force.

S

Sabotage: To destroy military or industrial facilities.

Second-degree murder: An unplanned or accidental killing through a desire to cause serious bodily harm.

Securities: Stocks or bonds.

Securities fraud: An individual or organization falsely manipulating the market price of a stock or commodity by deliberately providing misleading information to investors.

Self-incrimination: Offering damaging information about oneself during a trial or hearing; a person cannot be made to testify against him or herself and has the right to remain silent during a trial or interrogation.

Serial killer: A person who kills multiple people over a period of time.

Shield laws: Legislation prohibiting rape victims from being questioned about their prior sexual history unless specific need for the information is identified.

Shoplifting: A common form of petty larceny; taking merchandise from a store without paying for it.

Slave patrols: Groups of white volunteers assembled in the 1740s to police the black slave populations with the intent of protecting white citizens from slaves, suppressing slave uprisings, and capturing runaway slaves. Slave patrols are considered an early form of organized policing.

Sociopathic: A personality disorder characterized by antisocial, often destructive, behavior with little show of emotion.

Sovereignty: A government largely free from outside political control.

Speakeasy: A place where alcoholic beverages were illegally sold during Prohibition.

Stalking: The act of repeatedly following or spying on another person or making unwanted communications or threats.

Status offenses: Rules that apply only to juveniles such as unapproved absence from school (truancy), running away from home, alcohol and tobacco use, and refusing to obey parents.

Statutory rape: Rape without force involving an adult and teenager under the age of consent who has apparently agreed to the act; it is a crime because it is established by statute, or law.

Stranger violence: A crime in which the victim has had no previous contact with his or her attacker.

Strike: A work stoppage intended to force an employer to meet worker demands.

Subversive: Political radicals working secretly to overthrow a government.

Supermax prisons: Short for super-maximum-security prisons. Supermax prisons are designed to keep the most violent or disruptive inmates separated from other prisoners and correction staff, often in a special area within an existing prison.

T

Temperance: The use of alcoholic beverages in moderation or abstinence from all alcohol.

Terrorism: The planned use of force or violence, normally against innocent civilians, to make a statement about a cause. Terrorist attacks are staged for maximum surprise, shock, and destruction to influence individuals, groups, or governments to give in to certain demands.

Three-strikes laws: Laws that dictate that a criminal convicted of his or her third felony must remain in prison for an extended period of time, sometimes for life.

Toxicity: The degree to which a substance is poisonous.

Toxicology: The study of toxic or poisonous substances that can cause harm or death to any individual who takes them, depending on the amount ingested.

Trace evidence: Microscopic or larger materials, commonly hairs or fibers, transferred from person to person or object to object during a crime; examples include human or animal hair as well as wood, clothing, or carpet fibers.

Treason: An attempt to overthrow one's own government.

True crime: Stories in books, magazines, or films or on television programs that are based on actual crimes.

Trusts: Organizations formed by combining several major industries together to stifle competition and run smaller companies out of business.

V

Victim compensation: Payment of funds to help victims survive the financial losses caused by crimes against them.

Victimization: The physical, emotional, and financial harm victims suffer from crime, including violent crime, property crime, and business corruption.

Victimless crime: Crimes often between two persons who agree to the activity, leaving no immediate victims to file charges; such crimes are considered crimes against society and are defined by law or statute.

Victims' rights: A guarantee that victims of crime be treated with dignity and fairness by police, prosecutors, and other officials and be protected from threats and harm; victims may be notified about the progress of their case and informed of upcoming court dates such as parole hearings.

Vigilantes: A group of citizens assembled on their own initiative to maintain order.

Violent crime: Crimes against the person including murder, robbery, aggravated assault, rape, sniper attacks, crimes of hate, and stalking.

Virus: A computer program that disrupts or destroys existing computer systems by destroying computer files. Viruses often cost companies and individuals millions of dollars in downtime.

W

Warrant: An order issued by a judge or magistrate to make an arrest, seize property, or make a search.

White-collar crime: A person using a position of authority and responsibility in a legitimate business organization to commit crimes of fraud and deceit for his or her personal financial gain.

Work release: The release of selected inmates from a prison or community residential center for work during the day, returning at night.

Research and Activity Ideas

The following research and activity ideas are intended to offer suggestions for complementing crime and punishment studies, to trigger additional ideas for enhancing learning, and to provide cross-disciplinary projects for Internet, library, and classroom use.

Crime Statistics: The following annual publications can be found either online or in the reference section of local libraries: the Federal Bureau of Investigation's Uniform Crime Reporting Program (UCR) yearly report (http://www.fbi.gov/ucr/ucr.htm) or the National Crime Victimization Survey (NCVS), an ongoing study by the U.S. Bureau of the Census and the Bureau of Justice Statistics, an agency in the U.S. Department of Justice (http://www.ojp.usdoj.gov/bjs/cvict.htm). Divide the class into two groups and assign one statistic publication to each. Members of the groups should explore and analyze the statistics and report to the class on what they've found.

Three-Strikes Laws: As a class, research the three-strikes law in your state or a nearby state. Have a debate on the pros and cons of having such a law. Each student make a pro-con chart listing arguments for each side.

Neighborhood Watch Programs: Research neighborhood watch programs in your community. Students who live in a neighborhood with a program should interview its organizers and learn what is expected of participants in the program.

Map of Correction Facilities: Using a map of your state and some pushpins, locate federal, state, and county correction facilities. Explain to others the different roles of the facilities in housing convicted offenders.

Causes of Crime: Create a visual diagram illustrating the leading causes of crime. Place the word "crime" at the center of the diagram and surround it with words or pictures that convey the various causes.

Types of Crime: Create a visual diagram illustrating the various types of violent crimes, crimes against property, and public order crimes (such as substance abuse, prostitution, and pornography). Place the word "crime" in a circle at the center of the diagram, surround it with three more circles representing each general crime category, and then surround each category circle with words that describe the types of crime within that category. Be sure you can explain terms that many people find confusing. For example, what is the difference between murder and manslaughter? What are the definitions of robbery, burglary, and larceny? What does aggravated assault mean?

Newspaper Reports: Scan your community's newspaper for stories about crimes committed in your locality. Place them into a specific crime category—violent, property, public order, white collar, environmental, or cyber crime. For a well-publicized crime, attempt to follow court proceedings for as long as possible.

AMBER Alert: Research the history of AMBER Alerts. Learn the specifics needed to call an AMBER Alert in your state. How is the public notified of an alert and what should each individual do when they hear an alert called? Research actual AMBER Alerts in your state and find out their success rates or outcomes.

White-Collar Crime: Divide the class into eight groups and assign each group to learn about one type of white-collar fraud: healthcare, government, financial institution, loan, telemarketing, insurance, stock market (securities), and corporate fraud. Find actual high-profile examples of fraud cases. Each group then explains the specific type of white-collar fraud so the rest of the class can readily understand what is involved.

Car Theft Poster: Explore the Web site of the National Insurance Crime Bureau (NICB) at http://www.nicb.org for information on car theft. Create an informational poster on some aspects of car theft, such as illustrating where areas of car theft are likely to occur, the types of cars most often stolen, or ways to prevent car theft.

Organized Crime: In 2002 the FBI reported that U.S. organized crime activities brought in between $50 and $90 billion dollars, more income than any major national industry. The stories of real-life mobsters and street gangs have always captivated the American public. While throughout the twentieth century Americans thought organized crime meant only the American Mafia, by the twenty-first century street gangs had become dangerous and profitable organized crime groups. Many foreign organized crime groups also operate in the United States. Research one of the legendary American Mafia families—Colombo, Bonanno, Genovese, Lucchese, or Gambino. Alternatively, research a street gang—Hell's Angels, Bloods, Crips, Green Light Gangs, Gangster Disciples, or Latin Kings. Finally, examine a foreign crime unit operating in the United States—Japanese Yakuza, Chinese Triads, Hong Kong Triads, Russian Mafia, South American drug cartels, or Mexican Mafia.

Driving Under the Influence (DUI): Research and report on your state's DUI laws. Explore three organizations either through local chapters or through the Internet: Mothers against Drunk Driving (MADD; http://www.madd.org); Students against Destructive Decisions (SADD, http://www.nat-sadd.org); and Remove Intoxicated Drivers (RID, http://www.crisny.org/not-for-profit/ridusa).

National Institute on Drug Abuse: The National Institute on Drug Abuse (NIDA), a department of the National Institutes of Health, keeps up-to-date information on eighth through twelfth graders' alcohol and drug use. Go to their Web site, http://www.nida.nih.gov/Infofax/HSYouthtrends.html, and report to the class on the various trends.

School Violence: Research and then have a class discussion regarding the many possible causes that might push a young person to shoot his teachers and classmates. Be sure to include bullying and what your school is doing to combat bullying.

Death Penalty: Study all sides of the death penalty issue and check to see if the death penalty is legal in your state. Divide into two groups and have a debate on the use of the death penalty. Each student make a pro-con chart listing arguments for each side.

Juvenile Justice System: Explore the juvenile justice system in your state. Locate a nearby facility for youthful offenders. Make an appointment and interview an official at the facility. An administrator, juvenile probation officer, counselor, or clergy all would have available information for you to take back to the class. Also, check up-to-date juvenile justice statistics at the Web site for the National Center for Juvenile Justice, http://www.ncjj.org.

Environmental Crime: Using your favorite Internet search engine, identify recent environmental crimes prosecuted in your state. Also, explore cases at the U.S. Environmental Protection Agency's Criminal Enforcement division's Web site, http://www.epa.gov/compliance/criminal/index.html. What are the dominant types of environmental offenses? Do not confuse environmental crime with environmental terrorism such as setting gas-guzzling vehicles on fire or tree-sitting to prevent logging.

Careers: Find out what the qualifications are in your state or locality for becoming a law enforcement officer. Look into the departments of city police, sheriffs, and state police. Learn how their duties differ. Also check into the careers of probation officers and correctional facilities officers. Is there an FBI office in your state and, if so, where is it located? There are fifty-six FBI field officers spread across the United States, plus a number of small offices. What are the qualifications to become an FBI agent? How long is the training and where is the training facility?

Cyber Crime: Discover the latest information about cyberspace offenses from the Federal Bureau of Investigation's (FBI) Cyber Educational Letter at http://www.fbi.gov/cyberinvest/cyberedletter.htm.

Forensic Science: Every year the Federal Bureau of Investigation (FBI) publishes the *FBI Laboratory* yearbook, which is also available online. Within the publication the FBI explains each unit in its forensic laboratory. Research one type of forensic service in detail such as latent prints (finger-, palm-, and footprints), firearms and toolmark identification, documents, trace evidence, and so on. Find out where the nearest forensic laboratory is in relation to your community. What services does it provide? If possible, schedule a tour for the class.

Terrorism (part 1): The U.S. Congress requires the U.S. State Department to provide an annual assessment of significant terrorist actions in foreign countries. U.S. law also requires the report to describe how countries cooperate with the United States to apprehend, convict, and punish terrorists who attack U.S. citizens or interests. The report also addresses other countries' attempts to prevent future terrorist acts. This report, called "Patterns of Global Terrorism," is issued every year, and can be found at the U.S. State Department website (http://www.state.gov/s/ct/rls/pgtrpt). Go to this site and find the latest report. This report reflects the official State Department's words on the latest attempts to halt terrorism. Pull out the most important points and report to the class.

Terrorism (part 2): Each year the Secretary of State designates certain foreign organizations as terrorist organizations and puts them on the Foreign Terrorist Organization List (FTO). Find this updated list at the U.S. State Department's Office of Counterterrorism website (http://www.state.gov/s/ct/rls/fs/2003/12389.htm). Detailed information on each listed group may be found on the Center for Defense Information (CDI) website at http://www.cdi.org/terrorism/terrorist-groups.cfm. Choose several groups from countries that you are interested in and research them as fully as resources will allow. What is their goal, where do they operate, and what terror tactics have they used? Report to your class.

Crime and Punishment in America

ALMANAC

13

Crime Victims

According to the National Crime Victimization Survey (NCVS) almost twenty-three million Americans over twelve years of age were victims of violent crimes, property crimes, or both, in 2002. The term "victimization" is often used to describe the physical harm victims suffer from assault, rape, or murder, or financial loss due to theft, vandalism, or business corruption. Some 5.3 million crimes in 2002 were violent and 17.5 million were property crimes. Statistics from 1999 when crime rates were slightly higher showed there were 33 violent crime victims and 198 property crime victims for every 1,000 people over the age of twelve. The value of stolen property in 1999 was just less than $15 billion including $4.7 billion from theft and $7 billion in stolen vehicles.

For the first half of the twentieth century, crime victims received little attention in the criminal justice system. After the U.S. Supreme Court strengthened the constitutional rights of defendants in the 1960s, it seemed victims had fewer legal rights than criminals. Some victims became so distressed by the justice process they refused to testify in trials.

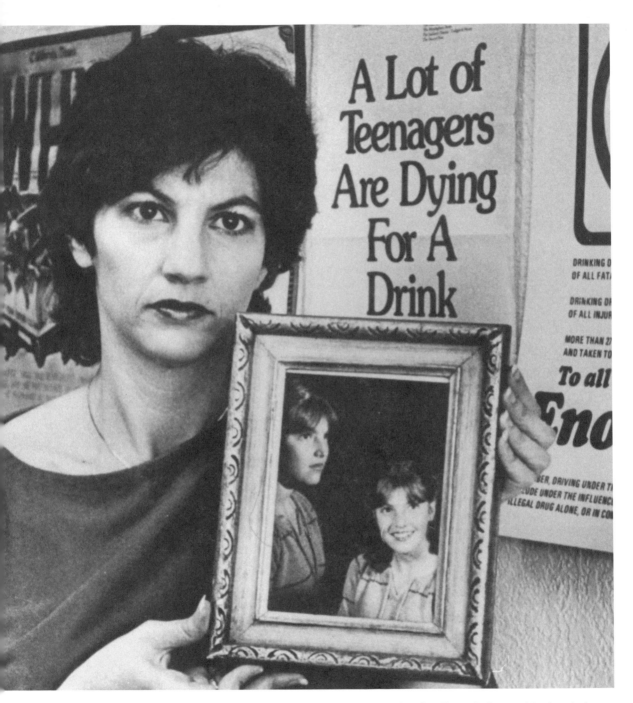

Families and friends are often deeply affected along with the victims of a crime. Candace Lightner founded Mothers Against Drunk Driving (MADD) in 1980 after her daughter was killed by a drunk driver.

(AP/Wide World Photos)

During the 1970s a number of states began establishing victim compensation funds to help victims survive the financial losses caused by crimes against them. In the 1980s a growing victims' rights movement brought change to the criminal justice system, and victims had an active role in the prosecution of their offenders. Society also came to believe it had an obligation to provide services to victims and help them recover from the effects of crime. By the early twenty-first century, over ten thousand victim assistance programs existed across the nation. Victims had finally gained significance in the criminal justice process.

Victim rights

For most of history prior to the eighteenth century, the victim was the primary focus of the criminal justice system. The main goal of justice was restitution (compensation or payment for damages) to the victim by the person who committed the offense. The victim, not the government, was responsible for initiating an investigation and played a key role in determining the fate of the defendant. In general, an offender's family had to provide long-term support to the victim or the victim's family. Overall, the victim held distinct rights and had the most power in the criminal justice process.

Not long before the American Revolution (1775–83; a war fought between Great Britain and the American colonies in which the colonies won their independence) emphasis in the American colonial justice system began changing. Crimes were considered offenses against society in general, rather than only against the victim. Crime became less of a personal dispute between the victim and offender as the colonial governments took over the primary responsibility to prosecute crimes. Public prosecutors were appointed and removed the sometimes costly responsibility of victims to pursue trials and seek justice. The new legal system, however, largely removed the victim from the center of the criminal justice process. The state became the system's focal point rather than the victim and any fines owed by defendants were no longer paid to the victims but to the state.

By the time the United States was founded, criminal justice had changed significantly. The Bill of Rights, added to the U.S. Constitution in 1791, provided protection only for

Women Victims

Though women are victimized by crime much less than men, the character of their victimization is quite different and generates much more fear. Men may have a 42 percent greater chance of becoming crime victims overall, but women experience the violent crimes of rape and sexual assault much more. Statistics indicate some five million women and girls over the age of twelve are victims of violent crime in the United States every year. One out of every six women is a victim of rape or attempted rape at some point in their lives. Some 870,000 rapes occur every year. Women between the ages of sixteen and twenty-four are more likely to be raped, with most raped prior to eighteen years of age.

Crimes against women are usually committed by a person they know well—a spouse or former spouse, boyfriend, family member, or friend. These attacks are the hardest to live with due to the personal nature of the crime. Only 16 percent of rapes are committed by strangers; over 30 percent of murders are committed by someone with whom the victim had a close relationship. The same pattern of familiarity follows in other crimes. Between 20 and 50 percent of women experience domestic abuse at least once in their lives. Statistics show that if a woman tries to leave an abusive relationship, it often turns more violent.

Studies have also shown women live with a greater fear of crime, especially rape. As a result, victim legislation often singles out female victims. In 1994 Congress passed the Violence Against Women Act (VAWA) providing federal funding for victim assistance programs directed toward female victims of rape, stalking, domestic abuse, and sexual assault. In 1998 VAWA provided $172 million to women's programs.

defendants in criminal proceedings. Evidence seized illegally could not be used in a trial, defendants had to be advised of their rights upon arrest, and the poor could have legal counsel provided free by the state. No mention of victim rights appeared; victims were simply evidence of a crime.

The right to sue and bear witness

The minor role of the victim in criminal justice remained largely unchanged through the 1960s. The victim only held the right to report crimes, serve as a witness, and sue in civil court for damages. Of course, first the criminal had to be caught. If the offender was never apprehended, the victim had

A rape victim being interviewed. In 1975 the first rape crisis center opened in Berkeley, California, to help victims through the legal process. *(© Richard T. Nowitz/Corbis)*

no options. As in earlier times when victims had to pay to pursue a civil lawsuit, the twist was that even if the victim won the court case, if the offender had no money there was nothing to collect. This was often the case, especially involving street criminals.

Through a series of studies in the late 1960s, the federal government discovered many victims did not report crimes and others refused to cooperate with police and prosecutors. Victims experienced poor treatment by authorities, long waits for trials, and no transportation or childcare while participating in the criminal justice process. This insensitivity on the part of the criminal justice authorities made victims feel "victimized" all over again. In response to the studies, law enforcement agencies and other criminal justice authorities began promoting victim assistance programs to address the needs of victims. With more victim cooperation came higher conviction rates.

The extreme stress faced by rape victims, who often did not report the crime because of the ordeal of going through the criminal justice system, was finally recognized. In 1975 the first rape crisis center opened in Berkeley, California, to help victims through the legal process.

Victim compensation laws

The financial well-being of victims was the first concern addressed in meeting the needs of crime victims. In the mid-1960s courts began ordering victim compensation in criminal sentencing. Direct restitution from the criminal to the victim became a condition of probation, mostly in property crimes. Poor offenders, however, often made such compensation impossible. To address this problem, California established the first victims' compensation program in 1965. Throughout the 1970s more state legislatures passed victim compensation laws, which established pools of public funds available to crime victims to ease the losses brought about by crime.

Many believed society owed victims something for their ordeal, so money was put aside from state revenues and penalties assessed against offenders. The funds could be used to pay for lost earnings, medical expenses, funeral expenses, counseling, and property loss or damage. Though payments to individual victims can go up to $25,000, this money is not intended to provide total compensation, but to help victims survive sudden losses.

During the 1970s over forty states made any profits earned from criminals' crimes—such as the publication of a book or selling movie rights—go to their victims. The idea of seizing such funds came from a highly publicized serial murder case in New York City. Convicted murderer David Berkowitz, known as "Son of Sam," was supposed to receive profits from a book about his crimes. In 1977 the New York legislature passed a law to seize any profits related to a convicted criminal's crimes and placed them in a special fund to pay any victims who might sue the criminal for damages. Through these Son of Sam laws, states are able to regulate money made from crimes and encourage victims to sue their attackers.

Congress passed Victims of Crime Act in 1984 setting up a similar fund for federal criminal cases. The act also provides money for state compensation funds using funds from penalties against federal criminals. The government gives states 40 percent of whatever the state paid to crime victims the previous year. In 1996 Congress passed the Antiterrorism and Effective Death Penalty Act that increased assistance and compensation to victims of terrorism.

Who qualifies

Each state varies how its funds are applied and who qualifies. For many states only low-income victims are considered; other states allow any victim to apply as long as the individual in no way contributed to the crime, such as picking a fight. Some states only provide payment for those physically injured or to families of victims who were killed. They do not compensate for property losses. For property crimes, victims who have insurance will be compensated through their insurance company. Those who do not have insurance must rely on offenders or their insurance to pay, or in rare cases a state that allows for property loss compensation.

To receive funds, victims or their families must file an application to state officials immediately after the crime occurs, identifying their loss or injuries. Funds are available to help victims even if the criminals are not caught or successfully prosecuted.

Studies at the end of the twentieth century indicated only about 15 percent of victims who report crimes receive compensation, usually those considered the most in need. Those who did not apply probably had strong support from family and friends, while others may not have been aware of the services and money available, especially in the more rural areas.

Victim rights

By 1975 only twenty-three programs existed around the country to provide direct assistance to victims. Through the 1970s, however, victim advocacy groups were quickly gaining membership and attention from state legislatures and the federal government. In 1975 the National Organization for Victim Assistance (NOVA) was formed to coordinate the different groups and increase their effectiveness. One of the most successful groups was Mothers Against Drunk Driving (MADD). MADD was founded in 1980 by Candace Lightner, whose daughter was killed by a drunk driver. Other groups included the National Coalition Against Domestic Violence, founded in 1978, and Parents of Murdered Children.

In 1982 the President's Task Force on Victims of Crime reported a need for more victims' services beyond compensation programs, so Congress passed the Victim and Witness Protection Act (VWPA). The act protected victims, witnesses, and informants and provided compensation to victims of federal crimes. The federal act served as a model for state victim protection laws. The 1984 Victims of Crime Act (VOCA) provided $150 million to support state compensation funds as well as victim assistance programs. The federal funding programs encouraged the growing number of local victim assistance groups to work with criminal justice agencies.

Victims' bill of rights

The victims' rights movement successfully pushed for legal protections for victims similar to those of defendants. By the twenty-first century every state either passed laws or adopted constitutional amendments to support victims in criminal prosecution. Wisconsin was the first state to establish a bill of rights for victims in 1980, which also provided funding for victim assistance programs. California followed in 1982. Crime victims and victims' rights organizations pushed for all states to protect victims' rights, believing many victims were ignored and even mistreated by criminal justice systems that seemed more focused on protecting the legal rights of defendants.

While victims' bill of rights varied from state to state, they each required that victims be treated with dignity and fairness by police, prosecutors, and other officials as well as provided with protection from threats and harm. Many also required the police to notify victims about the progress of their case, from the investigation phase to when criminals were released from prison, and to inform victims of upcoming court dates such as parole hearings.

In forty-one states, victims have the legal right to attend the trial of their offender. In twenty-two states prosecutors must notify victims of any plea bargains before agreements are reached. In twenty-three states the victim has the right to

Mediation

Another way victims can play an active role in resolving crimes against them is through a process called victim-offender mediation. In mediation, both the victim and offender must agree to meet and attempt to settle their dispute in a face-to-face manner, under the guidance of a mediator (a neutral party who helps resolve conflicts).

The mediation process predates the modern U.S. criminal justice system and was widely used in ancient times. Native American tribal justice systems have existed for centuries and still used this approach in the late 1990s. Several hundred mediation programs existed in the United States in the early twenty-first century. They can be found in the court system or the offices of sheriffs and prosecutors.

Mediation does require offenders to assume personal responsibility for their actions by admitting to the crime. The goal is to negotiate an agreement concerning the crime, with both parties having the opportunity to tell their stories and discuss what can be done to resolve the issues facing them. If the mediation is successful, the victim and offender write an agreement and sign it. The offender usually agrees to pay some compensation, perform services, or seek counseling. Mediators assign someone from their office to make sure both parties carry out terms of the agreement.

Occasionally, no agreement can be reached through mediation and the case returns to the usual criminal justice process. By this time, however, offenders have already admitted to their crimes as part of the mediation process. In some situations, the criminal justice system may still prosecute the case, even after an agreement is reached.

Mediations of more serious crimes, including murder, do occur though not as often. These cases, however, are more likely to be pursued after criminal prosecution has been completed and are usually conducted within a prison.

Mediation poses some risks to victims. If the offender fails to carry out the terms of the agreement, the victim may feel victimized once again. Most agreements, however, are honored; in these cases victims find their fears decrease while offenders often make positive changes in their lives as well.

speak in a hearing concerning a judge's acceptance of a plea bargain. Victims are also allowed the opportunity to write statements about how the crime affected them and their families. These statements are presented when the offender is sentenced and also at parole hearings. Forty-eight states must notify victims if their offender escapes from prison or a mental health facility.

Congress continued to find ways to increase victim rights while not restricting the rights of defendants. Following the lead of the various states, Congress passed the Crime Control Act and the Victims' Rights and Restitution Act both 1990. The Crime Control Act provided a federal bill of rights for victims of federal crime; the Restitution Act confirmed that victims had a right to compensation and use of federal services offering help to crime victims.

Congress passed other laws such as the Victims of Child Abuse Act of 1990, which provided a wide range of rights and protections for victims and witnesses of abuse; the Violent Crime Control and Law Enforcement Act of 1994, which provided domestic violence victims the right to testify at the sentencing and release hearings of their offender. The Violent Crime Control Act also offered counseling and restitution for victims of sexual assault, domestic abuse, and child abuse.

The Mandatory Victims' Restitution Act of 1996 further strengthened the requirements for defendants, including drug defendants in particular, to compensate victims for losses. The Victim Rights Clarification Act of 1997 reaffirmed the right of victims to attend the trials of their offenders.

Supporters or advocates for victims' rights pointed out that federal law protected the rights of victims, but the Constitution protected the rights of defendants. This meant defendants had more protection than victims should a case ever pit victim rights against constitutional rights. In an attempt to increase victim rights, a Victims' Rights Amendment to the Constitution was introduced in the mid-1990s and endorsed by President Bill Clinton (1946–; served 1993–2001). Following heated debate in Congress in April 2000, however, the amendment was dropped. If crime victims ever do receive protections equivalent to those of crime offenders, the criminal justice system would probably be forced to make major changes.

Protecting victims

Many of the federal acts, beginning with the Victim and Witness Protection Act of 1982, not only recognized a victim's rights but provided protection to those who might feel threatened by the offender. Through these acts the U.S. attorney general had the authority to assist crime victims or witnesses

A member of the witness protection program is allowed to keep his face covered as he testifies in court. The FBI helps create new identities and relocate people whose testimony puts their lives in danger. *(© Bettmann/Corbis)*

and their families in relocating to a new place of residence and to provide a new name and new identity. This included state as well as federal witnesses, and these responsibilities were carried by U.S. marshals.

Protection by marshals proved crucial to obtaining testimony from victims and witnesses, especially in organized crime, drug trafficking, and terrorism cases. It also protects victims and witnesses from pressures not to testify, such as bribery and threats of harm. By the early twenty-first century some seven thousand witnesses had been protected or relocated. Each state has similar laws, often leaving protection services to state police instead of U.S. marshals.

The ability to protect victims and witnesses became more difficult in the late 1990s. New computer technology made public and private records much more accessible to those who have the skills to search the Internet and hack into public sites. Witnesses and victims felt much less secure by the early twenty-first century.

Victim advocates

As support for victim rights grew, the role of victim advocates rose in criminal justice systems. Use of victim advocates first began in the 1970s in rape and domestic abuse cases. Advocates are trained to assist with the physical, emotional, and psychological trauma of victims and their families. An advocate advises victims of their rights in the criminal justice process, counsels them during the investigation, prepares them for trial, refers them to social services if needed, acts as a contact for state and local agencies, and provides personal support.

Police will often call an advocate to the scene of a crime, particularly in cases involving sexual assault and domestic abuse. How much a victim participates in the criminal justice process is often influenced by the speed and responsiveness of the police and the amount of sensitivity shown. With advocates assisting the victims and their families, law enforcement and prosecutors can focus on catching criminals and putting them on trial. Advocates establish a relationship of trust with victims and eventually help them return to normal lives.

Advocates assist victims in completing application forms for state compensation programs or to obtain restraining orders to keep abusers away. Advocates can also help victims replace lost documents, provide emergency food, clothing, and cash, temporary housing when needed, and improve security of a home or assist in relocating to another area. The advocate can also help with landlords, doctors, and bosses, as well as retrieve personal property from authorities when it is no longer needed for evidence.

Increased professionalism

Originally, advocates were simply individuals working out of their own personal interest, sometimes through local community organizations. Many were crime victims at one time themselves. For example, female victims of violence have provided counseling for rape and domestic abuse victims at shelters. Early advocates were not connected in any way to the criminal justice system. Eventually, states were able to hire victim advocates through federal funding.

Advocates became more widely available and integrated into the criminal justice system. During the 1990s, training programs and increased educational opportunities became available for advocates. NOVA provided training programs and began establishing standards for advocates.

At times victims have preferred advocates not officially connected to law enforcement agencies, to avoid pressure to prosecute or testify against their offenders. In addition, advocates who were not hired by law enforcement agencies were less likely to share a victim's personal information with authorities if the victim was against it.

In addition to individual victim advocates, other advocacy groups formed including the National Victim Center, Victim Assistance Legal Organization, and the National Center for Missing and Exploited Children. Many of these organizations were established by past victims of crime. Besides providing assistance directly to victims, these advocacy organizations also try to influence state and federal legislatures to emphasize the rights of victims. They also seek tougher penalties for crimes and provide public education programs to better inform the public on injustices in the criminal justice systems.

Becky Comeaux and her son, who were separated for twelve years, talk to reporters at the National Center for Missing and Exploited Children in Arlington, Virginia, in 1997. *(AP/Wide World Photos)*

The study of victims

Increased concern over crime victims in the 1970s not only led to victim compensation and assistance programs, but also to studies of victims and their roles in the criminal justice process. These studies formed a new area of criminology

Victim Statistics

Two major sources for statistics concerning victims are available. The Federal Bureau of Investigation (FBI) releases an annual report called the Uniform Crime Report (UCR). The Bureau of Justice Statistics (BJS) conducts an annual National Crime Victimization Survey (NCVS). The FBI reports have been produced every year since 1930 and collect information from seventeen thousand law enforcement offices.

The UCR reports on serious crimes including murders, rapes, aggravated assaults, robberies, burglaries, larcenies, and automobile thefts and provides statistics nationally and by state, county, and community. These statistics include only crimes reported to the police. Aside from murder cases, however, information on victims was not collected until the 1990s. The FBI also reports on college campus crime, terrorism, and hate crimes.

Created in 1973, the NCVS collects data from a large sample of the population to estimate how many physical and sexual assaults, robberies, automobile thefts, and other thefts have actually occurred. The survey collects data on victims such as sex, age, race, ethnic affiliation, income, amount of education, and residence. These statistics provide useful information on how certain groups of people are more susceptible to crime. Citizens wishing to minimize their chance of being victimized or victimized a second time, can use these statistics to change their behavior patterns.

called "victimology." Researchers look at the physical, financial, and emotional harm suffered by victims of crime, as well as how victims react—from seeking retaliation against their offenders to trying to get on with their lives. Such research helps shape future policy and programs to assist crime victims.

The studies also hoped to identify behavior or situations that might put people at higher risk of becoming crime victims. Some were simple: flashing a large wad of money in public could certainly attract a robber. Other studies were controversial or upsetting, such as stating that some females were more likely to be attacked or raped based on the way they dressed. A study concerning murders in Philadelphia found over one-fourth of all murders were caused by the victim in some way—including knowing an offender, as well as drinking alcohol, arguing, or fighting with the offender.

Other studies found that victims might provoke crimes through carelessness, like walking in a dark area at night. Even where a person works, shops, lives, goes to school, or socializes can be factors in a crime. Though many consider it important to determine the role victims play in crime so future attacks can be avoided, it does not remove any degree of responsibility from the criminal.

For More Information

Books

Austern, David. *The Crime Victims Handbook: Your Rights and Role in the Criminal Justice System.* New York: Viking, 1987.

Belknap, Joanne. *The Invisible Woman: Gender, Crime, and Justice.* Toronto: Wadsworth Thomson Learning, 2001.

Elias, Robert. *Victims of the System: Crime Victims and Compensation in American Politics and Criminal Justice.* New Brunswick, NJ: Transaction Books, 1983.

Gordon, Margaret, and Stephanie Riger. *The Female Fear.* New York: Free Press, 1989.

Jerin, Robert A., and Laura J. Moriarty. *Victims of Crime.* Chicago, IL: Nelson-Hall Publishers, 1998.

Karmen, Andrew. *Crime Victims: An Introduction to Victimology.* 4th ed. Belmont, CA: Wadsworth, 2001.

Stark, James, and Herman Goldstein. *The Rights of Crime Victims.* Chicago, IL: Southern Illinois University Press, 1985.

Web Sites

"Helping Crime Victims Rebuild Their Lives." *The National Center for Victims of Crime.* http://www.ncvc.org (accessed on August 19, 2004).

National Organization for Victim Assistance (NOVA). http://www.try-nova.org (accessed on August 19, 2004).

U.S. Department of Justice, Office of Justice Programs, Office for Victims of Crime (OVC). http://www.ojp.usdoj.gov/ovc/welcome.htm (accessed on August 19, 2004).

Policing

Policing in the United States is highly decentralized, meaning the legal authority to police is split among federal, state, and local forces. Most police forces largely operate independently, unlike policing in other countries. Many nations including European countries have strong national police forces. In the United States, a number of federal agencies have their own police powers. At the beginning of the twenty-first century some seventeen thousand police organizations existed in the United States, all operating with some degree of independence.

The U.S. policing system is highly decentralized, meaning its forces are widely spread throughout the states and each with varying amounts of power and independence. This kind of policing system was created by early American colonists who opposed having an authoritarian (highly centralized government power) police force, the kind they had while under British rule. The decentralized structure of the U.S. system, however, meant it evolved very slowly for the next century and beyond.

For much of U.S. history, few rules existed to guide policing. Not until the early twentieth century did police reform-

A fingerprint seen on a wireless device that can send the print via a
wireless connection to be immediately checked against a database.

(AP/Wide World Photos)

ers and the courts begin setting strict rules about police procedures. In the 1960s, the most active period during which courts established guidelines, new rules guided key police activities such as identifying suspects, arrest procedures, searching for evidence, and interrogation. Much of this court activity resulted from minorities seeking protection from police abuse.

Police in modern society look after the health, safety, welfare, and general morals of society. They maintain social order in communities and protect people's civil liberties (protections from unreasonable government actions). Police are responsible for solving crimes; enforcing traffic, drug, and firearms laws; carrying out routine patrols; and working with communities to prevent crime of all kinds.

Early policing

Though societies have had codes of behavior for thousands of years since ancient Babylon and the later civilizations of Rome and Greece, the existence of professional police forces to enforce the codes has a much shorter history. The term "police" comes from a Greek word *politeia* meaning business concerning the order of the state.

France established police including constables and night watchmen over a thousand years ago but did not create a central police force until much later in the seventeenth century. Similarly, the English had created policing roles in the eleventh century. The constable position is considered the first formal type of police officer. Next came sheriffs, who policed county-like areas of England. By the early fourteenth century a justice of the peace position was established in England to serve judicial duties and support policing activities.

During the American colonial period prior to the American Revolution the first type of police in the colonies were county sheriffs. The sheriffs not only kept the peace and fought crime, but also performed various legal functions such as serving court papers, collecting taxes, maintaining jails, and supervising elections. To assist sheriffs were undersheriffs, jailers, county clerks, and deputy sheriffs. The towns, still small in size, had volunteer constables and night watchmen.

Night watchman in London, England, 1608. (*The Granger Collection*)

Colonial governors often appointed the sheriffs and constables. Boston was the first colonial settlement to use night watchmen beginning in the 1630s. Besides watching for crime and spotting fires, night watchmen would also announce the time and weather conditions. Constables delivered warrants, supervised the night watchmen, and carried out the routine local government functions of the community. Over time, cities added town marshals, city councils, and justices to backup the constables and watchmen.

The southern colonies, where slavery was a key part of the region's economy, created slave patrols by the 1740s to police the black slave populations. They protected white citizens from slaves, fought slave uprisings, and captured runaway slaves. All capable men between eighteen and fifty years of age were expected to serve for a certain time. Historians consider the slave patrols the first modern police force in the United States.

Few changes occurred in colonial policing until later in the eighteenth century. Following the French and Indian War

(1756–63), in which the British defeated the French on the American frontier to seal their control of North America, an economic depression hit the colonies. A major rise in crime followed, primarily involving property and street crimes. Each colony and settlement responded individually to needs for improved policing with little or no coordination of efforts.

Even the new U.S. Constitution adopted in 1787 following victory over British forces did not specifically mention policing. The first ten amendments to the U.S. Constitution adopted in 1791, known as the Bill of Rights, did set important limitations on governmental police powers.

Founding Father and future U.S. president James Madison (1751–1836; served 1809–17) powerfully argued for the adoption of these criminal justice protections. For example, the Fourth Amendment guarded against unreasonable search and seizure. It required search and arrest warrants issued by a magistrate (judge) before police could conduct a search or make an arrest. The warrants had to be based on probable cause (sufficient evidence to support an arrest) identifying where the police could search and had to define what they were looking for.

The Fifth Amendment stated that an official could not force a person to be a witness against him or herself. This rule limited what police could do during an interrogation or questioning of a suspect. It also grants due process of law, meaning everyone must be treated fairly and their civil liberties respected regarding interrogations, undercover operations, and identification procedures that in modern days includes the use of fingerprinting, lineups, blood types, and DNA testing. Due process means the police cannot use torture, threats against family members, or deprive suspects of basic needs. The Sixth Amendment guaranteed a person the right to have an attorney present during any questioning and court proceedings.

Immediately following adoption of the new U.S. Constitution, the first U.S. Congress passed the first laws of the new nation. One act created federal marshals, the first federal police officers. The marshal was responsible for seeing that federal court orders were carried out and to enforce the first few criminal laws created in 1790. Communities still relied on volunteer constables and night watchmen.

On the western frontier, few federal or local police could be found. Order was maintained by groups of citizens, called vigilantes, beginning in the 1790s. As the frontier moved westward toward the Pacific Ocean over the next sixty years, vigilantism moved with it.

Policing developments that developed in Europe in the early 1800s eventually influenced America. Napoleon Bonaparte, leader of France from 1799 to 1815, expanded the duties of the French national police force to gather intelligence information. By the 1820s the growing industrialized city of London, England, was facing increased social and economic problems. With high unemployment, crime was on the rise. In 1829 under the direction of Sir Robert Peel (1788–1850), the city established its first professional police department, the Metropolitan Police Force of London, to keep order.

The London police, called "bobbies" after Robert Peel's first name (Bobby, short for Robert), wore uniforms and had military-like discipline. They considered themselves full-time civil servants. Their main responsibility was to conduct "preventive patrols" to discourage crime simply by their presence or being seen around their communities.

Professional policing

Through the first decades of the nineteenth century U.S. communities were growing into cities with rapid industrial growth. Along with larger populations and increased crowding came civil disorder. The volunteer system of constables and night watchmen were soon outmatched by growing crime rates. Various cities tried new arrangements of replacing volunteer constables and night watchmen with more formal, paid police forces.

In the 1830s a series of riots occurred primarily in Boston, often involving groups of Catholics and Irish immigrants. In response, some of the larger cities such as Philadelphia, Boston, and New York began moving toward professional policing. New York City was the first American city to establish a professional police force and other cities gradually followed. These included Chicago (1851), New Orleans and Cincinnati (1852), Philadelphia (1855), St. Louis (1856), Newark and Baltimore (1857), Detroit (1865), and Buffalo (1866). Modeled after the London police force, they also

Allan Pinkerton (seated at left), head of the Federal Secret Service, poses with his fellow Secret Service agents in 1862. *(© Medford Historical Society Collection/Corbis)*

adopted a preventive patrol approach. Once established in the larger cities, the development of police forces spread quickly to smaller communities.

During the American Civil War (1861–65; war in the United States between the Union [North], who was opposed to slavery, and the Confederacy [South], who was in favor of slavery) federal policing expanded. A priority for U.S. marshals was arresting Southern sympathizers in the Northern states. In 1865 Congress created the Secret Service to combat counterfeiting, a major problem since the country first began making its own currency. The assassinations of U.S. presidents in 1865, 1881, and 1901 led to the Secret Service becoming responsible for the protection of the U.S. presidents as well.

Important differences from the London police existed; the newly created U.S. police answered to local political leaders instead of being an independent police department. As a result, city councilmen often appointed friends into key police positions as rewards for support. Since they were not a part of city government, police related to the local public on an individual basis, building personal working relationships, and following community standards. As a result, enforcement varied from neighborhood to neighborhood.

Such a loose system of policing meant police were vulnerable to corruption. They often patrolled on foot alone, out of contact from the police sergeant in a time before officers carried two-way radios. Telegraph technology arrived in the 1850s and connected police stations by their typed messages, but telephones were not available until the late 1800s. Corruption involved almost all police departments, from chiefs to patrolmen. Police shared in the gains of thieves and received regular payoffs from criminals. Policemen often bought their promotions within a police department, paying thousands of dollars.

Much of policing in the nineteenth century involved community service activities such as assisting the homeless and poor, maintaining order, making arrests for drunkenness, or returning lost children to their homes or orphanages. In the 1890s with the further growth of industrial cities and the arrival of thousands of immigrants from east European countries, the police began handling more serious crime like murders, assaults, and burglaries as crime rates grew along with the city populations.

Private police

The increased crime rates following the Civil War led businesses such as banks and railroad companies to hire private police services. The private agents not only protected cargo and property, but also actually pursued criminals and broke strikes by employees of the companies that hired them.

Unlike local police they had no particular jurisdiction and could pursue suspects from town to town and across state lines.

The Pinkerton National Detective Agency was formed in the mid-nineteenth century and its agents even served as spies during the Civil War. By the 1870s the Pinkertons had established the first nationwide criminal database for its agents. More private police organizations appeared over the next few decades including the Burns National Detective Agency in 1904 by William J. Burns, a former Secret Service employee.

Seeking reform

By the end of the nineteenth century, politicians and the public pushed for reform to make police departments more professional and part of the city government. As part of the city, police forces would no longer be controlled by political leaders such as mayors and councilmen. The reformers wanted training programs, increased standards for recruits, and focus more on crime and less on civil service.

One of the lead reformers in New York City in the 1890s was future U.S. president Theodore Roosevelt (1858–1919; served 1901–09). He served as the newly created city police commissioner. Roosevelt believed in promotions based on merit (the performance of the individual) and tougher physical and mental requirements. Unfortunately, little came from these reform efforts.

In the first decades of the twentieth century patrol officers still worked twelve-hour days and were poorly paid. Most police departments did not even require their officers to have a high school degree. As employees in other workplaces such as factories began to form labor unions (organizations that sought better working conditions), police attempted to create their own unions. This trend, however, was short-lived; in 1919 most of the Boston police force went on strike for the right to form a union. While the officers were on strike a crime wave hit Boston and police lost all public support to improve their working conditions. Most of the strikers were fired and the police union movement disappeared until well after World War II.

Counterterrorism

Following the terrorist attacks on the World Trade Center in New York City and the Pentagon in Washington, D.C., on September 11, 2001, killing some three thousand people, policing in the United States experienced major new challenges. Intelligence gathering gained greater attention and counterterrorism led to much greater cooperation among police organizations of all levels of government.

Police resorted to a range of investigation tools from high tech monitoring devices to consulting with psychologists about the behavior of terrorists. Police found that terrorists were quite different than usual criminals; street criminals often acted on impulse taking advantage of opportunities and were untrained and undisciplined. Terrorists, driven by strong political and religious beliefs, carefully planned their activities, sometimes over long time periods.

In October 2001, just over a month after the terrorist attacks in New York and Washington, Congress passed the Uniting and Strengthening America by Providing Appropriate Tools Required to Intercept and Obstruct Terrorism Act (more commonly known as the Patriot Act). The act loosened the restrictions on police for obtaining personal information about citizens. People no longer needed to be suspects in a crime for the police to access information about them.

Under the act, the FBI could deliver a letter to a doctor's office or librarian demanding the personal records of a specific individual without a warrant. Warrants could also be obtained for electronic surveillance without naming specific individuals. Warrants had to identify only what area or electronic system was to be tapped. The act was the subject of much debate. It spelled out that the greatest challenge for police was to prevent future terrorist attacks while protecting the civil liberties of its citizens.

National crime spree

Through the 1920s crime became a national issue for the first time. Prohibition, which banned the sale, manufacture, possession, and transportation of liquor, brought crime syndicates, gangsters, and bootleggers (those who sold liquor illegally) plenty of business. The U.S. Bureau of Alcohol, Tobacco, and Firearms (ATF), first formed in 1862 during the Civil War, had much of the responsibility for tracking bootleggers.

The U.S. Customs Service was in charge of guarding the nation's borders to keep smugglers from bringing liquor (and

Policing was revolutionized with the widespread use of police cars and two-way radios. *(© H. Armstrong Roberts/Corbis)*

later drugs) into the country illegally. Even the Internal Revenue Service (IRS) went after criminals—by charging them with tax evasion (not paying taxes). After other law enforcement agencies tried and failed numerous times to convict notorious gangster Al Capone (1899–1947) of various crimes, the IRS nailed him for tax evasion and sent him to prison.

Still, crime was out of control. In 1929 President Herbert C. Hoover (1874–1964; served 1929–33) appointed U.S. attorney general George Wickersham (1858–1936) to head a national commission to study crime and punishment in the nation. The commission produced fourteen volumes by 1931. The volumes addressed various issues related to policing, including police corruption and the use of too much force, which lead to violence against suspects. Much of the policing sections was written by Los Angeles police chief August Vollmer (1876–1955).

Reforms

Major steps toward professionalism were led by a number of prominent police chiefs around the nation including Vollmer. Police departments adopted codes of ethics to combat corruption and established education requirements for recruits. Police academies were established and San Jose State College offered the first training program for professional policing in 1931. Police departments adopted formal rules and hiring practices to further separate themselves from political influence.

Police departments also adopted modern technologies such as establishing forensic laboratories. The biggest technological change had come by the 1920s with the automobile. Policing was revolutionized with the widespread use of police cars and two-way radios. The radios put officers in continuous contact with their sergeants at the police station and allowed them to be much more responsive to calls from the public. Unfortunately, patrol cars also served to separate police from the community as they were no longer on foot patrols. Nonetheless police were more efficient, responded faster, and had new technologies to help them solve and prevent crimes. These tools led to greater professionalism and a drop in corruption.

During this time J. Edgar Hoover (1895–1972) overhauled the U.S. Bureau of Investigation into a top notch professional federal police agency. Hoover and his G-Men, as the agents were called, became famous with their capture and killing of several notorious crime figures in the early 1930s. As a result Congress gave the bureau expanded crime fighting responsibilities such as kidnappings, crossing state lines to avoid prosecution or testifying, carrying stolen goods across state lines, and drug enforcement. In 1935 the agency changed its name to the Federal Bureau of Investigation (FBI) and established an academy to train local police officers.

Like other federal agencies, the FBI grew throughout the 1930s with its new responsibilities—which in turn led to a decline in the role of U.S. marshals. Marshals, however, contin-

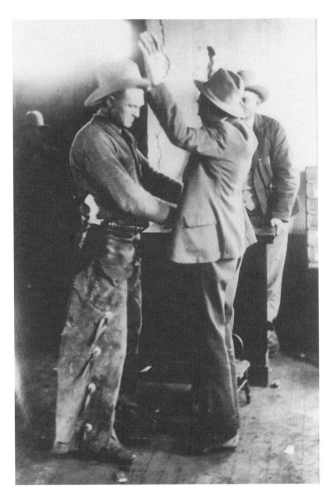

The Texas Rangers had existed off and on through the 1800s and were officially established in 1874.

(© Underwood & Underwood/Corbis)

ued to serve court papers and to patrol the courts. The federal government had also expanded its policing powers with the addition of the Immigration and Naturalization Service (INS) in 1940 as part of the Department of Justice.

Changes in police agencies

A trend toward forming state police organizations grew throughout the 1920s and 1930s. Fifteen states established state police forces by World War II. State police forces first appeared in Texas and Massachusetts during the previous century. The Texas Rangers had existed off and on through the 1800s and were officially established in 1874. Massachusetts also experimented with a state police force beginning in 1865, primarily aimed at Irish immigrants and Irish Americans and enforcing liquor laws.

Following World War II the steady progress toward increased police professionalism continued through the 1950s among the nation's police departments as standards continued to rise. A leader at this time was Chicago police commissioner Orlando W. Wilson (1900–1972) who established a criminology program at the University of California at Berkeley.

Then came the 1960s, a traumatic period in U.S. history in many ways. Policing in the United States changed dramatically. Civil rights demonstrations were increasing, antiwar protests grew, and race riots erupted. These events brought new and staggering demands on police forces. The general crime rate doubled during the decade including a particularly steep increase in violent crime. Not only was the existing police system unable to deter crime, but police actions often triggered riots.

Beginning in the mid-1950s the Civil Rights movement involved black Americans fighting discriminatory laws and city ordinances limiting their use of public places like restaurants and hotels. The movement's civil disobedience (challenging rules of public behavior) included "sit-ins," which blocked access to places like offices, sidewalks, or streets; boycotts (getting groups of people to stop buying certain goods or services); and demonstrations in the streets. These activities led to direct confrontations or clashes with local police. They even led to conflicts between state police enforcing local laws and U.S. federal marshals enforcing federal court rulings. By being forced to uphold discriminatory laws passed by local politicians, the police themselves became a symbol of inequality.

By the late 1960s, race and antiwar riots erupted in various U.S. cities. The antiwar movement adopted many of the civil disobedience measures practiced by the supporters of civil rights. Well-known battles between police and antiwar protestors became common. The notable example was the Chicago riots in the summer of 1968 during the Democratic National Convention. An investigative commission after the riots was so critical of police reaction that they called the Chicago conflict a "police riot."

A number of race riots erupted in various cities across the nation including New York in 1964, Los Angeles in 1965, Newark and Detroit in 1967, and Washington, D.C., in 1968. Race riots were started by routine police traffic stops in the Watts neighborhood of Los Angeles and in Newark, New Jersey, while a police raid on a bar started a riot in Detroit. Police lost considerable respect among the public during the decade.

Support for police

Two national commissions on crime were established in the mid-1960s to determine how to improve policing in America—President Lyndon Johnson's (1908–1973; served 1963–69) Crime Commission on Law Enforcement and the Administration of Justice, and the National Advisory Commission on Civil Disorders. The commissions found major police weaknesses including abuse of power, brutality, harassment, and a lack of training on how to control riots. They also noted the poor relations between police and com-

Well-known battles between police and antiwar protestors became common in the 1960s. A notable example was the Chicago riots in the summer of 1968 during the Democratic National Convention. *(AP/Wide World Photos)*

munity members, racial discrimination in arrests and hiring, and continued problems of corruption in some departments including New York, Denver, and Chicago. Among some two hundred recommendations, the commissions called for improved training programs and the hiring of minorities.

To bolster local police departments, Congress created the Law Enforcement Assistance Administration (LEAA) in 1965 to provide federal funding to improve policing. Over a ten-year period billions of dollars went to the various states to improve police departments. Part of the funding purchased new weapons including tanks, armored cars, computer systems, helicopters, and riot control equipment. Funding available through LEAA quickly rose from $63 million in 1969 to $700 million in 1972.

U.S. Supreme Court justice Earl Warren made several landmark decisions between 1961 and 1966 affirming the rights of suspects.
(AP/Wide World Photos)

Protecting civil liberties

During the 1960s police also saw increased restrictions on their activities. Congress passed the Omnibus Crime Control and Safe Streets Act of 1968 requiring warrants for any kind of electronic eavesdropping (like tapping someone's phone to listen in on conversations). The U.S. Supreme Court under Justice Earl Warren (1891–1974) made several landmark decisions between 1961 and 1966 affirming the rights of suspects to be advised of their rights before questioning (Miranda Rights) and to prevent police from illegal searches and the seizure of a suspect's property without proper cause and the necessary court-approved documents (the exclusionary rule).

The Supreme Court expanded a much earlier decision issued in 1914 about search and seizure rules. Until 1914 search and seizure was handled more through a trespassing law rather than as a constitutional protection. But in *Weeks v. U.S.* (1914), the Court ruled that any evidence obtained in violation of a suspect's Fourth Amendment rights could not be used as evidence against him or her in court proceedings and must be excluded.

In short, the "exclusionary rule" states that evidence obtained illegally by the police cannot be used in a court of law. Since the Bill of Rights only applied to the federal government and federal law officers, however, evidence gained illegally by state or local police could still be used in a federal court. Supreme Court Justice Warren extended the exclusionary rule to include search and seizures by state and local police in addition to federal authorities.

The Fifth Amendment provided the basis for Miranda Rights, established in a 1966 Supreme Court ruling. According to the decision, police must advise people being arrested that they have the right to remain silent, that anything they say can be used against them, they have a right to a lawyer, and that a lawyer will be provided if they cannot afford one. Many foreign countries have adopted some form of the Miranda Rights.

Despite the increased police patrols and presence through the late 1960s and early 1970s the crime rate stayed high. Police considered the restrictions on their tactics by the Supreme Court a major problem. Many criminologists attributed the high crime rates to the number of seventeen to thirty-four-year-olds in the population at the time.

Changing views

The increased professionalism of public police departments in the 1930s led to their dominance over private police organizations until the 1970s. The high crime rates of the 1960s and 1970s, however, led to the rapid growth of private security firms. By 1975 there were twice as many private police as public. By 1990 two million private security officers

A major change in policing brought back practices of the nineteenth century, such as the use of foot as well as bike patrols. Known as community policing, police began to partner with community members to prevent crime and increase the chances of catching criminals. *(© Kelly-Mooney Photography/Corbis)*

(like bodyguards) were employed in the country compared to six hundred thousand in public police agencies. This trend toward private policing continued into the twenty-first century as security from terrorism became a greater concern.

By the 1980s with a strong public push to "get tough on crime," police forces saw a change in support and respect from their communities. Retiring members of the Supreme Court brought in new justices who were more conservative or traditional in their thought and decisions. The Court made rulings favoring the prosecution of crime rather than protecting the rights of the accused. Restrictions were eased on searches and stopping suspicious persons. The exclusionary rule was relaxed making it easier to obtain warrants.

Police in cities, such as New York, performed shakedowns or pat-down searches of suspicious people on the sidewalks, reducing the number of illegal firearms. Most searches occurred without warrants in situations outside of homes where a warrant was not needed, such as traffic stops or on the streets while in pursuit of a criminal. Roadblocks and searches only required reasonable suspicion, not probable cause and a warrant. Flying over property in a helicopter or small plane did not require warrants, so police could keep an eye out for suspicious activity by air. Also, if a person agreed to a police search, then Fourth Amendment protections were not involved.

Another major change brought back policing practices of the nineteenth century. These were foot as well as bike patrols. Known as community policing, the overall police strategy changed from reacting to calls for assistance to working in partnership with community members to prevent crime and increase the chances of catching criminals. Citizen cooperation was encouraged and programs like Neighborhood Watch and Drug Abuse Resistance Education (DARE) helped heal relations between police and the public. By the end of the twentieth century, well over half of all U.S. communities had adopted some form of neighborhood policing.

Another major change came with adoption of a new theory in policing to control crime known as "Broken Windows." Police focused on stopping minor or lesser crimes, which in turn restored order to the streets. As a result, major crimes also decreased in those areas.

The 1990s proved a better period for policing in America. Crime rates went down and stayed down, particularly for violent crimes, which fell 30 percent in New York City in 1995. The drop in crime was probably due to more police, increased tactics to seize illegal guns, longer prison sentences, more prisons, more jobs, and a decline in drug use. Perhaps the biggest factor was the aging population: males between seventeen and thirty-four years of age had grown up and settled down.

Major challenges

In the twenty-first century policing in the United States remained divided between a number of agencies with differing powers and jurisdictions. Local police forces answered to their communities; police chiefs were elected and the public had the power to reelect or deny them another term. City councils, made up of elected officials, created laws and determined how they would be enforced. A major police responsibility remained the protection of civil rights and the freedom of every community's citizens. All citizens were to be treated fairly and equally regardless of economic status, race, or religion.

Police challenges in the new millennium include random crimes that seem to have no motive or intent; monitoring gang activities; using video surveillance equipment that many believe threatens privacy; and guarding against possible terrorist attacks.

For More Information

Books

Conser, James A., and Gregory D. Russell. *Law Enforcement in the United States*. Gaithersburg, MD: Aspen, 2000.

Gaines, Larry K., Victor E. Kappeler, and J. B. Vaughn. *Policing in America*. Cincinnati, OH: Anderson, 1994.

Miller, Wilbur R. *Cops and Bobbies: Police Authority in New York and London, 1830–1870*. Chicago, IL: University of Chicago Press, 1977.

Morn, Frank. *"The Eye That Never Sleeps": A History of the Pinkerton National Detective Agency*. Bloomington, IN: Indiana University Press, 1982.

Oliver, Willard M. *Community-Oriented Policing: A Systematic Approach to Policing*. Upper Saddle River, NJ: Prentice Hall, 2001.

Walker, Samuel. *The Police in America: An Introduction*. New York: McGraw-Hill, 1992.

Web Sites

Court TV's Crime Library: Criminal Minds and Methods. http://www.crimelibrary.com (accessed on August 19, 2004).

"LAPD Had the Nation's First Police Woman." *Los Angeles Almanac*. http://www.losangelesalmanac.com/topics/Crime/cr73b.htm (accessed on August 19, 2004)

15

Crime Laboratories

Crime laboratories offer forensic science services to the criminal justice system. Forensic science applies scientific testing methods and the latest technologies to collect, preserve, process, and analyze evidence. Proof of guilt or innocence is frequently determined by the results of forensic evidence.

Forensic science is a combination of many kinds of knowledge, some of which have existed, however primitive, for centuries. These include weapon identification, fingerprinting, document analysis, chemical identification, and trace analysis of hair and fibers. Two newer disciplines that have become major components of the twenty-first century crime laboratory are DNA analysis and explosive investigation.

The leading forensic laboratory in the world is at the Federal Bureau of Investigation (FBI), located 50 miles outside of Washington, D.C., in Quantico, Virginia. The FBI Laboratory moved from its site in downtown Washington, D.C., to its newly built facility in early 2003. The FBI Lab, with approximately 650 employees, partners with state and local crime laboratories throughout the country to solve criminal cases.

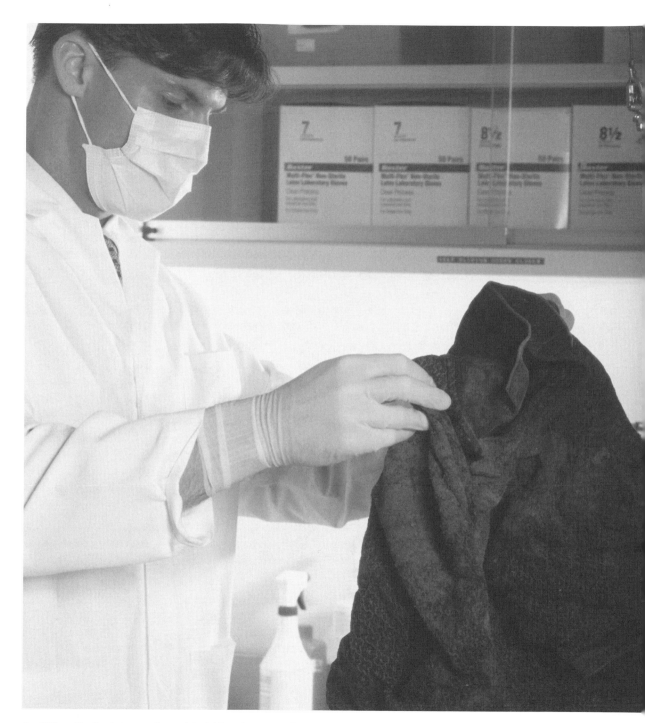

An FBI pathologist examines dried blood on a jacket.

(© Anna Clopet/Corbis)

In this chapter a brief history of forensics is presented, followed by a description of the major types of forensic investigation used in crime labs at the local, state, federal, and private levels. Next is an in-depth look at the FBI Lab, followed by details of how crime lab investigations identified the individuals responsible for a series of sniper attacks that paralyzed the Washington, D.C., area in October 2002.

Historical perspective

The word *forensic* comes from a Latin term meaning "in the court" or "public forum." Forensic science applies scientific knowledge within a court of law. Forensic science has existed for many centuries. Its beginnings can be traced to thirteenth-century China where in 1248 a scientist wrote a book called *Hsi Yüan Lu (The Washing Away of Wrongs)*. The author tell readers to not be surprised if solving a crime comes down to the difference between two hairs.

Although much of what the author discusses relies solely on superstition, *Hsi Yüan Lu* clearly demonstrates aspects of forensic detection that are still used today. For instance, the book discusses the importance of analyzing wounds inflicted on a dead body. Most importantly, the book talks about the need to study the scene of a crime. *Hsi Yüan Lu* teaches that to solve a crime, one must carefully observe all clues.

The Chinese first used fingerprint identification to match documents to their authors in the eighth century. By the nineteenth century four main types of fingerprints were identified: arches, loops, whorls, and composites. Fingerprint patterns proved to be unique to each person. By studying the arches, loops, whorls, and composites, criminalists could compare fingerprints to see if they matched. This idea has not changed and is still the fundamental basis of modern fingerprint technology.

An early famous case of firearm identification came from the Bow Street Runners, a group of policemen in England, who became famous because of their success in catching criminals. In 1835 one of the Bow Street Runners, Henry Goddard, was called to the scene of a shooting. After the lead bullet was removed from the dead man, Goddard examined it and found a distinctive ridge. By comparing the marks on bullets from the firearms from several suspects, Goddard determined the source of the bullet and arrested the guilty party. Following Goddard's lead, many cases involving firearms were solved by the careful analysis of the marks left behind on spent bullets or casings.

Another ancient scientific study involved poisons. The word toxicology comes from the Greek word *toxicon,* which means poison. Greek physician Hippocrates (c. 460–380 B.C.E.) introduced toxicology by describing the use and effects of poisons. In the Middle Ages (c. 500–c. 1500), an Italian noblewoman named Catherine de Medici (1518–1589) experimented with poisons by giving them to people of the lower class and then recording their reactions. In the nineteenth century a Spanish physician named Mathieu Joseph Bonaventura Orfila (1787–1853) was the first scientist to introduce chemical analysis as proof of poisoning in a court of law.

A criminal records specialist uses the computer to check fingerprints online. *(AP/Wide World Photos)*

Crime laboratories

In 1910 Professor Edmund Locard (1877–1966) of the University of Lyons, France, established the first crime lab based upon the idea that criminals leave behind traces of themselves with every crime. Using Locard's principles, Los Angeles, California, police chief August Vollmer (1875–1955) established one of the first modern crime laboratories in the United States in 1923.

Vollmer recognized the need to establish a reliable way of analyzing clues from a crime scene. Chief Vollmer modernized not only the Los Angeles Police Department but law enforcement in general by introducing the use of: (1) a crime investigation laboratory; (2) a fingerprint and handwriting classification system; (3) a workable system for filing information about the way a crime was committed; and, (4) the creation of a police school where scientists would teach courses in the study of criminal behavior or criminology.

The Bureau of Investigation, renamed the Federal Bureau of Investigation in 1935, continued Vollmer's work in 1932 with the creation of the first national crime lab in Washington, D.C.

Modern forensic investigations

Firearms and toolmark identification

The identification of firearms and weapon-related evidence has played a critical role in crime investigation throughout the twentieth century. Firearms investigations involve the examination of fired bullets to determine what kind of weapon they were fired from. Examinations can eliminate various firearms until a match between bullet and weapon is made. All pistols, revolvers, and rifles contain "rifling" in the bore, the long protruding part through which a bullet travels. Rifling consists of grooves and markings on the inside surface of the bore. These markings have a right or left twist that varies with each manufacturer.

Rifling studies the path of a bullet according to each weapon's bore. A raised marking on the bullet will correspond to a groove in the bore. In addition to rifling characteristics, each fired bullet has tiny imperfections that reflect the imperfections in the bore. A test bullet fired from the gun investigators believe has been used in a crime must be identical to the bullet taken from the crime scene. If the test bullet and evidence bullet have the exact markings, then the crime weapon has been found. Together rifling and imperfections on the bullet can positively identify the weapon used to fire the bullet. These microscopic, or tiny, characteristics are as individualistic as human fingerprints.

Toolmark identification also falls to firearm specialists. Tools such as prying instruments, screwdrivers, and metal bars, or weapons like knives or axes leave identifying marks. Whether on a safe, a door, or a body, toolmarks help identify specific weapons. Tools generally have trace evidence, such as metal shavings, paint, or in the case of a human victim, blood or other biological substances. In assisting the investigation of a crime, both firearms and tool identification add specific information to a body of evidence.

A firearm and toolmark examiner shows an extracted bullet that was fired into a bullet recovery tank. *(AP/Wide World Photos)*

Latent prints

Latent prints refer to fingerprints, palm prints, and the footprints that are not visible to the unaided eye but can be recovered from a crime scene for study. Forensic print specialists retrieve the prints using powders, chemicals, or special lighting. Gathered latent prints are compared against those of suspects, or if no suspects have been identified, they are compared to hundreds of thousands of prints in a computer database.

Fingerprint identification and comparison has been widely used in criminal investigations since the 1920s and early 1930s. A young J. Edgar Hoover (1895–1972), who worked at the Bureau of Investigation, created a fingerprint database in 1924. At that time 810,188 fingerprint records from Leavenworth Penitentiary in Kansas and the National Bureau of Criminal Identification were combined to form the first FBI file.

Questioned Documents

Identifying who wrote a document and the time a document was written depend on analyzing writing characteristics, ink types, and typewriter, printer, and photocopy characteristics. The Questioned Documents department of the crime laboratories also restores documents that are damaged or have faded over time. One major function of document analysis is to determine forgeries, copies or imitation documents created with the intention of pretending they are authentic documents. Log books, letters, diaries, various legal contracts, checks, wills, notes left at a crime scene, and medical records are typical documents that are analyzed. Chemical analysis of ink, including its age, is used to determine changes, additions, or the rewriting of documents.

Chemistry

One of the oldest and largest sections of a forensic crime lab is the chemistry department. The chemistry department undertakes the demanding task of identifying most solids or liquids crime investigators ask them to analyze. Bullet lead, metals from a disaster scene, paint chips from automobiles and structures, dyes, and biological specimens to test for illegal drugs, prescription drugs, alcohol, poisons, and food products all are examples of substances analyzed.

Crime labs generally divide the chemistry department into various parts. Metallurgy units analyze metals for strength, corrosion, or evidence of being tampered with. Paints are analyzed in another unit. Most chemical analyses are preformed on a wide array of instruments that must be maintained and quality controlled to assure accurate results. Maintenance and quality control are carried out by yet another chemistry section. These chemistry sections provide key pieces to crime puzzles.

The toxicology unit, one of the largest chemistry sections, analyzes biological specimens. Toxicology is the study of toxic or poisonous substances, substances that can produce harm or death to any individual who takes them. The toxicity, or deadliness, depends on the amount ingested by the victim. For example, prescription drugs taken as directed do not generally cause a toxic effect, but overdoses of the same drug can lead to death. Toxins or poisons can be manmade or occur naturally in nature like arsenic.

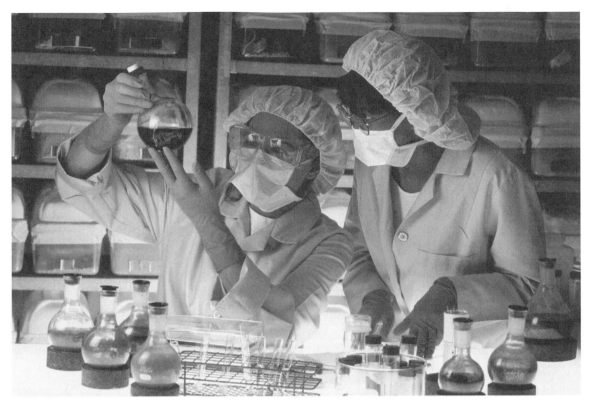

One of the oldest and largest sections of a forensic crime lab is the chemistry department. The chemistry department undertakes the demanding task of identifying most any solid or liquid crime investigators ask them to analyze. *(© Steve Chenn/Corbis)*

For centuries, poisoning was a favored method of murder, and the study of poisons has gone on just as long. In the twentieth and twenty-first centuries, although poison is still used in a few murders and suicides, accidental poisonings are more common. The American Association of Poison Control Centers states that approximately two million poisoning accidents occur every year.

Trace evidence

Trace evidence refers to microscopic or larger materials, commonly hairs or fibers, which are transferred from person to person or object to object during a crime. Examples include human hair, animal hair, wood fibers, clothing fibers, carpet or car seat fibers, rope, and feathers. Also analyzed in a trace

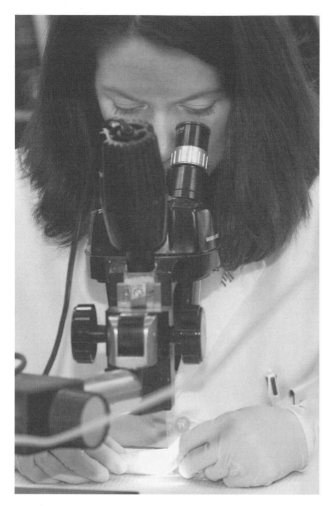

A forensic scientist examines traces taken from a suspect vehicle in a hit-and-run fatality case. Trace evidence refers to microscopic or larger materials, commonly hairs or fibers, which are transferred from person to person or object to object during a crime. *(AP/Wide World Photos)*

evidence laboratory are dental specimens. Forensic dentistry is known as odontology. Physical anthropologists, who study the physical makeup of humans through millions of years, analyze skeletal remains in the trace evidence lab.

DNA

Deoxyribo**n**ucleic **a**cid, or DNA, is the substance that chromosomes are made of. Chromosomes are long connected double strands of DNA that have a structure resembling a twisted ladder. Along the chromosome strands are genes, or the genetic code unique to every person (except in special cases such as identical twins who have the same genetic code). Individuals inherit one strand of the DNA chromosome from their mother and one strand from their father. The paired chromosomes, one from the mother and one from the father, are located in the nucleus of each individual's cells.

After specific laboratory treatment, DNA double strands separate into single strands. When photographed with the aid of high power microscopes and computers, a single DNA strand appears as a long row of light and dark bands that look something like the bar codes on items for sale. The end result is that scientists can compare two DNA samples to see if the bands line up. If there is an exact match, the two samples came from the same person.

When samples from a crime investigation include blood, saliva, and other body fluids, chromosomal DNA is separated into single strands and the bar code of each strand becomes a DNA profile. If the evidence includes tiny or damaged quantities of DNA from hair, bones, teeth, and body fluids then

A DNA lab worker performing the early stages of mitochondrial DNA extraction. *(AP/Wide World Photos)*

another kind of DNA testing can be analyzed and will also produce a unique banded DNA profile.

Explosives

Explosive experts respond to the scene of an explosion or investigate the discovery of an undetonated (unexploded) bomb. They examine and identify parts of bombs. Even if an explosion occurred, the components used to build and detonate the bomb, although damaged, often can still be identified.

Chemicals, switches, wires, and detonators are all characteristic of the builder. The builder may be an individual or a terrorist group. The number of bomb response units has multiplied across the United States since the bombings in Oklahoma City in 1995 and the World Trade Center Towers in

New York City in 1993. The FBI estimates that 85 percent of terrorist activities attempted toward U.S. citizens or interests at the beginning of the twenty-first century involved explosive devices.

FBI crime laboratory

The Federal Bureau of Investigation Laboratory is the most advanced and comprehensive crime laboratory in the world. Not only does it provide scientific evaluations of evidence for U.S. law enforcement agencies, but it also cooperates in sharing information worldwide. The FBI is a federal government agency under the U.S. Department of Justice.

The FBI Lab is made up of twenty-five departments called units organized in two branches, the Forensic Analysis Branch and the Operational Support Branch. The units serve such functions as forensic analysis, scientific analysis, forensic science support, operational response, and operations support. The FBI Lab includes units for firearms and toolmarks, latent prints, questioned documents, chemistry, trace evidence, DNA, and explosives, as well as a wide array of specialized units needed in the twenty-first century. For example, one unit carries out forensic examinations of hazardous materials —chemical, biological, and nuclear. Another unit sends out bomb and crisis response teams that collect and preserve evidence under the most difficult conditions.

There is also a specialized photography unit in the FBI Lab, and a graphics and design unit that recreates exact or scaled down replicas of crime scenes. The FBI Lab Outreach provides educational and training opportunities for lab staff, FBI special agents, local and state law enforcement agencies, and persons involved with forensic laboratories throughout the country.

Forensic analysis

The Latent Prints Unit has two categories of fingerprint holdings, criminal and civil. The criminal fingerprint file contains print records of about 47 million individuals who have been arrested and charged with a crime. The civil files have about 30.7 million print records. Civil prints are made of all employees of the federal government, all members of the U.S. military, those seeking employment in the banking and stock

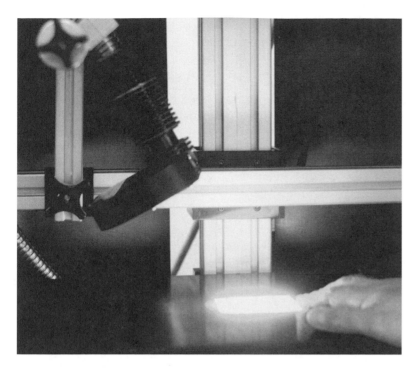

A forensic scientist studying latent fingerprints in front of a filtered green xenon light that is used to highlight chemical images captured on a digital camera. *(AP/Wide World Photos)*

market industry, individuals applying for U.S. citizenship, adopting a child, or working or volunteering at a child or senior daycare center.

The purpose of keeping the civil print database is to perform background checks searching for a criminal history. The FBI shows an average annual hit of 900,000 checks—or 900,000 prints each year submitted to the civil databases are identified persons with a criminal history record. Civil submissions also are checked against wanted persons files and a terrorist watch list.

The FBI receives approximately fifty thousand fingerprint submissions every day. It received a total of 17,736,541 submissions in 2003. Some 48 percent of these submissions were civil and 52 percent criminal. In July 1999 the FBI revolutionized its databases with the Integrated Automated Fingerprint Identification System (IAFIS). Previously, all prints arrived on paper fingerprint cards that had to be processed by hand. With the introduction of IAFIS, prints and pictures can be submitted electronically.

The IAFIS allows personnel of the Latent Print Unit to quickly process requests from law enforcement agencies all over the country for criminal background checks of people arrested or to check prints recovered at crime scenes against those on file. Many identifications have been made when law enforcement had no suspects. Other times suspicion can be lifted from innocent people and the real offender captured.

The Questioned Documents Unit also compiles a number of databases that can be crosschecked. These databases include a Fraudulent (bad) Check File, Bank Robbery Note File, Anonymous Letter File (threatening unsigned letters), and even a Shoeprint File. Three units provide laboratory analysis of evidence: Firearms-Toolmarks, Latent Prints, and Questioned Documents. The Firearms-Toolmarks Unit provides extensive firearm and toolmark identifications on weapons and tools used in crimes. They also restore serial numbers that have been altered or filed off of firearms to hinder identification.

Scientific analysis

The newest unit in the FBI Lab is the Chem-Bio Sciences Unit. Chem-Bio was added in 2003 for the forensic examination of hazardous materials. This unit works closely with the U.S. military, analyzing chemical and biological, even nuclear, substances and is developing portable identification systems to be taken to field locations where incidents have occurred.

The Chemistry Unit is one of the largest with secondary sections consisting of General Chemistry, Toxicology, Paints, Metallurgy, Elemental (analysis of elements such as lead, arsenic, and silicon in glass), and Instrumentation Operation and Support. The Paint Unit has samples of every color of paint used on U.S. automobiles dating back to the 1920s. Every auto manufacturer in the United States must send in paint samples every year. Most foreign manufacturers also submit samples. From tiny smudges of paint the FBI paint sleuths can identify the make, model, and year of any automobile.

DNA profile matches and checks identify murderers and sex offenders often when there had been no suspect. They also release innocent persons from suspicion. The three DNA divisions are the CODIS Unit, DNA Analysis Unit I, and DNA

Analysis Unit II. CODIS stands for Combined DNA Index System. The several CODIS indexes provide (1) a database of DNA profiles from crime scene investigations, (2) a database of DNA profiles of persons convicted of felony sex and other crimes, and later added, (3) a missing persons DNA profile database.

Federal, state, and local forensic laboratories exchange DNA profiles of convicted offenders using CODIS's National DNA Index System (NDIS). The NDIS contained 1,566,552 DNA profiles of convicted offenders as of October 2003. DNA Analysis Unit I (nuclear DNA) and DNA Analysis Unit II (mitochondrial DNA) analyze samples from body fluids such as blood, saliva, semen, and from hair, bones, and teeth.

Forensic science support

The Counterterrorism and Forensic Science Research Unit carries out research activities for all units of the FBI Lab, introducing new and more precise scientific techniques. The constantly evolving methods of this unit help solve crimes and thwart terrorist actions.

The Special Photographic Unit provides a wide range of services such as crime scene photography, surveillance, photography from the air, and aerial mapping. The unit works with traditional photographic processes as well as with digital imaging. In addition, it provides maintenance for photographic equipment throughout the FBI Lab and supports personnel with ongoing training classes.

Operational response

Three units provide some of the FBI's most dramatic services: Bomb Data Center, the Evidence Response Unit, and the Hazardous Materials Response Unit. The Bomb Data Center provides the latest training, techniques, and equipment to local law enforcement bomb squads—those who are the first to respond to threats of explosive and biological weapons.

The Evidence Response Team Unit organizes the activities of Evidence Response Teams (ERTs), made up of FBI special agents trained in evidence recovery from incident sites. ERTs traveled halfway across the world to Piyadh, Saudi Arabia, after vehicle bombs destroyed residential buildings there on May 12, 2003. Twenty-three people, including nine Americans, died in those bombings. ERTs are available to assist foreign

Members of the FBI Evidence Response Team prepare to make their way to a campsite believed to have been used by a bombing suspect. *(AP/Wide World Photos)*

countries when specially requested. ERTs carry out crime scene investigations including evidence collection, the preservation and documentation of that evidence, and also provide photography and fingerprinting.

The Hazardous Materials Response Unit coordinates specialized response teams trained to handle chemical, biological, radiological (radioactive), and nuclear substances. It also oversees national and international training to respond to such materials, and supports FBI response programs located throughout the country. The unit also deals with an increasing caseload of environmental crimes such as the illegal dumping of waste into the nation's waterways.

Operational support

Two units that provide operational support develop fascinating recreations of crime scenes by reconstructing not only buildings, but providing drawings of suspected individuals. The Investigative and Prosecutive Graphics Unit surveys crime scenes, then produces computerized animated scenarios of human movements and actions during a crime. They provide maps, floor plans, diagrams, and timelines, and they are the unit responsible for composite drawings of suspects from victim interviews. The unit can also reconstruct the appearance of individuals from skeletal remains.

The Structural Design Unit supports expert testimony in trials by providing three-dimensional models of crime sites, scale models of vehicles, and models of bomb devices. This unit also provides mannequins of victims for wound locations.

Examples of investigative aids from the Structural Design and Graphics units include the composite drawing of Timothy McVeigh, who bombed the Murrah Federal Building in Oklahoma City; a model of the Murrah Building before and after the bomb blast; a map of Columbine High School in Littleton, Colorado, site of a mass shooting in April 1999; and a model of the cabin where Ted Kaczynski, the notorious "Unabomber," lived in Montana. Until captured Kaczynski mailed sixteen bombs between 1978 and 1995 to selected individuals across the United States killing three and injuring twenty-nine.

Engineering Research Facility

In response to rapidly advancing computer and telecommunications technology, the FBI separated the Forensic Audio, Video, and Image Analysis Unit and the Computer Analysis and Response Team into a new division called the Engineering Research Facility in 2002. The new division is the FBI's cornerstone for counterterrorism and cyber crime (crimes committed by computer, involving the Internet).

The Computer Analysis and Response Team trains and assigns computer specialists to FBI field offices throughout the country. These specialists focus on searching and gathering computer data evidence. The Forensic, Audio, Video, and Image Analysis Unit examines audio, video, and photographic evidence to help solve and prevent crimes.

Solving Old Mysteries

John Wilkes Booth (1838–1865) assassinated U.S. president Abraham Lincoln (1809–1865; served 1861–65) at Ford's Theatre in Washington, D.C., in April 1864. Booth dropped his gun, a single-shot pistol, as he leapt onto the stage and escaped out the back of the theatre. The pistol was put on display in 1940 at the theatre's museum.

In 1997, following the death of a suspected thief, records were discovered that he had stolen Booth's pistol in the 1960s and replaced it with a fake. The U.S. National Park Service, which runs the Ford Theatre Museum, asked the FBI to determine if the museum's pistol was real. Using a photo of the original pistol taken prior to 1960 and the pistol on display, the FBI's Firearms-

Toolmarks Unit and the lab's Special Photographic Unit analyzed the pistol itself, the photograph of the pistol, and historic photographs of other pistols of this type.

The lab compared the museum's pistol to other pistols of the same time period and used a dental material to make a cast of the inside of the gun barrel. The FBI determined that the pistol had a number of unique markings and characteristics including a crack in the wooden part of the gun. These characteristics confirmed the pistol that was in the museum was from the time period of Lincoln's assassination, was not a replica made in later years, and was the actual gun that had killed the president.

Sniper attacks

In October 2002 two individuals carried out sniper attacks in the Washington, D.C., area as well as in Virginia and Maryland. Millions of residents were gripped by fear, worrying that their community would be the next to suffer a deadly sniper attack. The offenders were seventeen-year-old Lee Boyd Malvo and forty-one-year-old John Allen Muhammad.

Between the time Malvo and Muhammad were first identified as the offenders and the conclusion of their trials at the end of 2003, six FBI Lab units cooperated to bring the criminals to justice. The units involved were Latent Prints, DNA Analysis, Trace Evidence, Questioned Documents, Structural Design, and Investigative and Prosecutive Graphics.

Around October 23, 2002, the police department of Montgomery, Alabama, decided to submit fingerprints gathered from the murder of a convenience store clerk to the FBI Latent Print Unit. They suspected whoever carried out the shoot-

An ATF agent searching for evidence in the 2002 Washington, D.C.-area sniper case. *(AP/Wide World Photos)*

ing spree in the Washington, D.C., area might be the same individuals involved in the convenience store murder. FBI personnel entered the fingerprints into the Integrated Automated Fingerprint Identification System (IAFIS) and got a match. The prints belonged to Malvo, who had once been arrested on an immigration violation. Further examination of Malvo's records found another name—John Allen Muhammad. The Latent Print Unit matched Malvo's and Muhammad's fingerprints to items left at the crime scenes. Twelve hours later Malvo and Muhammad were apprehended at a highway rest stop in Maryland.

The FBI's DNA units matched DNA from the crime scenes and from the car of the snipers. The samples matched Malvo and Muhammad and included such evidence as bags, notes, a brown glove, and hairs found in a duffel bag and on a coat from crime scenes, as well as the weapons recovered from the car.

The Trace Evidence Unit matched blue, gray, and white fabric fibers to the car seats of the snipers. Trace Evidence also found brown fibers collected at the crime scenes matching brown gloves, one of which was left at a crime scene, the other one from the car. Questioned Documents analyzed notes written and left at two crime scenes and determined that they were written by the same person who wrote in a manual found in the suspects' car.

Both the Structural Design and Graphics units provided visual reconstructions used as exhibits in trials. Structural Design built a full-sized replica of the snipers' trunk, complete with the specially made hole from which shots could be fired. Graphics produced digital images of the white van and truck originally thought to belong to the suspects; made diagrams of crime sites, their victims, and possible positions of the shooters; and provided a timeline of the sniper attacks.

Both Malvo and Muhammad were found guilty of carrying out the sniper attacks. Malvo, largely because of his young age, received life in prison without parole. Muhammad was sentenced to death.

The FBI Lab units played a major role in the arrest and conviction of Malvo and Muhammad. Many criminal cases, like the D.C. sniper case, involve the cooperation of many departments and units on local, state, and federal levels. They all have the same goal of collecting, preserving, and analyzing all kinds of evidence to bring criminals to justice.

For More Information

Books

Federal Bureau of Investigation. *FBI Laboratory 2003*. Quantico, VA: U.S. Department of Justice, 2003.

Inman, David, and Norah Rudin. *Introduction to Forensic DNA Analysis*. Sarasota, FL: CRC Press, 1997.

Lane, Brian. *Crime and Detection.* New York: Alfred A. Knopf, 1998.

Smyth, Frank. *Cause of Death: The Story of Forensic Science.* New York: Van Nostrand Reinhold Company, 1980.

Web Sites

American Association of Poison Control Centers. http://www.aapcc.org (accessed on August 19, 2004).

Federal Bureau of Investigation (FBI). http://www.fbi.gov (accessed on August 19, 2004).

Human Genome Study Information. http://www.ornl.gov/sci/techresources/ Human_Genome/home.shtml (accessed on August 19, 2004).

16

Criminal Courts

Federal and state governments each consist of three sections: the legislative branch to make laws, the executive branch to carry out the laws, and the judicial branch or court system to resolve legal disputes and administer justice. The U.S. Constitution developed a delicate balance of power between the three branches so one cannot hold sway over either of the other two.

The three branches, however, did not develop equally after the U.S. Constitution was adopted in 1787. The court systems, including criminal courts, were the slowest part of the U.S. government to take form. This lag in development can be traced back to the colonial period prior to the American Revolution (1775–83).

Over the next two centuries, the federal government changed a great deal. By the twenty-first century, criminal courts were the centerpiece of a complex U.S. justice system. With federal courts limited to matters involving federal law, including federal crimes and constitutional issues, state courts enjoyed broader jurisdiction and were the location of most criminal trials. State court decisions could be appealed to

Philadelphia's first city hall, which held the first Supreme Court of the
United States. *(© Bettmann/Corbis)*

federal courts only if they involved questions concerning the U.S. Constitution or federal law.

Criminal courts not only serve to determine guilt or innocence, but also often provide rehabilitation programs and other social services for offenders as well as victims.

Early American courts

During the earliest period of European settlement in North America, the colonial legislative and judicial bodies were not separate. Legislative bodies often judged major cases; as a result, the same assembly that made laws also heard cases challenging those laws. No separation of power existed between these two governmental functions.

Local magistrates (officers of the court) heard lesser or minor cases. Magistrates were usually prominent people from within the community, though not legally trained judges. This judicial arrangement was quite different from England and Europe where criminal courts were well established.

Throughout the eighteenth century the colonial legal system, including the courts, developed more completely though were still not politically independent from other parts of government. Sometimes the colonial legislatures would overrule court decisions. Appeals of colonial court decisions also often went back to England for review. Improvement of the court system was not a major issue with colonists.

The Articles of Confederation, written in 1781 to form a temporary government until the U.S. Constitution could be adopted, did not even mention a national court system. Similarly, most of the thirteen newly forming state governments focused more on the duties of the executive and legislative branches of government. State courts seemed less important, and some even argued against creating independent courts.

The Constitution and the courts

Following independence from Great Britain in 1783, the U.S. Constitution finally established a national court system. It called for a U.S. Supreme Court and gave Congress the power to establish lower courts as it saw fit. Federal judges served the courts for life and could only be removed if impeached (put on trial for specific crimes against the government) and convicted by Congress. The U.S. president had the responsibility to make selections for federal judge positions and send the nominations to the Senate for approval. The Senate Judiciary Committee carried out an investigation of the nominees and heard arguments for and against each selection.

The Constitution also determined what cases federal courts would have authority to hear. These included all cases raising issues over constitutional or federal law, federal treaties, or cases between people in different states, between a state and a person in another state, or between two states. Courts did not serve in an advisory role to the legislature as courts do in other countries. Some foreign courts review proposed laws before they are enacted to determine their constitutionality. In addition, if a U.S. federal court determines a court issue is primarily political, known as a political question, then the court refers the case to the other two branches to resolve the case if they choose.

Creating a national court system

After the American Revolution, the new U.S. Congress adopted the Constitution and immediately passed the Judiciary Act of 1789. The act defined the role of the Supreme Court and its six justices. It also created three federal circuit courts and fourteen federal district courts. Each state had at least one federal district court with one district court judge. The circuit courts did not have their own judges; instead, two Supreme Court justices "rode the circuit," or covered the area along with a local district court judge. Major cases went straight to the circuit courts while district courts heard the lesser cases.

The act gave state courts jurisdiction to hear cases involving federal law issues. If a state court ruled a federal law unconstitutional, then the case could be appealed to a federal court. The act also created the positions of U.S. Attorney, Attorney General, and U.S. Marshals. Marshals were charged with providing security in federal courts and carrying out court orders.

Developments in the court system were limited for the next century. With new states joining the union, the number of federal circuit courts increased to ten by the American Civil War (1861–65). After the war the U.S. court system began

In 1789 President George Washington appointed Edmund Jennings Randolph the first attorney general of the United States. *(The Library of Congress)*

changing more substantially. The Removal Act of 1871 expanded federal court jurisdiction over all cases involving federal issues. What had become the controversial requirement that Supreme Court justices sit on circuit courts finally ended in 1891.

Congress replaced the original circuit courts with nine circuit courts of appeal with their own judges. In 1925 Congress reduced the number of appeals the Supreme Court was required to hear in a year. Establishing a formal screening process, it required petitioners (those wishing to be heard by the courts on some issue) to obtain a *writ certiorari,* or court order, from the Supreme Court to have their case accepted.

By the late twentieth century federal and state court systems were much more complex including highly specialized courts. Courts held an important position in the criminal justice system. Much of this distinction came following a series of Supreme Court decisions in the 1960s protecting the civil liberties of defendants (persons accused of a crime). Federal and state courts became much more active in supervising procedures used in other parts of the criminal justice system. These included how law enforcement agencies searched properties, seized evidence, conducted interrogations, and even how inmates were treated in correctional facilities. Criminals could be tried in state or federal courts, or both since they could appeal state court decisions to federal courts if federal laws or constitutional issues were involved.

Federal courts

The modern federal court system consists of: (1) the U.S. Supreme Court with one chief justice and eight associate justices; (2) twelve regional circuit courts of appeals and a court of appeals in the District of Columbia that reviews rulings of the district courts; and, (3) ninety-four federal district courts where original criminal cases involving federal law or other jurisdictions established by the Constitution are heard.

In 2004 there were 679 district judges and 179 circuit judges. Federal judges are often former state judges, legal scholars, or state and federal prosecutors. U.S. presidents select federal judges based on political party membership or for gender or race considerations. In addition, Congress used its constitutional authority to establish a series of lower federal courts such as the U.S. Court of Claims, the U.S. Tax Court, and the U.S. Court of Military Appeals.

District courts

District courts are trial courts for both criminal and original civil suits. Each state has at least one district court, and some—including New York, Texas, and California—have as many as four. No state boundary divides a district court jurisdiction, since they hear both jury trials and bench (where the judge determines guilt) trials. Jury trials make use of a jury formed from members of the public who determine guilt or innocence. Judges make rulings on legal questions that arise during the trial, but otherwise they remain impartial unless it is a bench trial.

Structure of Federal Courts

Ninety-six federal district courts exist throughout the United States. Twenty-six states have one district court, twelve states have two, nine states have three, and three states have four.

For the federal courts of appeal, the First Circuit Court of Appeals includes Maine, Massachusetts, New Hampshire, Rhode Island, and Puerto Rico; the Second Circuit Court includes Connecticut, New York, and Vermont; the Third Circuit Court covers Delaware, New Jersey, Pennsylvania, and the Virgin Islands; the Fourth Circuit Court covers Maryland, North Carolina, South Carolina, Virginia, and West Virginia; the Fifth Circuit Court covers Louisiana, Mississippi, and Texas; the Sixth Circuit Court covers Kentucky, Michigan, Ohio, and Tennessee; the Seventh Circuit Court covers Illinois, Indiana, and Wisconsin; the Eighth Circuit Court covers Arkansas, Iowa, Minnesota, Missouri, Nebraska, North Dakota, and South Dakota; the Ninth Circuit Court covers Alaska, Arizona, California, Hawaii, Idaho, Montana, Nevada, Oregon, Washington, Guam, and the Northern Marianas; the Tenth Circuit Court covers Colorado, Kansas, New Mexico, Oklahoma, Utah, and Wyoming; and the Eleventh Circuit Court covers Alabama, Florida, and Georgia.

During the 1960s crime rates including violent offenses greatly increased. To help with the growing caseload, Congress created magistrate judges to assist district court judges. Magistrates were appointed by district judges for eight-year terms. Each district judge determined the responsibilities of its magistrates. In general, magistrates have issued arrest and search warrants, set bail, conducted pretrial hearings, and heard misdemeanor cases. By the late 1990s, federal district courts were hearing from 295,000 to 320,000 cases per year. About 20 percent, or 62,000 cases, were criminal, which included some 50,000 felony cases and 12,000 misdemeanor cases.

To assist judges, federal district courts have law clerks, attorneys, marshals, secretaries, and probation officers. Each federal district has a U.S. attorney and a number of assistant U.S. attorneys. The U.S. president nominates the U.S. attorneys and the Senate confirms them. Each U.S. attorney then selects assistant attorneys, and they usually change every time a new president is elected and comes into office. The U.S. attorney is the top federal law enforcement officer in the district and is directly involved in any court cases of which the United States is a party.

Each federal district also has a U.S. marshal, who like U.S. attorneys are nominated by the president and confirmed by the Senate. The marshals provide court security, deliver court papers, transport federal prisoners, operate the federal witness protection program, and enforce federal court orders.

Built in 1772, the Olde Colonial Courthouse, in Cape Cod, Massachusetts, is the site of the famous protest march of September 1774 held in opposition to the king's court. (© Lee Snider/Corbis)

Appeals courts

The appellate courts do not hear original cases, they only review lower court decisions. Appeals court judges determine which cases they will accept and how they will proceed, either as full trials or through a more limited review process. Normally a panel of three appellate judges hears a case, and then, after discussion, makes a ruling. There are no juries. Each federal appellate court includes several states. No state is divided between appellate circuits.

The Supreme Court is the last resort in the appeals process. It often makes case decisions, known as landmark rulings, directly affecting how federal and state courts conduct their proceedings.

(AP/Wide World Photos)

The Supreme Court

The Supreme Court is the last resort in the appeals process. It often makes case decisions, known as landmark rulings, directly affecting how federal and state courts conduct their proceedings. The Supreme Court receives around eight thousand cases a year for review but actually hears full oral arguments for less than one hundred.

State courts

State courts systems operate independently of federal courts, but are structured much like the federal system with the multiple levels of trial courts, appellate courts, and a high court, usually called a state supreme court. States also have more specialized courts than found in the federal system.

Most cases in the United States, including criminal cases, go to state courts. State courts hear almost one hundred million cases annually. They decide disputes between individuals, between an individual and the state or local government, and between different governmental agencies. State court decisions cannot be reviewed by federal courts unless some federal or constitutional question is involved.

Each state court system is different, influenced by each state's unique history and society. The state's constitution and laws establish the structure and operation of its courts, all within general limits set by federal law and the U.S. Constitution. The court systems of forty-nine states are based on English common law like the federal government, however Louisiana is not. Due to its French history, Louisiana's criminal justice system is based on civil laws that operate quite differently including a more active role of judges during trials. Despite their independence, some common features do exist among the court systems of all U.S. states.

Lower courts

Most state courts are lower courts with limited jurisdiction. They deal with both criminal and civil matters that are neither serious nor complex. These courts are less formal, normally do not record their proceedings, rarely have juries, and do not have attorneys involved.

Lower courts hear a high volume of cases including minor criminal cases. These are usually misdemeanors for shoplifting, traffic violations, vandalism (damaging property), and writing bad checks. Lower court judges do not have to be licensed lawyers. Decisions from the lower courts can be appealed to district courts, and in some cases, a new trial will be ordered.

Trial courts

Trial courts frequently have general jurisdiction and hear all cases not reserved for other special state courts with limited jurisdiction. The general trial courts, known as superior courts in many states, hear the more serious criminal and civil cases including most felony criminal cases. In these courts, the judge must be a licensed attorney, court records are kept, the proceedings are formal, and most trials use juries.

As in federal district courts, many people assist the judges. Court reporters produce transcripts (a written record) of court proceedings. Court clerks perform such tasks as issuing marriage licenses and automobile registrations. Law clerks work for state court judges and staff attorneys work at larger courts. Bailiffs and court officers maintain order as well as custody of the jury and the prisoners.

Appellate courts

All states have at least one high court or supreme court to hear appeals. Texas and Oklahoma both have separate high courts for criminal and civil cases. State supreme courts have from five to nine members on the bench, with most having seven.

Most states also have appellate courts, though eleven states do not. Like the federal appeals courts, the state appeals courts usually have three judges sit as a panel to hear and decide cases. The number of appellate court judges varies from three in a few states to eighty-eight in California.

Parts of a trial are often recorded by a court reporter on a stenographic machine, seen here. *(AP/Wide World Photos)*

Selecting state judges

The process for selecting state trial and appellate court judges varies greatly among the states. Some are elected by political party and others are appointed by a state's legislature. The same is true for selecting state high court judges. The terms of office can also be quite different among states and between court levels. Appellate court judges usually enjoy longer terms than trial court judges.

State trial court judges generally serve from four- to six-year terms though in some states they can serve until seventy years of age. Some states have life-long terms for high court judges like the federal government. Because of the elected and political appointment processes used for selecting state court judges, these court systems often play a major role in state politics.

Special state courts

In addition to the basic system of lower, superior, appellate, and high courts, states have added special jurisdiction courts through the years. These include juvenile courts, drug courts, and domestic violence courts.

Juvenile courts

Illinois was the first state to establish a separate court system for juveniles in 1899, influenced by social worker Jane Addams (1860–1935). In the following decades other states followed. During this period, the courts and the public favored rehabilitation or treatment over punishment for young offenders. Juvenile state courts became increasingly involved in family issues. The main goal of juvenile courts has always been to do what is best for the child; for this reason the courts are less formal, judges have more flexibility, and the records of juvenile offenders are usually kept confidential or "sealed."

Most juvenile courts have jurisdiction over cases that would be crimes for adult offenders, as well as various other violations. Since most states set the age at which a person becomes an adult as eighteen, juvenile courts are for offenders seventeen and under in most states. An offender's age sometimes becomes a factor depending on the kind of crime committed.

In the 1960s the U.S. Supreme Court issued several rulings to further protect the rights of offenders in adult courts. Many feared juveniles were not receiving the same benefits because of the more informal nature of juvenile courts. By protecting juveniles from the harshness of the adult criminal justice system, young offenders were sometimes denied due process protections as well. As a result, adults had more constitutional safeguards than juveniles yet could endure much harsher sentences, including the death penalty in some states.

By the late 1960s the Supreme Court made three decisions to protect juveniles. The decision gave youthful offenders the right to be informed of charges against them, the right to a lawyer, the right not to incriminate themselves (to withhold information that indicates their guilt), and the right to cross examine witnesses.

The courts also increased the level of evidence needed to convict youths in criminal cases, from simply needing a preponderance (a large amount) of evidence to actually being able to prove guilt beyond a reasonable doubt, as in adult criminal courts. Jury trials, however, were still not required for juveniles. Despite the increased legal protections in juvenile courts, many judges still maintained a less formal process.

As the fear of youth crime increased through the 1980s, many people believed dangerous youngsters were too protected by the juvenile justice system. More and more youthful offenders started being transferred to adult criminal courts. The public was repeatedly exposed to the highly publicized occurrences of tragic school shootings across the country in the 1990s. As a result, the public perception of rising youth crime remained throughout the decade, even though youth crime actually decreased substantially during this period. The result was that juvenile courts were less distinct from adult criminal courts than earlier in the twentieth century.

Social worker Jane Addams had a strong influence in the development of a separate court system for juveniles. *(AP/Wide World Photos)*

Drug courts

During much of the 1970s the federal government fought rising drug use in the nation through treatment programs and discouraging drug use among youth. When Ronald Reagan (1911–; served 1981–89) entered the White House, however, the emphasis switched from treatment to prosecution. The number of arrests, prosecutions, and imprisonments rose dramatically and continued throughout the 1990s. The number of criminal arrests increased 168 percent from 1980 to 1998, while the number of prison inmates increased 300 percent. Drug cases swamped the criminal courts.

To relieve the high caseload, states created drug treatment courts for nonviolent offenders with no previous criminal record. The first drug court was established in Miami, Florida, in 1989, followed by another in Oakland, California, in 1991.

Drug courts operate with the belief that drug addiction is treatable. In criminal courts, judges cannot address defendants directly; yet in drug courts judges personally supervise their defendants and are involved in their treatment. Judges even check on their defendants during treatment.

Drug courts provide psychological support while helping individuals take responsibility for their own recovery. If an offender relapses back into use, drug courts increase punishment and require additional treatment programs. This can happen several times with a single case. If the offender successfully completes a treatment program, they will not have a criminal record. If an offender fails to complete a treatment program, however, a criminal conviction will go on his or her record. For cases that do end up in criminal court, if the offender pleads guilty and still successfully completes a drug treatment program, the sentence will be reduced.

By 2000 some five hundred jurisdictions had drug courts. Between 1989 and 2000 approximately two hundred thousand drug offenders participated in court sponsored treatment programs. The effectiveness of drug courts has been proven through several studies which found that participants had much lower relapse (falling back into bad habits) rates than those who went through standard criminal courts.

Domestic violence courts

By the late twentieth century domestic violence became one of the major issues facing criminal courts. Domestic violence, or abuse by one's partner, is one of the leading causes of injuries in women between the ages of fifteen and forty-four. By the early 2000s domestic violence courts were the fastest growing kind of specialized courts in the United States.

International Criminal Courts

Atrocities of World War II such as the death camps in Nazi Germany raised the issue of creating an international criminal system in the late 1940s. The United Nations created the Genocide Convention, which in turn established genocide as an international crime. It was illegal to destroy a group of people based on national, ethnic, religious, or racial criteria.

During the Cold War, however, interest in international war crimes declined until ethnic-based killings occurred in the former Yugoslavia in the early 1990s. The UN Security Council established a court or tribunal to try Yugoslavian war crimes. In 1994 it created another court to prosecute those involved in mass killings in Rwanda, Africa.

These tribunals increased the debate once again about establishing a permanent world court, rather than creating new tribunals whenever a crisis occurred.

In 1998 over one hundred members of the United Nations approved the new International Criminal Court (ICC). The ICC was to be located in The Hague, Netherlands. The process to ratify or approve the ICC by a required number of nations ran into the early twenty-first century. The court was originally supposed to have criminal jurisdiction over genocide (the attempt to kill or wipe out an entire ethnic group), crimes against humanity, serious war crimes, and other undefined criminal aggression.

As domestic violence cases multiplied, Congress passed the Violence Against Women Act in 1994. The resulting Domestic Violence Task Force assisted state courts in addressing this complex issue and helped raise public awareness of the problem. From 1989 to 1998 domestic violence cases increased 178 percent. Using drug courts as a model, states created the specialized courts to handle the various dimensions of domestic violence cases in a coordinated manner, offering a range of services to both offenders and victims.

Courts monitor domestic violence cases to establish priorities. Social workers are involved to rehabilitate offenders, provide assistance to victims, and make sure children are not placed in dangerous situations. Other aspects such as divorce, child custody and support, drug dependency, juvenile delinquency, and criminal prosecutions are all addressed by the court. Various local organizations such as shelters for battered women and counseling agencies are brought into the legal proceedings.

Judges believed bringing all aspects of a domestic violence case into one court would prove more efficient and less painful for the victim. Offenders were more likely to obey court orders knowing they would face the same judge again if they failed to comply. In addition, judges set up monitoring programs to review offenders and their progress on a regular basis.

Prosecutors and defenders

Federal and state criminal courts follow precise rules of law to ensure the fairness of their proceedings regardless of a defendant's race, religious or political beliefs, or who they associate with. The courts do, however, have flexibility. Judges make decisions at every step on how a trial will proceed. Such decisions include how and where a defendant is held, jury selection, the trial itself—including what evidence may be allowed—and sentencing. Two defendants charged with similar crimes may have totally different experiences due to the details of their case and the judge presiding over their trial.

Criminal trials are based on an adversarial system, which means the prosecutor and defense attorney present their arguments and evidence concerning the guilt or innocence of the defendant within the framework of very precise rules. The adversarial process is designed to ensure fairness, giving both sides the opportunity to make their case.

Prosecutors, often known as district attorneys or prosecuting attorneys in federal courts, are public officials who represent the government in criminal cases. They are often elected or appointed to their positions. In state courts, prosecutors may be the state attorney general. Prosecutors are responsible for guiding a case from beginning to end; they start by filing charges against a defendant, attend the arraignment (a formal reading of the charges before a judge), participate in bail hearings, present the case at trial, and attend sentencing if the defendant is found guilty. Since the court system could not handle the caseload created if every case led to charges and a trial, prosecutors must decide what charges will be filed, if any, against whom. They usually select cases with the best chances of conviction.

The person charged with a crime, the defendant, is represented by a defense attorney. The defense attorney is respon-

A lawyer addressing the jury. Judges make decisions at every step on how a trial will proceed. Such decisions include how and where a defendant is held, jury selection, the trial itself—including what evidence may be allowed—and sentencing. *(© Steve Chenn/Corbis)*

sible for seeing that the constitutional rights of the defendant are protected and for presenting the best possible defense. The defense attorney represents the person from the time of arrest through sentencing (if found guilty) and may decide to appeal the case.

The Sixth Amendment to the Constitution provides anyone accused of a crime the right to a defense attorney in federal cases. If a person cannot afford to hire a defense attorney, then the federal government provides one. States also provide attorneys for the poor if the criminal charges lead to imprisonment. Public defenders are attorneys appointed by the court for offenders who cannot afford their own lawyers. Sometimes public defenders are well-known private defense attorneys who provide services for free, known as working "pro bono."

A defendant accompanied by his court-appointed defense lawyer. If a person cannot afford to hire a defense attorney, then the federal government provides one. *(AP/Wide World Photos)*

Bringing a case to trial

A criminal case normally proceeds through several stages. Following arrest, a defendant is held in custody and booked, meaning personal information is recorded about the individual including fingerprints and a photograph. The defendant is usually questioned or interrogated, probably with a lawyer present. The police then turn any evidence they have over to the prosecutor.

If the case involves a serious felony federal crime, the U.S. Constitution requires that a prosecutor presents the evidence to a grand jury. Grand juries are composed of citizens chosen from the community who determine in a closed (not open to the public) hearing if there is probable cause or enough evidence to have a trial. Only prosecutors present evidence in grand jury hearings; lawyers are not allowed nor do they try to defend their clients.

About half the U.S. states hold grand juries while the others hold preliminary hearings before lower court judges. In preliminary hearings, the defendant may be present and contest the prosecutor's charges. Grand juries and preliminary hearings are not held for lesser crimes or misdemeanors.

Court proceedings begin when a prosecutor files a complaint (if a misdemeanor) or submits a bill of indictment from a grand jury (for felonies) to the court with jurisdiction. The complaint or indictment formally asks the court to take the case. If the court accepts the case from the prosecutor, the defendant is brought in for an arraignment before the court that will try the case. The charges are read, the defendant is advised of his or her rights, a trial date is set, and bail is considered.

Bail is the money defendants pay to ensure their appearance for trial, allowing them freedom until then. If the defendant does not appear for trial, he or she loses the money (the court gets to keep it). If the defendant cannot afford bail or the judge refuses bail, then the defendant remains in custody or jail until trial. If the defendant is considered a respected member of the community, he or she is usually released on his or her "own recognizance," meaning the defendant is released from custody on the merits of his or her honor or good character and not forced to post bail.

Seeking a decision

After arraignment, the prosecutor usually meets with the defendant and defense attorney to discuss a possible plea bargain. In a plea bargain, the defendant pleads guilty in return for reduced charges, a smaller sentence, or some other consideration. Throughout the process the judge, prosecutor, and public defender or defense attorney work together to help the case move as quickly as possible. Plea bargains are reached in over 90 percent of criminal cases, few actually go to trial. This is one point in the system where fairness between wealthy and poor defendants is difficult to achieve. Wealthy defendants can afford more than one defense attorney, often putting together a team of attorneys who work aggressively on their behalf.

If a plea bargain cannot be reached, a case goes to court. The process of deciding a case in court is called adjudication. The defendant can be found guilty or innocent, or if no verdict can be reached, it is called a "hung jury." With a hung jury, the defendant may face a retrial. If the defendant is found guilty, the judge determines if the defendant will go to jail (if the sentence is less than one year), prison (if the sentence is over one year), pay a fine, or get court supervision known as probation (no jail or prison time). In the early 2000s less than 40 percent of all defendants convicted of a crime in state and federal courts were sent to jail or prison.

Once sentencing is complete, the defendant can appeal the case to an appellate court. The appeal must be based on trial procedures, such as improper use of evidence or some other point on which the presiding judge might have made an error. In general, if a defendant is found guilty, he or she is turned over to correctional authorities after the verdict is read. In some special courts, a judge may stay involved in the case even after the sentencing phase.

For More Information

Books

Baum, Lawrence. *American Courts.* 5th ed. Boston, MA: Houghton Mifflin, 2001.

Buzawa, Eve, and Carl Buzawa. *Domestic Violence: The Criminal Justice Response.* Thousand Oaks, CA: Sage, 1996.

Carp, Robert A., and Ronald Stidham. *The Federal Courts.* Washington, DC: CQ Press, 1998.

Carp, Robert A., and Ronald Stidham. *Judicial Process in America.* 5th ed. Washington, DC: CQ Press, 2001.

Mays, G. Larry, and Peter R. Gregware. *Courts and Justice.* Prospect Heights, IL: Waveland Press, 2000.

Patrick, John J. *The Young Oxford Companion to the Supreme Court of the United States.* New York: Oxford University Press, 1998.

Web Sites

"Domestic Violence." *U.S. Department of Justice.* http://www.usdoj.gov/domesticviolence.htm (accessed on August 19, 2004)

National Center for State Courts. http://www.ncsconline.org (accessed on August 19, 2004).

U.S. Courts. http://www.uscourts.gov (accessed on August 19, 2004).

17

Corrections

Apprehension, examination before a judge, and correction are the three components of the U.S. criminal justice system. Apprehension, the investigation and arrest of an individual suspected of committing a crime, is the responsibility of police and other law enforcement agencies. Once apprehended, an individual moves to the court system where a judge or jury listens to all sides of the case and decides on guilt or innocence. If found guilty, the convicted defendant is sentenced by the judge to some form of punishment. Once sentenced, the defendant enters the correctional process for punishment.

The legal term for sentence is "disposition." Disposition ranges from fines to imprisonment in a large, tightly guarded correctional facility. The history of an individual's behavior and the seriousness of the crime are significant factors used in determining the type of punishment.

Courts look carefully at a defendant's past criminal behavior. A first-time offender may be given a lighter sentence than a habitual or repeat offender. For example, if a gun was used in a robbery, placing victims at considerable risk of bod-

Entrance to the Valley State Prison for Women in Chowchilla, California. The prison was the site of a 2000 state hearing over inadequate medical treatment for women inmates in California prisons. *(AP/Wide World Photos)*

ily harm, a tougher sentence would be handed down than for robbery without using a gun.

Fines, restitution, and community service are common punishments for minor crimes. Fines are based on and taken from an offender's daily income. Restitution is a cash amount paid by the offender to the victim to make up for the victim's loss, like making an offender pay a portion of an injured victim's medical expenses. With community service, offenders pay back the community rather than a specific victim. Courts may order offenders to work for a certain number of hours in local public service organizations or for charitable groups that help their community.

Disposition for more serious crimes called felonies falls into several categories: probation, incarceration (confinement) in a jail or prison, or time in a community-based correctional facility or program. The final two stages of the correctional process are parole or release at the end of a completely served sentence. Most convicted individuals do not serve out their full correctional sentence but are paroled earlier. Parole allows an inmate to leave a correctional facility before serving out his or her full sentence. Upon returning to the community, the parolee is supervised by a parole officer for the remaining sentence period.

Probation

Probation is the most common form of correctional punishment for criminal activity. It allows an offender to stay within the community, but under the supervision of a probation officer. Approximately 61 percent of convicted individuals are sentenced to probation. In 2002, there were 3,995,165 adults on probation in the United States.

A judge is never required by law to issue a sentence of probation; it is only given after all aspects of a crime have been considered. Sentencing laws demand that judges make specific determinations about each convicted defendant, such as if this person is a danger to the community. If not, and the judge believes the offender is sorry for his or her crime and will be a law abiding citizen in the future, probation is an appropriate sentence.

Once an offender receives probation, he or she is immediately assigned a probation officer. Conditions of probation

Rich Crawford, North Dakota chief federal probation officer. Probation is the most common form of correctional punishment for criminal activity, allowing an offender to stay within the community under the supervision of a probation officer. *(AP/Wide World Photos)*

are set down by the judge in a contract the offender must agree to and sign. The contract lists the kind of behavior (both prohibited and required) the offender must follow during the probation period. Examples of probationary conditions include not owning or possessing a firearm or drinking alcoholic beverages; meeting with the probation officers at assigned times; attending counseling or drug therapy sessions; reporting any changes of address or in living arrangements; and submitting to regular drug testing. Failing to follow the conditions of probation or committing another crime can result in its withdrawal and the offender being sent to jail or prison.

The advantages of a probation sentence over incarceration include allowing the offender to work in the community, earn

Famous Prisons

Leavenworth Federal Penitentiary is the largest maximum-security prison in the United States. Located fifteen miles north of Kansas City in Leavenworth, Kansas, it began accepting inmates in 1903. Leavenworth was the first federal penitentiary. During its century of use, Leavenworth has housed such famous outlaws as "Machine Gun" Kelly and Robert F. Stroud, who later became known as the "Bird Man of Alcatraz" where he was later moved.

Alcatraz, meaning pelican, is located on an island in San Francisco Bay. It was the first permanent U.S. Army military fort on the West Coast beginning in the early 1850s, then became a military prison in the early 1860s. In 1933 and 1934 it was transformed into a prison for the nation's most dangerous criminals. Alcatraz, also known as the Rock, was essentially escape-proof because it was surrounded by shark-infested waters. Alcatraz operated until 1963 when it was closed. In 2000 it became part of the Golden Gate National Recreation Area and a major tourist attraction.

San Quentin State Prison, located in Marin County, California, just north of San Francisco, is California's oldest prison. Pris-

money to support his or her family, and to have the support of friends and family while attending counseling sessions. Probation costs the state only a fraction of what a jail or prison term costs. Offenders are also spared exposure to the harshness of prison life and the hardened criminals who live there.

Disadvantages of probation include the fear of community residents who believe convicted criminals should not be back on the street because they might commit other crimes. Another concern is how inconsistent probation sentences and probation officers can be in their treatment of offenders. Some counties may send offenders to jail for the same crime where others are given probation. Similarly, probation officers may be very strict in one area and very lax in another. While one officer might report the failure to attend a therapy session as a probation violation, another might overlook the absence.

Incarceration

Persons sentenced to jail or prison are imprisoned within the U.S. penal system. Jails are generally operated locally by oners finished building San Quentin in 1854. They were housed offshore on a boat while constructing the prison. In 1893 it became California's execution site. Hanging was the standard means for execution until 1938 when the gas chamber came into use. Although a maximum security prison for over one hundred years, by 2000 San Quentin was serving as a medium security facility for six thousand inmates.

Sing Sing Correctional Facility is a state prison located in Ossining, New York, and took its name from that village. Built in 1825, Sing Sing became known for executing death row prisoners by electrocution. Between 1914 and 1971 all of the state of New York's executions took place in the prison's electric chair. Sing Sing remained a maximum security facility for male offenders.

Attica Correctional Facility, a state prison located in Attica, New York, has held many of New York's worst criminals since it opened in 1933. It is best known for a bloody prison riot in 1971 that resulted in forty-two deaths—thirty-one inmates and eleven prison guards. It is the only U.S. prison that uses a tear gas system piped throughout the facility to quiet conflicts. Attica holds many criminals who have been sentenced to lengthy prison terms—often twenty-five years to life—for committing murder.

counties or cities; they confine offenders convicted of misdemeanors (minor crimes) whose sentences are for less than one year. They also hold persons awaiting court proceedings such as a trial. There are approximately three thousand jails in the United States, some confine only a small number of prisoners while others hold thousands. Prisons are operated by federal and state authorities plus a few private corporations. They hold offenders convicted of felonies (major crimes) whose sentences are more than one year.

State and federal prisons—called minimum, medium, or maximum-security prisons—vary in their characteristics. Minimum-security prison camps may have no walls or fences and hold only nonviolent offenders who do not pose much of an escape risk. In maximum security facilities, prisoners spend up to twenty-three hours of each day in their individual cells, are heavily guarded, and are considered "escape proof." These prisons hold America's most dangerous and violent criminals.

Beginning in the mid-1980s private corporations provided a new source of prisons. Federal and state governments signed

Boot Camp Prisons

Boot camp prisons, often referred to as shock incarceration camps, provide intense short-term (from 90 to 120 days) incarceration for young, generally nonviolent, offenders. Just as the name "boot camp" implies, the centers employ strict military drills, discipline, and require hard physical labor. They also provide special education, counseling, and drug treatment. Boot camps are another type of alternative incarceration relieving prison overcrowding. Their effectiveness in deterring repeat offenders was still under study at the beginning of the twenty-first century.

contracts with these private companies to house offenders, usually for minimum and medium security facilities, but not maximum-security prisons. The two best-known private correction companies that run over half of the private facilities are Wackenhut Corrections Corporation and Corrections Corporation of America. At the beginning of the twenty-first century private companies accounted for approximately 5 percent of the prison population.

Growing jail and prison populations

According to the U.S. Department of Justice, Bureau of Justice Statistics, there were 2,033,331 inmates incarcerated in local jails and federal, state, and private prisons in 2002. This figure represented a rate of 701 persons in custody for every 100,000 persons in the United States. Federal prisons held 151,618 individuals; state prisons held 1,209,640; local jails held 665,475; and inmates in privately operated facilities numbered 6,598. In 1990, there were 1,148,702 inmates in federal state prisons and local jails, representing a rate of 458 for every 100,000 persons. In 1980, however, there were only 329,821 total incarcerated persons.

The rapid increase in prisoners directly relates to the "Get Tough on Crime" legislation passed on both the federal and state levels. In the early 1990s both federal and state governments began what came to be called a "War on Drugs." This "war" was a reaction to a huge increase in drug related offenses throughout the United States. Many states passed legislation to lengthen prison stays for drug offenders, for both first-time and repeat offenders. In 2002 approximately 58 percent of prison inmates were convicted on drug related charges.

States also passed guidelines limiting parole for convicted criminals, creating minimum prison sentences for certain violent felonies, and establishing long required prison time for offenders with three convictions. All of these mandatory requirements contributed significantly to the rise in prison pop-

President George W. Bush outlining his new battle plan in the "War on Drugs," 2002. *(AP/Wide World Photos)*

ulations and the overcrowding of correctional facilities. At the start of the twenty-first century the United States had the highest incarceration rate per its population in the world.

Prison construction

Both federal and state governments constructed new correctional facilities to ease overcrowding. Congress passed the 1994 Violent Crime Control and Law Enforcement Act authorizing $7.9 billion for prison construction, then quickly added $2.3 billion more as costs and prison populations continued to increase. Large prisons called "megaprisons" were built for up to 20,000 prisoners.

Megaprisons are run on very tight budgets and, in keeping with "Get Tough" policies, many offer no or few rehabil-

New Treatment: Prisoners and Animals

Animal assisted therapy (AAT) involves using highly trained animals to help promote emotional, physical, and mental well-being. In a prison, using animals can be very helpful, especially to inmates who have never experienced the unconditional love of a pet. Incarceration can be a very stressful time for inmates given the fear of attack from other inmates, detachment from friends and family, and guilt for not providing for their children. The animals used in AAT receive special training to function in an institutional setting. Many inmates who have been through AAT respond very positively, finding the animals provide a safe outlet for their emotions. Studies have shown that prisoners who go through AAT are often calmer, more relaxed, and get along better with their fellow inmates.

Aside from therapy animals, some animal shelters have begun allowing inmates to work with orphaned pets. Carefully chosen inmates take care of a specific pet, including brushing, cleaning, and training the animal. Prisoners are given the opportunity to care for a pet, and the animals begin to trust humans again so that they may be adopted into a loving home.

itation programs. Many prisons have dropped vocational and technical education programs such as welding or car repair, the very programs that might offer prisoners a chance to succeed after release. Even though studies show 80 percent of offenders have some form of substance abuse problem—drug and alcohol treatment programs are also frequently cut to save money.

Supermax prisons

Supermax prisons, short for super-maximum security prisons, are designed to keep the most violent or disruptive inmates separated from other prisoners and correction staff. Supermax prisons are generally a special area within an existing prison. In 2002 most states had supermax units, while some prisons such as the federal penitentiary in Florence, Colorado, are designed entirely as supermax facilities.

Inmates are not assigned to supermax incarceration when they enter prison; only extremely disruptive or violent prison behavior such as injuring other inmates or staff, or attempting to escape will get a prisoner sent to supermax. Prisons with these units confine an average of 8 to 10 percent of their prison population in supermax.

Life in a supermax is bleak. Twenty-three hours a day are spent in windowless cells made completely of concrete and steel. One hour is spent showering, in solitary recreation, or in visitation. Anytime prisoners leave their cells, they must wear wrist and ankle irons and are accompanied by several guards. Many supermax units are entirely automated so prisoners never come into direct contact with another human being. Although many prisoners spend only limited time in a supermax unit, returning to the general prison population by

Death row inmates, or those who have been sentenced to death and are awaiting execution, play basketball in San Quentin Prison.
(AP/Wide World Photos)

good behavior, some prisoners spend their entire sentence in supermax.

Death row

Death row refers to locations where inmates sentenced to death await execution. In 2001 thirty-eight states and the federal government allowed the use of the death penalty. Many states keep death row inmates separate from others, in special wings or in an entirely different building. Most convicts sentenced to death are men, although there are a growing number of women. In 2001, there were 3,539 males and 54 females on death row awaiting execution. Thirty-seven of the thirty-eight death penalty states had one or more prisoners on death row.

The conditions on death row vary from state to state and prison to prison. The average length of time a prisoner is on death row is about twelve years. The reason inmates spend so long on death row is because of the appeals process, or the opportunity all inmates are given to challenge a court's decision. Working through the appellate system is a lengthy process and can take many years.

There are three types of death row: unreformed, reformed, and mainstream. Unreformed death row prisoners are held in their cells in isolation and let out only for short periods of individual recreation or visitation with friends or relatives. Reformed death row facilities allow their inmates to work and have recreational time with other death row inmates. Mainstream death rows occur only in the Missouri state prison system, where inmates are housed with the general prison population. They are given the same work, recreation, and counseling opportunities as other maximum security prisoners.

Parole

Parole is the process of releasing inmates from prison to serve the remainder of their sentence in a community. The decision to parole an inmate is made by a parole board after considering information about inmates and their record during incarceration. Parolees are supervised by parole officers. Parole is often used to control prison overcrowding, to reward good behavior, and to help prisoners reenter their community with supervision. In 2002 out of a total estimated correctional population of 6,732,400, the number of adults on parole was 753,141. The 2002 rate of adults on parole in the United States was 350 for each 100,000 persons.

Parole boards generally hold parole release hearings at the prison. Prison officials participate in the interviews, and in many states the inmates and their relatives or friends may also play a role in the parole process. Most parole boards also allow a written statement from the victim. Information from police and any opposition to an inmate's release are also considered. Some parole boards make their decisions only from written reports. An inmate's personal information such as age, prior criminal record, prison record, and most importantly the amount of time already served are factors related to the board's decision.

The decision to parole an inmate is made by a parole board after considering information about an inmate and his or her record during incarceration. *(AP/Wide World Photos)*

After being paroled, offenders are assigned a parole officer who sets up the conditions for the parole agreement. Much like probation, parole requirements often include counseling or drug therapy programs, getting a job, restricted travel or changes of address, a ban on owning or possessing weapons. Failure to meet parole terms or further criminal activity will send the offender back to prison.

Community-based corrections

Community-based correction programs began in the 1970s, 1980s, and 1990s. The programs offer an alternative to incarceration within the prison system. Many criminologists believed a significant number of offenders did not need in-

Women in Prison

At the beginning of the twenty-first century, the fastest growing group in prison and jail population was women. According to the U.S. Department of Justice's Bureau of Justice Statistics, there were 91,612 women in state and federal prisons at the end of 2000, or 6.6 percent of the nation's total prison population. Ten times that many or about 900,000 were on probation or parole. Back in 1970 there were just 5,600 incarcerated women, 12,300 in 1980, and in 1990 approximately 40,000. From 1990 until the end of 2000 the number of imprisoned women grew by 125 percent.

Eighty-five percent of women prisoners committed nonviolent crimes, mostly drug offenses and theft. The astounding increase in the number of incarcerated women in the 1990s was largely due to drug arrests. In the early 1980s federal and state governments initiated a "War on Drugs," in reaction to a huge increase in drug related offenses throughout the United States.

Most incarcerated women are poor, undereducated, and women of color. Black American women are three times more likely to be in jail or prison than Hispanic women, and six times more likely than white women. Most female inmates are young (between twenty-four and twenty-nine years of age); raised in a single parent home; experienced violence or sexual abuse at home; started using drugs in their early teens; and were unemployed or in a low paying job at the carceration in high security prison cells. Some inmates, who might otherwise have been ready to turn away from a life of crime, instead became like the hardened criminals they associated with in prison.

In response, states, counties, and cities established local correctional facilities and programs that became known as community-based corrections. These facilities, located in neighborhoods, allowed offenders normal family relationships and friendships as well as rehabilitation services such as counseling, instruction in basic living skills, how to apply for jobs, and work training and placement.

Some offenders are placed in community-based corrections without ever going to jail or prison. Others are assigned to these correction programs after serving part of their prison sentence to learn how to rejoin community life. These programs include strict supervision, house arrest and electronic

Former Olympic figure skater Tonya Harding performing community service work after serving three days in jail on a disorderly conduct charge. *(AP/Wide World Photos)*

time of their arrest. Eighty percent are mothers leaving approximately 250,000 children under eighteen years of age to the care of others.

Most women in prison do not receive proper healthcare or drug treatment and are often sexually abused or assaulted by male corrections officers. Medical care in a system designed primarily for men does not provide the kinds of testing, treatment, and medication needed by women and often leaves them with recurring health problems. Most women sentenced for drug crimes do not receive drug treatment therapy while incarcerated, and once released they are unable to receive federal assistance such as food stamps and student loans because of their drug convictions. Roughly 80 percent of female drug users released after serving time will return to prison on new convictions.

monitoring, halfway houses, boot camp prisons, and work-release programs.

The popularity and growth of community-based programs nationwide is based on five factors: (1) the programs provide closer supervision than regular probation sentences; (2) major cost savings compared to full incarceration; (3) flexibility for judges to sentence to community correction programs instead of incarceration in a jail or prison; (4) a more gradual reentry into community life after prison or jail time; and, (5) less overcrowding in jails and prisons.

Intensive probation supervision

Intensive Probation Supervision (IPS) is the most frequently used community-based corrections program. It is an intermediate program with more supervision than with ordinary probation but does not lock an offender up in a jail or prison. It gives judges another option besides the often too light probation sentence or too harsh prison sentence. IPS relieves prison overcrowding, saves taxpayer dollars, protects the community better than usual probation due to closer supervision, and provides rehabilitation services to offenders within normal community surroundings.

Offenders are evaluated to determine their risk to the community and an individualized IPS program is developed. Offenders convicted of violent offenses or those with long criminal histories usually do not qualify for IPS and are incarcerated. Individual IPS programs combine a variety of community-based correction programs including house arrest, electronic monitoring, strict curfews, drug counseling and drug testing, employment or preparation for employment, community service, and strict adherence to meeting with an assigned IPS officer.

Unlike probation officers who may have a caseload of several hundred offenders, each of which can be met with only once a month, IPS officers try to keep small caseloads of approximately twenty offenders. They meet once a week for intensive sessions. Offenders just starting in IPS may meet once or twice daily with their IPS officer. Some offenders are placed in IPS without ever being incarcerated while others are released into IPS programs after serving their minimum sentence time in prison.

House arrest and electronic monitoring

House arrest involves court-ordered confinement in an offender's home. House arrest relieves prison overcrowding and allows the offender to stay connected to familiar surroundings, family, and friends. House arrest is maintained at several different levels depending on an offender's individual program. Curfew is the lightest form of house arrest; under curfew offenders are confined to their house only certain hours of the evening or at night. Home detention means offenders must remain at home except for time at employment, school, medical appointments, or religious services. Home incarceration confines the offender to home at all times except for court-ordered counseling or treatment.

Electronic monitoring (EM) is commonly used along with home detention or incarceration. As electronic surveillance

Lakeview NeuroRehabilitation Center's halfway house in New Hampshire. Halfway houses are rigidly controlled rehabilitation homes for inmates who have been released early from prison or are on parole. *(AP/Wide World Photos)*

technology improves so does electronic monitoring; EM devices are active, passive, or use global tracking. An active EM system makes use of a small transmitter strapped to an offender, which constantly emits a signal to a receiver-dialer placed on the offender's telephone. Should the offender move too far from the receiver-dialer the signal is interrupted and a central monitoring computer is notified.

Passive EM involves a device strapped to offenders and their phones, but a constant signal is not emitted between them. Instead, IPS officers periodically call the specially designed phones and offenders must make voice contact and insert their tracking device into the phone itself to verify their whereabouts. Global tracking or Global Positioning Systems (GPS) make use of U.S. government-owned satellites. Offenders wear a transmitter that emits a constant signal to a satellite; their exact location can be checked at any time by IPS officers.

Halfway houses

Halfway houses, renamed Community Residential Treatment Centers, are rigidly controlled rehabilitation homes for offenders. Relieving prison overcrowding, the centers house inmates who have been released early from prison or are on parole. Their services vary widely from a full range of counseling, treatment, and education programs to no direct services, only a place to live under supervision. The centers can host a few residents or several hundred. Residents are generally allowed to leave unsupervised each day for specific hours for work, school, or treatment programs.

Residential centers provide a practical solution to the public's demand for criminals to remain in prison longer despite a shortage of prison and jail space. By the year 2000, keeping an offender at a residential center cost must less than in a prison. Residential Treatment Centers are considered similar to minimum security prisons.

Work release programs

Work release programs, also known as furlough, day parole, and day release programs, allow selected inmates release from a prison or community residential center for work during the day. The Department of Justice estimates 40 percent of released prison inmates are returned to prison for new convictions within three years. A major reason is the lack of employment opportunities for ex-prisoners. In work release programs, inmates can learn skills needed for employment and put those skills to use in jobs before their release from prison. The goal of work release is to give released prisoners a smoother transition back into their communities, in hopes they will be less likely to return to criminal behavior.

Inmates selected for work release are those least likely to commit further crimes while in the community. They must have served the majority of their sentences, be on minimum-security status, and their conviction cannot be for murder or rape. The number of offenders actually placed in work release is very small, about 3 percent of incarcerated individuals. Few employers are willing to accept offenders for training, and most communities continue to view work release offenders as dangerous. Although work release offenders rarely cause problems, a few highly publicized escapes and violent incidents keep public opinion unfavorable.

For More Information

Books

Beck, Allen, and Paige Harrison. *Prisoners in 2001*. Washington, DC: Bureau of Justice Statistics, 2001.

Schiraldi, Vincent, and Jason Ziedenberg. *America's One Million Non-Violent Prisoners*. Washington, DC: Justice Policy Institute, 1999.

Siegel, Larry J. *Criminology: The Core*. Belmont, CA: Wadsworth/Thomson Learning, 2002.

Silverman, Ira. *Corrections: A Comprehensive View*. 2nd ed. Belmont, CA: Wadsworth, 2001.

U.S. Department of Justice. *A Profile of Female Offenders*. Washington, DC: Federal Bureau of Prisons, 1998.

Web Sites

"Correction." *U.S. Department of Justice, Office of Justice Programs, National Criminal Justice Reference Service*. http://virlib.ncjrs.org/Corrections.asp (accessed August 20, 2004).

"Corrections Connection." *The Official Home of Corrections*. http://www.corrections.com (accessed on August 20, 2004).

U.S. Department of Justice, National Institute of Corrections (NIC). http://www.nicic.org (accessed on August 20, 2004).

18

Military and Native American Criminal Justice

In the early twenty-first century multiple criminal justice systems existed in the United States. Two major kinds of systems—in addition to the civilian U.S. criminal justice system—were the military justice system and numerous American Indian or Native American justice systems. The military judicial system balances the rights of military service members with the need to maintain strict discipline. It has jurisdiction (legal authority in a geographic area) over all military members accused of criminal conduct no matter where they are stationed in the world.

Military justice is one part of military law; another is martial law, which is when the military exerts police power in politically unstable areas. The military justice system changed through time from being strictly run by military commanders who exerted considerable influence over proceedings of each trial to a more formal, standardized process that included protection of the constitutional rights of accused service men and women and provided them an opportunity to appeal decisions. Since the mid-twentieth century, fairness in the judicial process has been considered important in maintaining

The military judicial system balances the rights of military service members with the need to maintain strict discipline. *(AP/Wide World Photos)*

high morale in the military. Military courts are administered by the Department of Defense, not the Department of Justice.

Hundreds of Native American governments formally recognized by the U.S. government maintain sovereignty (a government free from outside control) over their lands and tribal members within the borders of the United States. In 2000 some 1.4 million Native Americans lived in the United States, or about 1.5 percent of the total population, many of whom claim tribal affiliations. Only the U.S. Congress can make decisions restricting tribal sovereignty.

American Indian reservations and other lands controlled by tribes are known as Indian Country in legal terms. Indian Country amounts to some 56 million acres within the United States, scattered in small areas around the country. As part of their sovereignty, tribes maintain their own criminal jurisdiction on these lands. Over two hundred tribal justice systems operate independently of each other and the U.S. criminal justice system. Given the poverty of many tribal communities in the late twentieth century, criminal justice in Indian Country was poorly coordinated.

Early military justice

The first federal courts in the United States were military courts created to maintain discipline and order in the American Revolutionary Army during the war for independence from Great Britain. In 1775 the Continental Congress created Articles of War patterned after the British military legal system. The articles emphasized discipline more than justice. In addition to the more common types of crimes such as murder, robbery, and rape, the military also added insubordination (disobeying someone of higher military rank), poor performance of duties, and absenteeism. Federal civilian courts did not come into existence until the late 1780s, following the adoption of the U.S. Constitution in 1787.

The two justice systems remained separate even though the Constitution gave responsibility for military matters to the civilian side of government. The Constitution named the U.S. president as commander-in-chief of the armed forces. It also gave Congress responsibility to raise and fund the armed services for the common defense of the nation. The U.S. Supreme Court stayed away from accepting appeals from military cases,

The trial of Caption Henry Wirz, the only person to have been tried for war crimes following the American Civil War. *(The Library of Congress)*

except where the cases protected civilians (nonmilitary people) from prosecution in military courts.

One main difference between the two criminal justice systems was that the military system did not have an appeals process with appellate courts. A military member convicted in a court proceeding had no means of appealing the decision. Even the U.S. president, who could pardon (grant exemption from punishment) the defendant, could not actually reverse the decision.

With limited revisions through the years, the system remained largely unchanged until after World War II (1939–45; war in which Great Britain, France, the Soviet Union, the United States, and their allied forces defeated

The military police are responsible for the enforcement of military codes and discipline. *(National Archives and Records Administration)*

Germany, Italy, and Japan). The emphasis remained on discipline. Public concern over justice within the military system was rare; military justice was considered primarily a tool for commanding officers to maintain discipline. To ensure military order, the military system had to operate swiftly and harshly when necessary, quite different from the much slower civilian criminal system.

It was common knowledge that when citizens joined the military, they gave up a certain degree of their constitutional rights, such as freedom of speech. The authority of the military command had to be reinforced. Military society was clearly different than civilian society.

One change did come in 1863 during the American Civil War (1861–65) when Congress more clearly defined the court-martial process, reaffirming the authority of the military to prosecute the crimes and conduct of its personnel. During this early period, commanders held considerable influence over the military criminal justice system. Commanders accepted cases, selected members of the court from those under their command, and had to approve sentences before they went into effect. Commanders could alter punishments either by influencing court members or by simply changing them, making sentences harsher or lighter if they chose.

Military defendants did not have the right to an attorney like in civil criminal cases. Instead, the judge advocate general (JAG) would both prosecute the case on behalf of the military and provide limited legal advice to the defendant. The person JAG assigned to advise the defendant might not even be a lawyer; they mostly followed instructions from a booklet about court-martial proceedings.

Military Police

The enforcement of military codes and discipline is a necessity within the U.S. armed forces. Military police generally capture deserters (those who run away from their post), arrest service personnel accused of criminal activities, and control rowdiness.

During the American Revolution, the Continental Army copied the British system of police units called provosts (soldiers assigned solely to keep order). However, following the Revolution until the Civil War, the army simply assigned regular troops to perform these policing duties, but during the conflict the large armies of the North and South were particularly unruly while in camp and away. Soldiers looted and fought frequently, so both sides adopted systems creating provost marshals, who had police powers. The marshals assumed important responsibilities after the war as well, overseeing the temporary local governments setup in the South.

During World War I (1914–18) the U.S. Army established the Military Police Corps with soldiers wearing "MP" armbands. Their roles included rounding up soldiers who had abandoned their duties, guarding enemy prisoners and prisoner-of-war camps, and investigating cases of desertion (leaving without permission) and draft evasion (avoiding a national call to duty). The navy had a similar program called Shore Patrol, in which sailors maintained order and discipline particularly between off-duty sailors and civilians. None of these programs were permanent parts of the military.

As the United States got ready for World War II, the U.S. Department of War created a permanent Military Police Corps in September 1941, less than two months before the Japanese attack on Pearl Harbor. This was the beginning of a permanent military police force with an MP training program. Over two hundred thousand military personnel served as MPs during the war.

Military police were responsible for keeping order and enforcing discipline throughout the remainder of the twentieth century and into the new millennium. MPs also provide security for military facilities, including those near combat zones, and guard prisoners of war.

To operate swiftly wherever military personnel were stationed, the system had to be mobile and function in combat conditions. Given these various characteristics of the military justice system, one major result was how the same crime might have very different punishments based on the location where the offense was committed and the military offender's commanding officer.

Military justice reform

During World War II the public often viewed military justice as unjust, too harsh, and following no set pattern. Many wanted military justice to be more like civilian procedures and Congress reorganized the military in 1947 into a department of the federal government, called the Department of Defense. Instead of separate justice systems for the army, air force, navy, and marines, there would be one military justice system run by the Department of Defense. During this time, European countries also reorganized their military justice systems, to be more like civilian courts.

Congress passed the Uniform Code of Military Justice (UCMJ) in 1951, a common criminal code for all military services. The military courts, also known as tribunals, explain and enforce these laws. The new codes took away some of the influence of military commanders over the judicial system. Over the next several decades the military system became more like civilian courts, however, the UCMJ maintained the important need for conducting speedy trials and handing out clear and predictable rulings to maintain order.

According to the codes, crimes such as murder, robbery, assault, and rape by military personnel against civilians are tried in the civil criminal justice system. If a military person commits a crime against another military person, the case is tried in military courts. If the crimes are committed against citizens of other countries when the United States is stationed abroad, the U.S. military tries to maintain jurisdiction through treaties with foreign countries.

Throughout the second half of the twentieth century the U.S. Supreme Court still rarely interfered with the military process. One unusual instance was a ruling in 1969 when the Supreme Court overturned a court-martial verdict, stating that the military did not have jurisdiction over a soldier who committed a felony against a civilian away from a military base. In most cases though, the Supreme Court almost always lets military decisions remain in effect due to what it considers "military necessity."

A key ruling came in 1981 by the U.S. Court of Appeals for the Armed Services. The court ruled that the protections of the first ten amendments of the U.S. Constitution, known as the Bill of Rights, fully applied to military service members. These protections included freedom of speech, freedom from illegal search and seizure, and freedom from self-incrimination. The courts, however, have defined these protections to military justice only in very general ways instead of specific findings.

Like the Supreme Court, Congress has rarely used its constitutional authority to interfere with the military justice system. Public interest in military law only occurs during controversial or highly publicized cases. One such case came in 1971 when Lieutenant William Calley was convicted in the killing of five hundred unarmed civilians in the village of My Lai during the Vietnam War (1954–75; a controversial war in which the United States aided South Vietnam in its fight against a takeover by Communist North Vietnam). Calley was sentenced to life in prison, though he was paroled a short time later (some people felt that he was unfairly singled out and blamed for the killings). Otherwise the public pays little attention to the military judicial system, so there has been little pressure to reform. Military justice is relatively free of public scrutiny or interest.

Court-martials

A court-martial is a military court of officers appointed to try a person accused of seriously violating military law. The offender appears before a court of several military officers who will decide his or her case. There are three different types of court-martial—summary, special, and general.

Summary court-martials hear minor offenses committed by enlisted men and women, not officers. Sentences cannot exceed one month of confinement, forty-five days of hard labor, limited pay loss, or a reduction in military rank. The process is simple and does not provide legal safeguards for the accused such as an attorney. For this reason, summary court-martials can only be conducted if the accused has agreed to the proceedings.

In summary court-martials, the trial is conducted by one military officer. This kind of proceeding has declined in recent years and been replaced by administrative proceedings before the defendant's commander. The commander can impose fines or a reduction in rank.

The proceedings of a court-martial, a military court of officers appointed to try a person accused of seriously violating military law.
(The Library of Congress)

The second type or special court-martial can hear all types of offenses and be assembled by lower ranking commanders. These cases are run by a military judge and three military service members, unless the accused requests only a judge alone. The three members serve as a jury to determine guilt and decide a penalty. Penalties from special court-martials can include imprisonment up to six months, three months of hard labor, a fine, or a "dishonorable discharge." Dishonorable discharges force defendants to leave the military, often with the loss of military benefits such as special insurance policies and retirement funds.

The third kind of court-martial is the general court-martial, which tries major felonies and hands down the harshest punishments. By the early twenty-first century, general court-martials were the most frequently used proceedings, consisting of a military judge and five military members as a jury. Like special court-martials, defendants can request a judge with no jury.

Unlike other court-martials, however, general court-martials can only be convened by high-ranking government officials such as the U.S. president, the secretary of a federal department (like the secretary of defense), or a commander. Defendants are allowed an attorney, who must be a military lawyer, and a detailed record of the court proceedings is kept like in civil courts. General court-martials can impose the death penalty, high fines, imprisonment, and dishonorable discharges.

The court-martial process

The modern court-martial process still relies heavily on a military commander's decisions. The commander can order criminal investigations, issue search warrants, send the case to trial, select jurors, and change the court's results. The military judicial process also includes legally trained attorneys and judges, a jury, a thorough appeals review process, and allows a greater degree of legal representation than civilian courts.

To initiate a court-martial trial, a military commander receives a report of wrongdoing from military or civilian law enforcement. The commander decides whether to pursue a trial, dismiss the charges, or handle the alleged violation through a less formal process.

No bail (the money a defendant pays to be released while awaiting trial) exists in military courts. If the commander/judge decides to confine the accused until trial, the decision is reviewed in a hearing where the defendant and his or her attorney can participate. Military attorneys are provided free of charge to all defendants for every phase of a trial. Defendants can also hire private civilian attorneys to represent them.

If a commander decides to pursue a court-martial, a pretrial hearing (similar to a grand jury proceeding in civilian law) is held in which the prosecution's evidence is presented. In these hearings, a military defendant has greater rights than

A military policeman escorting a soldier to court.
(AP/Wide World Photos)

in civilian criminal law. Unlike civilian grand juries, military pretrial hearings are not closed to the defendants and his or her lawyer can cross-examine witnesses and introduce evidence as well. The commander then decides whether to proceed with a trial.

Court-martial trials begin within 120 days of initial imprisonment. The commander who ordered the trial also selects the five commissioned officers to compose the jury. The jurors must have a higher military rank than the defendant. Enlisted servicemen and servicewomen may request that part of the jury have enlisted personnel as well. The military judge is a senior judge advocate officer assigned by JAG. The process resembles a civilian trial except it proceeds much quicker.

Military judges can enforce the Fourth Amendment safeguard against unreasonable searches and seizures by ruling out certain evidence acquired by the prosecutor. In the military, however, evidence discovered during normal inspections of living quarters and duty stations can be used at trial. Unlike civilian judges, the military judge can also question witnesses during the trial. Another difference is that it takes just two-thirds of the jury to determine guilt, while it takes all jurors to agree on a verdict in a civil trial.

The punishment process in court-martials is different than in civilian court. The defendants are still protected against cruel and unusual punishment but sentencing normally occurs immediately upon the determination of guilt. No separate report is prepared for the sentencing phase like in civilian courts. Nonetheless, the defendant's background information is presented, including past arrests or disciplinary actions, and the defendant has a chance to speak. The same jurors who heard the case determine the sentence.

In military justice, there are no mandatory sentencing guidelines. The court has considerable flexibility in deciding a sentence. Choices include a prison sentence, the death penalty, a fine, loss of pay, or discharge from the service. There is no probation (a sentence other than imprisonment) in military justice, but there is parole (early release from serving a full sentence). Defendants given long prison sentences are sent to the military prison in Fort Leavenworth, Kansas, or to a federal prison; those with shorter sentences are held at U.S. military bases.

For all court-martial trials a judge advocate reviews the trial records to ensure the court followed proper procedures. At this time, defense attorneys can submit requests for lighter sentences or overturning convictions. For sentences longer than one year or for service discharges, the Court of Criminal Appeals automatically reviews the cases. Three judges hear arguments by both sides and once again the record is reviewed. Defendants may even appeal to the U.S. Court of Appeals for the Armed Forces and to the U.S. Supreme Court.

Military appeals courts

The original 1951 UCMJ codes created a civilian appeals court to hear military cases called the U.S. Court of Appeals for the Armed Forces. The court originally had three judges and later expanded to five. Like other federal judge positions, the U.S. president appoints these judges and the Senate approves them. This court hears cases sent by JAG, all death sentence cases, and some appeals submitted by those convicted in lower courts. It has worldwide jurisdiction since cases can come from any place around the globe where U.S. troops are deployed.

The U.S. Court of Appeals for the Armed Forces serves as a civilian safeguard on the military judicial process. Its decisions may be appealed to the U.S. Supreme Court. A major difference between this court and civilian courts is that the military judges do not have lifetime appointments. Instead they serve fifteen-year terms.

Congress passed the Military Justice Act of 1968 creating intermediate appellate military courts located in each military service. Originally called the Courts of Military Review, they were renamed Courts of Criminal Appeals in 1995. JAG appoints the judges, who are trained attorneys, not commanders, and who do not have fixed terms. The appellate courts review all cases where the accused was sentenced to over a year of confinement, was given the death penalty, lost his or her rank as a commissioned officer, or was discharge dishonorably. The courts can drop the charges, reduce the sentence, or order a new trial.

Native American justice systems

Prior to the European settlement of North America in the early seventeenth century, many long-established Native American groups handled justice through traditional means. Rather than two sides presenting arguments before a judge, Native Americans preferred both sides reach an agreement together. In the early twenty-first century, about 560 federally recognized tribes use traditional methods to resolve disputes and address criminal activity. The tribes are quite different in population size, structure, culture, language, available funding, and even traditions.

Limited criminal jurisdiction

Native Americans and white Americans do not use the same kinds of punishment, due to cultural differences. In the 1880s the Lakota tribe in South Dakota resolved a murder case through traditional tribal means. The murderer was required to provide the victim's family with goods and provisions. Though the family was satisfied with the outcome, the U.S. Department of the Interior, which oversees tribal matters, was not.

The Department of the Interior pressed for extending U.S. criminal jurisdiction into Indian Country for major criminal offenses. Congress passed the Major Crimes Act of 1885 to extend U.S. jurisdiction over seven major crimes committed in Indian Country. The crimes were murder, manslaughter, arson, burglary, and various forms of assault. The list of crimes was later expanded to include twelve crimes, including rape.

The General Crimes Act, first passed in 1834, established U.S. jurisdiction over crimes involving Native Americans and non-Indians. If an Indian robs a non-Indian on a reservation,

A U.S. Bureau of Indian Affairs police officer investigating a car accident in Montana. *(AP/Wide World Photos)*

U.S. criminal jurisdiction applies. If the Native American commits the same crime against another reservation member, then tribal courts handle the case.

The biggest change in tribal criminal justice came in 1934 when Congress passed the Indian Reorganization Act. The act encouraged tribes to establish governments modeled after the U.S. justice systems. These new governments replaced traditional tribunals and their practices, using the adversarial or two-party system of U.S. courts. Many of the tribes adopted new tribal constitutions but could not afford to operate as independent court systems. They relied on the U.S. Bureau of Indian Affairs (BIA) to provide a judicial system.

Tribal criminal justice

By the early twenty-first century, some 275 Native American tribes had their own formal tribal court systems. Each tribal court was unique in how it operated and the laws it enforced. Most tribal courts tended to be less formal than U.S. courts; many did not keep formal court records like U.S. justice systems.

Though tribal courts had been patterned after U.S. criminal courts, by the late twentieth century many had begun returning to traditional methods of solving disputes through tribal elders and other community-based approaches. Some tribes adopted a combination of the two systems, using tribal courts for more serious criminal offenses.

As some tribes gained greater economic standing through the twentieth century, they could afford to operate their own governmental services, including criminal justice systems, rather than relying on the BIA. Jurisdiction for criminal cases in Indian Country is determined by the race of the accused and the victim and whether the crime is a felony or misdemeanor. Tribal courts hold criminal jurisdiction over their own members and other Native Americans on their lands. In many cases, sentences are less than one year and fines are kept below a certain amount.

In addition to the crimes identified in the Major Crimes Act, the United States holds jurisdiction over non-Indians who commit crimes against Indians on reservation lands as well as crimes committed by Native Americans against non-Indians. The only authority a tribe has against a non-Indian is to banish the person from the reservation. State laws generally do not apply to tribal members in Indian Country. Similarly, tribes hold civil jurisdiction in almost all cases over Native Americans and non-Indians on reservations. In resolving cases, tribal courts first look to tribal codes, then to federal, and finally to state law for guidance if no tribal code applies.

High crime rates

In the late 1990s as violent crime was decreasing in the general U.S. population, it dramatically increased in Indian Country. Indian Country had almost twice the crime rate as the entire national population. The murder rate in particular was three times higher than for the U.S. population in general. The Fort Peck Reservation had a murder rate double that of the city of New Orleans, which had the highest murder rate among U.S. cities.

The swearing in of new Yavapai Indian tribal police officers, 1997.

(AP/Wide World Photos)

Gang and domestic violence, aggravated assault, sexual assault, and child abuse were also rising sharply on tribal lands. The U.S. Department of Justice called the situation a public safety crisis. Among the many different racial and ethnic groups in the United States, Native Americans had one of the lowest life expectancy rates, due in large part to violence and crime contributing to these numbers.

Law enforcement in the remote rural areas where most tribal lands are found was spread very thin. In 1996 Indian Country had a total of 135 tribal law enforcement agencies and over 1,700 officers, along with 339 full-time BIA officers. Indian Country had 1.3 officers for every one thousand tribal members compared to the national average of 2.9 officers for every one thousand U.S. citizens. Many of these officers patrolled remote areas alone, a very dangerous situation.

In addition to law officers, there were only 78 full-time BIA and 90 tribal criminal investigators and just over 100 FBI agents available nationwide to Indian Country. Some seventy poorly funded and aging jails were located on fifty-five reservations, most holding only between ten and thirty inmates. Most were built in the 1960s and 1970s and had major problems. The jails held some 1,700 inmates in 1999, with forty-eight operated by tribes and the remainder by BIA or private operators. Only ten of these facilities were for juveniles; most housed juveniles along with adults. Programs for education and substance abuse hardly existed. In some cases, jail staffers had to buy necessities such as soap and toothpaste for inmates out of their own personal funds. Few of these staff members ever received professional training.

Given the dire conditions in Indian Country judicial systems overall, Congress increased funding for a newly created Tribal Courts Program to improve tribal judicial systems. In some cases money was available for intertribal courts, so more than one tribe could share a judicial system. Other funding went to help with tribal caseloads; revise and update tribal criminal codes and operating rules; hire more investigators, prosecutors, defense lawyers, and judges; create better record-keeping systems and buy fireproof storage cabinets; purchase more legal library materials; and make training and technical assistance programs available to tribes.

For More Information

Books

Bachman-Prehn, Ronet D. *Death and Violence on the Reservation: Homicide, Violence, and Suicide in American Indian Populations*. New York: Auburn House, 1992.

Belknap, Michal R. *The Viet Nam War on Trial: The My Lai Massacre and the Court-Martial of Lieutenant Calley*. Lawrence, KS: University Press of Kansas, 2002.

Davidson, Michael J. *A Guide to Military Criminal Law*. Annapolis, MD: Naval Institute Press, 1999.

Davis, Mary B. *Native America in the Twentieth Century: An Encyclopedia*. New York: Garland Publishing, Inc., 1994.

French, Laurence, ed. *Indians and Criminal Justice.* Totowa, NJ: Allanheld, Osmun Publishers, 1982.

Lowry, Thomas P. *Don't Shoot That Boy! Abraham Lincoln and Military Justice.* Mason City, IA: Savas Publishing Co., 1999.

Wilkinson, Charles F. *American Indians, Time, and the Law: Native Societies in a Modern Constitutional Democracy.* New Haven, CT: Yale University Press, 1987.

Web Sites

National American Indian Court Judges Association. http://www.naicja.org/ (accessed on September 1, 2004).

National Institute of Military Justice. http://www.nimj.com/Home.asp (accessed on August 20, 2004).

U.S. Department of Tribal Justice, Office of Tribal Justice. http://www.usdoj.gov/otj (accessed on August 20, 2004).

19

Juvenile Justice

In the early twenty-first century most people assumed juveniles would be treated differently than adults in the U.S. criminal justice system. This distinction did not come to pass until the end of the nineteenth century. In criminal justice, juveniles are youths who are not old enough to be held fully responsible for their crimes. Juvenile justice is largely a state matter and is separate from the regular adult criminal justice system.

Most states set the age of eighteen as when a person assumes the responsibilities of being an adult in criminal law. Some states send youth as young as seven to juvenile courts. Though there are federal juvenile laws for persons under age eighteen, for youths accused of committing federal crimes, this is a very minor part of criminal law.

Juvenile courts have jurisdiction over children in three basic kinds of situations: (1) when they are accused of conduct that would be a crime by an adult; (2) when parents or guardians abuse or neglect them or when they are in need; and, (3) when they violate rules that apply only to juveniles, called status offenses. Status offenses include unapproved ab-

Officers arresting a juvenile delinquent. Until the nineteenth century, the public considered children to be young adults and fully responsible for their own actions. *(© Bettmann/Corbis)*

sence from schools (truancy), running away, alcohol and to-bacco use, or refusing to obey parents. Juveniles who commit acts considered adult crimes are referred to as delinquents.

Juvenile courts also perform duties such as determining paternity and child support, or custody in divorce cases (where a child lives and how often he or she visits the other parent). In adoption cases, the court grants parental rights to foster parents or guardians.

Juvenile court procedures are less formal than those in adult criminal courts. For status offenders and delinquents, rather than punish the offenders, juvenile courts seek to re-habilitate, supervise, or provide counseling. Treatment of ju-veniles is usually more lenient than for adults. The purpose is to protect youth and guide them to more productive lives while still holding them accountable to some degree for their actions.

Changing social attitudes toward children

Determining the minimum age of responsibility for crim-inal actions has been a problem throughout history. Until the nineteenth century the public considered children below seven years of age incapable of crime, while those above seven were considered adults and responsible for their actions. Chil-dren over seven years of age could face criminal charges and, if convicted, be placed in adult prisons. They faced the same punishment as adults including whipping, branding, and hanging. At times, however, courts informally considered an offender's age in their deliberations, especially those under fourteen.

Many social changes, however, occurred throughout the nineteenth century including perceptions of children and how they should be punished for committing criminal acts. Children began to be viewed as different from adults, since their thoughts and decisions were made in a different man-ner than adults. They were innocent and vulnerable to bad influences since they had not gained wisdom from experi-ence. Because of this innocence, it was believed states should not hold them accountable for their actions. Rather than be-ing punished, youthful offenders needed to be reformed and educated.

Reformers

In the 1800s the Child Savers Movement was dedicated to improving the conditions of children in America. They promoted free public education and child labor laws restricting the use of children in factories. Social reformers in the nineteenth century were distressed that youngsters charged with crimes were placed in facilities along with hardened adult criminals. Reformers claimed children who came out of prison were more likely to turn to a life of crime or be harmful to society. Most states created work farms and reform schools for children convicted of crimes.

During the nineteenth century, juvenile crime rates were low and not considered a major issue. With rapid population growth, however, both in city size and through east European immigration, children faced serious neglect and poverty. Uneducated children who lived in poverty were likely to commit crimes, and reformers believed they were a threat to not only themselves but to the nation as well.

Reformers hoped supervision of children whose parents worked long hours in factories would help prevent crime. They turned to the English common law concept of *parens patriae,* where the government had the right to become the parent of children in need, to save them from terrible living conditions and protect them from criminal influences. The government was responsible for shaping the habits and morals of juveniles.

Juvenile courts

Reformers including Chicago social worker Jane Addams (1860–1935) argued for a separate legal system for juveniles to teach them the proper way to behave. Some supported this idea for the sake of the children, others simply feared immigrant street youths. As a result, Illinois was the first state to establish a separate court system for juveniles in 1899. In these new courts, specially trained judges had many choices in how to deal with youthful offenders.

Judges acting like parents instead of doling out harsh punishment dominated for the next century. During this period, the law defined a juvenile as a person less than sixteen years of age. Rather than prosecute juveniles for a crime, courts

Juvenile Crime Statistics

The National Center for Juvenile Justice offered the following statistics on their Internet Web site for 1999: law enforcement arrested some 2.4 million juveniles, and for every 1,000 juvenile delinquency cases handled, 238 resulted in probation and 93 received residential placement.

On a given day, October 27, 1999, nearly 109,000 juveniles were held in residential placement nationwide. Of all juveniles who went to court, about 25 percent were charged with violent crimes. Fifty-seven percent of the juvenile cases were handled formally through court proceedings and 43 percent were handled informally by law officers or court workers.

Of the status offenses, about 25 percent of runaway cases, 40 percent of those judged unruly, 34 percent of alcohol cases, and 47 percent of truancy cases resulted in formal probation. For all offenses committed in the United States in 1999, juveniles placed them in reform schools or with foster parents. These juveniles then remained under court supervision until age twenty-one.

To further reduce the stigma of formal courts, the terms used in juvenile proceedings were borrowed from civil rather than criminal courts. For example, prosecutors charged juvenile offenders using petitions rather than indictments. Juveniles were not arraigned before the court upon their arrest, but given an intake hearing instead. In addition, court proceedings were not called trials, but hearings. Juveniles, rather than being found guilty, were ruled delinquent. Less proof was needed to find a youth delinquent, called a "preponderance of evidence," rather than the criminal court's requirement of an evidence level considered to be "beyond a reasonable doubt."

In determining treatment for young offenders, courts tried to take the best interest of the juvenile into account. Protecting the constitutional rights of the child was not a concern, since the court was supposed to be acting on his or her behalf. Rather than hearing arguments by attorneys, judges made decisions based on the facts presented by the plaintiff and a background investigation of the juvenile.

committed 16 percent of the violent crimes, or 68,000 arrests, and 32 percent of property crimes. Property offenses tended to occur in mid-teen years and violent offenses in later teen years. Juveniles comprised almost 28 percent of all arrests with juvenile males accounting for over 16 percent of total male arrests and juvenile females almost 22 percent of all female arrests.

About 1 percent of all juvenile cases are transferred to adult criminal court. Of those, 55 percent were black Americans and 90 percent were male. Of those transferred to adult courts, 75 percent resulted in prison sentences. Of those sent to prison 61 percent were for violent crimes, 22 percent for property crimes, and 16 percent for drug or other public disorder crimes. Approximately 2 percent of the adult prison population is teens, amounting to some 15,400 juveniles. Some states had only a few juveniles in prison, while Florida and Connecticut had over 500.

Black Americans made up 15 percent of the U.S. juvenile population in 1999 but accounted for 25 percent of all juvenile arrests, almost 41 percent of violent crimes, and over 27 percent of property crimes.

By 1925 almost all states had juvenile systems using the Illinois law as a model. Although varying slightly from state to state, eighteen generally became the age of transition from juvenile to adult criminal courts. Much of the twentieth century was a period in which the courts and the public clearly favored rehabilitation over punishment for youth. The states increasingly intervened in family issues, creating status offenses in addition to criminal laws. The government considered these lesser violations to be a stepping-stone to criminal behavior.

Into the 1960s juvenile justice remained informal and flexible, records were kept confidential, and the media was not allowed in the courtroom. The court kept only two records, the original police report and the report of a probation officer who interviewed anyone familiar with the juvenile and the case. During the hearing, the judge would question the juvenile defendant and witnesses; unlike other courts, however, the juvenile did not have the right to an attorney or to cross-examine witnesses.

In 1947 Congress passed the federal Juvenile Courts Act to establish a more consistent informal process for juveniles among the states and to emphasize treatment (rehabilitation) over punishment.

In the twentieth century, children began to receive special treatment in the judicial system. Here, a juvenile receives justice in the privacy of a judge's office rather than in a public courtroom. *(© Bettmann/Corbis)*

Changes in the system

Throughout the second half of the twentieth century, thoughts on how to treat juveniles in the criminal justice system changed as the public became increasingly concerned about delinquent behavior. Some states changed to a more formal and harsher process in the 1950s as criticism of the juvenile system increased.

In the 1960s, the U.S. Supreme Court issued several rulings strengthening civil liberty protections in adult criminal courts. Supporters of juvenile justice feared youthful offenders were not benefiting from such decisions because of the informality of the juvenile court system. By protecting juveniles from the harshness of the adult system, they were being denied their constitutional protections as well. As a result, adults enjoyed more constitutional safeguards than juveniles.

Concerns over the rights of youthful offenders led to a series of Supreme Court decisions affecting juvenile courts beginning in the late 1960s. In 1967 the Court ruled that constitutional protections were not only for adults but for juveniles as well. Parents had to be notified in a timely manner concerning charges against their child and juveniles had a right to a lawyer, the right of protection against self-incrimination, and the right to cross-examine witnesses.

These safeguards, known as due process requirements, also stated that the court had to notify juveniles of charges and hearings. In a 1970 case the Court increased the level of proof needed to find juveniles guilty. The level of proof changed from a preponderance (significant amount) of evidence to guilty beyond a reasonable doubt as in adult criminal courts.

Following the initial Supreme Court rulings on juvenile justice procedures, Congress passed the Juvenile Delinquency Prevention Act in 1972. The act set out general rules for state juvenile justice systems, such as keeping juveniles separate from adults in jails and prisons, and required juveniles to have a court-appointed guardian. In another case affecting juvenile justice, the Supreme Court ruled in *Breed v. Jones* (1975) that a person could not be tried for the same offense in both juvenile and criminal courts.

A New Justice Approach

General disappointment with the juvenile justice system in the early twenty-first century led to exploring alternative processes. One approach, called the "restorative justice approach," came into use in several countries including the United States. Called a community-based approach, in these cases the juvenile offender, the victim, their families, and several members of the community meet to repair the harm done. A person not associated with either of the parties guides the group to an agreed upon consequence or punishment for the juvenile. Positive results with this approach led to increasing interest and proposals that less serious juvenile offenders be treated through such community-based programs, leaving the more serious cases for the adult criminal justice system.

Getting tough on crime

By 1980 youth gangs coupled with gun violence caught the public's attention. In *Schall v. Martin* (1984) the Court

The Juvenile Delinquency Prevention Act reaffirmed that states had to keep juveniles separate from adults in jails and prisons, causing all-juvenile prisons, like this one in South Dakota, to open. *(AP/Wide World Photos)*

ruled that juvenile court judges could arrest and hold (detain) juveniles, but they must have a special hearing and inform parents of the date, charges, and reasons for detention. Juveniles were sent in greater numbers to adult courts to face more severe punishment, including possible execution. Some states even passed laws making parents legally responsible for their children's criminal acts.

Juvenile crime rates rose steadily from 1980 to 1994. A rash of fatal school shootings in the 1990s kept fear of juvenile crime high and many believed dangerous offenders were not punished enough in the juvenile justice system. Violent juvenile crime rates, however, declined after 1994 and by 2000 had fallen back to 1980 levels.

Despite lower crime rates, fear of juvenile violence remained high. As a result, the line between juvenile and adult criminal justice was less clear than in earlier decades—juvenile sentences were tougher, a higher number of cases were deferred to adult criminal courts, and youthful offenders were held to greater levels of accountability for their crimes.

Modern juvenile justice

In the early twenty-first century all states had juvenile courts and laws identifying the rights of juveniles and the options available to judges. Larger U.S. jurisdictions had full-time juvenile courts, while smaller ones were part time and often combined with some other form of court.

Juvenile judges were licensed attorneys in most states and often elected officials. Because of the large caseloads in some areas, experienced attorneys acted as assistant judges under supervision of the juvenile judge. The most frequent violent offense for juveniles is aggravated assault, while the most common property crime is larceny-theft.

Delinquency proceedings

Though juvenile justice procedures vary among the states, they do share certain basic features. For juveniles accused of criminal acts or status offenses, police often issue reprimands or notify parents instead of taking offenders into custody. If juveniles are taken into custody, they have a right to telephone their parents and an attorney. Juveniles in custody are usually separated from adults but some occasionally find themselves among adult defendants. Almost half of the states require a juvenile's school receive some form of notification.

Within hours of an arrest, a juvenile will be interviewed by an intake worker, a person trained to work with youthful offenders, such as a probation officer. Most jurisdictions have a detention center, which is used for intake interviews and houses juveniles awaiting hearings or serving short sentences. The worker also interviews the parents and the victim or person who filed the complaint.

After the hearing, the juvenile is usually released to a parent or guardian. The intake worker then decides whether the case should be dismissed, go to court for a hearing, or be han-

An attorney meets with her young client. Juveniles and their parents have a right to hear any pending charges and to have an attorney. The court will appoint an attorney if the juvenile's family cannot afford one. (© Shelley Gazin/Corbis)

dled informally with a warning to the offender or referring the family to a social worker. Many cases are dismissed or settled informally. If the intake worker decides the case should proceed, then the information is forwarded to a prosecutor. Parents are advised of the right to legal representation, if the prosecutor proceeds by petitioning (formally requesting) a hearing before the court to began prosecution.

Juveniles and their parents have a right to hear any pending charges and to have an attorney. The court will appoint an attorney if the juvenile's family cannot afford one. Youthful offenders cannot be made to testify against themselves and prosecutors must prove their guilt beyond a reasonable doubt, just like in adult criminal cases.

Like adult criminal court, a prosecutor presents evidence before a judge, the offender responds to the evidence and is able to question witnesses. Unlike adult cases, however, juveniles cannot have jury trials and their records are sealed (kept private) in most states. In addition, juvenile court proceedings are held in rooms separate from adult courtrooms.

If juvenile offenders are found delinquent, they face another hearing with a probation officer who prepares a more detailed report on the youth's background. The officer may require alcohol and drug tests, check for learning disabilities, and explore mental health needs. The report is shared with the juvenile and his or her lawyer before the sentencing hearing is held. During the hearing, the victim or a victim's family can talk about how the offender's crime has affected them.

Treatment of delinquent youths

Juvenile court judges have many sentencing choices, such as probation, issuing fines, sending offenders to juvenile correctional institutions or foster homes, referrals to day treatment or social skills classes, mental health programs, or community service. A combination of treatments is often ordered by the judge. These can include probation, community service, fines, or medical treatment. Repeat offenders can be declared juvenile delinquents and removed from their homes and placed in foster care or a state facility.

The harshest treatment a judge may order is commitment to a secure reform facility. In other words, the juvenile is locked into the facility for the duration of his or her sentence. These facilities are often called youth development centers. Though rehabilitation is the goal of juvenile justice, these centers resemble prisons and serve to protect the community from the juvenile.

The length of time juveniles serve in secure facilities can vary. Since offenders are only sentenced to confinement for more serious crimes, they often remain there until they reach eighteen years of age. Most states, however, allow juvenile courts to keep jurisdiction over the offenders beyond eighteen. Some states, like New Hampshire, place juvenile offenders in adult prisons if they commit a violent crime and are at least sixteen years of age.

First-time youth offenders cleaning the streets of New York instead of doing jail time. Juvenile court judges have many sentencing choices, such as probation, issuing fines, sending offenders to juvenile correctional institutions, and community service, among others.
(© Marc Asnin/Corbis)

Most youth offenders receive a sentence of probation. Probation means a juvenile is released back into the community under the supervision of a youth services officer. The juvenile has to meet certain conditions such as completing school with a good record and not using drugs or alcohol. If the juvenile does not fulfill these conditions, the judge can order him or her to be confined in a development center.

By the early twenty-first century the privacy of juvenile records was no longer assured. About half of U.S. states do not allow records of serious or violent offenses to be sealed or destroyed. Some thirty states grant access to sealed records under certain circumstances, as spelled out in state laws. Nine states allowed the release of juvenile court records without any restrictions, while thirteen permitted or required delinquency hearings be open to the public.

Juveniles in adult criminal court

Thousands of youths are transferred to adult courts every year. In the most serious cases, juveniles can be reassigned immediately, and in some states the move is automatic for certain offenses. Assigning juveniles to adult courts has always been controversial. As a result, state laws differ as to what offenses deserve to be transferred and how it should be handled. In 1997 forty-six states allowed reassignment. These offenses increased during the "get tough" period of the 1980s and 1990s.

In most states, cases involving murder, rape, aggravated assault, and armed robbery are transferable. Other offenses include drug violations, running away from juvenile facilities, stalking, and various sex offenses. Juveniles have the right to appeal court decisions to adult courts. In federal courts a juvenile can be sent to an adult criminal court for violating federal firearms laws or selling illegal drugs.

The process requires a prosecutor to request a transfer from juvenile to adult court and to show the juvenile is the one who committed the crime. The prosecutor may also say the juvenile is not likely to be helped by treatment and is a danger to the community. According to the 1966 Supreme Court ruling in *Kent v. U.S.*, juveniles have the right to be present at the transfer request with an attorney.

Juvenile offenders can provide evidence at transfer hearings and cross-examine witnesses to prevent moving to adult court. The decision often depends on the crime and the offender's prior offenses. If the decision is made to transfer the case, the prosecutor notifies the adult court in another hearing.

Juveniles tried in adult courts are considered first offenders and generally receive lighter sentences. The transfer of a juvenile to adult courts, however, can have serious consequences. The juvenile could be sentenced to life in prison or even execution. In 1988 the Supreme Court ruled that no juvenile younger than sixteen years of age at the time of the crime could be executed by a state.

The lawyers for a high-school shooting suspect try to prevent the boy from being tried as an adult. The transfer of a juvenile to adult courts can have serious consequences. The juvenile could be sentenced to life in prison or even execution. *(AP/Wide World Photos)*

As emphasis shifted from rehabilitation to crime control, most states passed laws in the 1980s and 1990s making it easier to send juveniles to adult courts. As a result, the number of cases transferred between 1988 and 1994 increased by 73 percent before declining in the late 1990s. Another consequence was that the number of juveniles in prison doubled between 1985 and 1998.

Cases of abuse or neglect

Besides handling cases of delinquency and status offenses, juvenile justice systems also deal with cases involving abuse, neglect, custody, adoption, paternity (identification of the biological father), and parental rights in general. Where abuse or neglect is a concern, a state agency or private citizen may petition a juvenile court to take action.

In cases of suspected physical or emotional abuse, the judge will assign a guardian or trained volunteer to serve as an advocate for the juvenile in court and in dealing with other services. This person may also prepare a report on the youth's living conditions to help the judge make a decision. The judge will usually place the juvenile in foster care or a state home, and keep certain people from having contact with the juvenile.

Removal of a juvenile from home may also occur when the court determines the parents do not have enough money to raise the child. In such cases, the parents have the right to be heard in court and the juvenile may also testify. Many times the judge will refer the juvenile or parents for counseling.

Reasons for juvenile crime

Various theories for juvenile crime have been offered through the years. Some researchers point to individual traits, such as neurological (brain) functioning, nutritional deficiencies, and psychological or emotional problems. Others point to the youth's living environment. Poor children often do not have educational, economic, and social opportunities. Drug use and other criminal activity may be occurring within the family. The juvenile may be hanging around with other delinquent youths, sometimes in gangs who offer alternative ways to gain social status.

Many still believe the major factor affecting delinquent behavior is poor parenting, with little or no control over the youth or worse, when parents simply do not care. The favored method to solving juvenile crime for some is not through harsh punishment, but in childcare and educational programs to address the issues of poverty, drug abuse, and neglect.

The future of juvenile justice

Public support for a separate juvenile system declined in the late twentieth century. Critics argued they should be abolished, claiming juvenile courts coddled youthful offenders and rehabilitation was ineffective in many individuals. Critics further claimed the courts were established only to handle status offenses such as truancy, not the violent mass murders of the late twentieth century.

Youthful offenders, critics believed, should be punished according to their crimes, just like adults. If offenders believed juvenile courts would not hold them fully responsible for their crimes, they would be more likely to commit serious crimes. Juveniles who were confined for serious crimes were released by age twenty-one or even eighteen, serving far shorter sentences than adults who committed the same offense. Critics of the juvenile justice system believed the age of an offender should be a factor, but only on an individual basis during sentencing.

Defenders of juvenile courts claimed youth crime rates have decreased and the court system should not be judged on the highly publicized violent acts of a few, such as the school shootings of the late 1990s. They claimed the court system allows judges to transfer the most violent offenders to adult courts, which did occur on an increasing basis by the early 2000s. Supporters further remarked that since children are treated differently than adults in every other part of society, it should be the same in the criminal justice system as well.

Juvenile justice defenders believed exposing youthful offenders to the violent world of adult prisons increased the potential of future criminal behavior. Rather than pay for a juvenile to be imprisoned, the funding would be better spent on rehabilitation programs, including education and job training. Instead of branding youthful offenders as adult convicted criminals, give them the chance to learn from their mistakes. Statistics showed youths who went through juvenile courts had lower rates of returning to criminal behavior than those who went through adult courts. Most importantly, supporters of juvenile justice believed society had to address the basic social and economic causes of juvenile crime while still holding violent offenders accountable for their actions.

For More Information

Books

Clement, Mary. *The Juvenile Justice System.* 3rd ed. Woburn, MA: Butterworth Heinemann, 2002.

Mones, Paul. *When a Child Kills.* New York: Simon & Schuster, 1991.

Platt, Anthony. *The Child Savers: The Invention of Delinquency.* Chicago, IL: University of Chicago Press, 1969.

Whitehead, J. T., and S. P. Lab. *Juvenile Justice: An Introduction.* 3rd ed. Cincinnati, OH: Anderson, 1999.

Web Sites

National Center for Juvenile Justice. http://www.ncjj.org (accessed on August 20, 2004).

National Center for Mental Health and Juvenile Justice. http://www.ncmhjj.com (accessed on August 20, 2004).

20

Children's Rights

From the late nineteenth century into the early twenty-first century, U.S. society increasingly became concerned about the welfare of the nation's children. Congress and the states passed special laws recognizing that children held a right to a healthful upbringing and are particularly vulnerable to being victimized by criminals. Children have a right to basic needs such as food, clothing, shelter, medical care, education, and safety from society's ills. All states have laws requiring biological parents to provide these basic needs. However parents are given much discretion on how they satisfy these responsibilities of providing nurturing and safety. Criminal penalties were provided for those who denied these rights through abuse, assault, abduction, or some other action. The laws addressed acts against children at home, in places of worship, at childcare facilities, and in the workplace. The laws also placed an emphasis on prevention as well as prosecution.

The basis for these criminal laws was the recognition that children have special needs separate from adults. By the twentieth century the public determined that to protect the long-term interests of society children must be provided the basic

Two young boys working in a textile mill. *(The Library of Congress)*

needs to develop into healthy and productive adults. At the same time the laws protect the parents' interests in raising their children as they see fit. Overall the United States gives parents greater flexibility than many other countries.

When a child faces hunger, abuse, or neglect, the state intervenes in family matters. Those who deny these basic rights to children can be charged with criminal offenses. In addition criminal penalties are particularly harsh toward those who abuse, sexually assault, murder, or kidnap children.

Protection of children

For centuries children over the age of seven were considered little adults, especially the poor who often had to work to help support their families. They were also considered as "property" owned by their parents with few rights. Fathers in particular had nearly total power in disciplining and working their children, especially in farming communities where children fed and tended livestock. The government stayed away from internal family relations. As a result, no specific criminal laws addressed child abuse or neglect. Assaults or kidnapping by others were treated by general criminal laws. Such was the legal status of children during much of the American colonial period prior to the American Revolution (1775–83).

By the late eighteenth century, public perceptions of children began to shift. American society changed throughout the nineteenth century as cities grew around newly developing industrial centers. Immigration was growing as well, particularly from eastern Europe by the late part of the century. With parents working long hours in factories, children were left alone and some citizens became concerned for their well-being, worried that they were susceptible to becoming crime victims. Others were concerned about the effects of so many unsupervised children on the streets, that they could enter into criminal activity making the streets less safe for others. In addition sociological perceptions of children continued to change.

As society realized children were not just little versions of adults, ideas about child development grew. It became known that children did not have the same reasoning abilities as most adults and could not be held responsible for all of their actions, especially if they did not have proper supervision. Early promoters of children's rights believed children needed proper legal protection and special consideration in the justice system.

Other changes in society also affected children in the country after the American Civil War (1861–65). With fathers increasingly away at factory work, mothers gained greater responsibility in raising children. This trend led courts to adopt the "tender years" policy, which recognized mothers as the primary caregivers for a child's early years.

With all of these changes in attitude and growing concerns over the welfare of the young, courts applied the concept of *parens patriae* more freely. The concept meant that the state could act as a parent if it was believed necessary. Under this concept, the government has the duty to intervene in families to make decisions in the best interest of the children when needed.

Childcare

Organized childcare outside of the home assists parents in providing the basic needs of a child. Though often controversial in much of the twentieth century, organized childcare has a long history in the United States. Infant daycare facilities have operated in parts of Boston and New York City since the early 1800s. The number of day nurseries increased by the late nineteenth century as industries grew and increasing numbers of immigrants, both men and women, sought jobs. These facilities were primarily for children of the working poor and run by private charities. For middle-class families, kindergartens became available in the mid-nineteenth century.

Publicly funded childcare programs did not come into existence until World War II (1939–45). Congress passed the Community Facilities Act in 1941 to create childcare centers for war industry workers. Many women worked in the war industries while their husbands were away in the military. This national childcare program ended after the war, though California kept some centers open through state support.

In place of a national childcare system, other programs were created throughout the postwar years to assist parents and fulfill the rights of children. These programs included Head Start for poor children under four years of age; Aid to Families with Dependent Children, which helped pay for daycare; the At-Risk Child Care Program, which gave assistance to families in need; income tax deductions for childcare expenses; and the 1993 Family Leave Act, which required large companies to grant unpaid leave to employees who needed time off to care for children or family members.

In addition to programs for younger children, all school-aged youngsters are provided free education at public schools. School aged children with disabilities are also provided access to education through the Individuals with Disabilities Education Act of 1975. The Medicaid program was created to assist the healthcare needs of the poor and their children.

Organized childcare continued as privately-owned businesses in the United States into the twenty-first century. To ensure the quality and safety of private childcare centers, states regulate these services. State agencies require childcare centers to screen workers for criminal records; facilities and workers who commit severe violations can be criminally charged.

Child labor

Another key concern over children's rights arose in the late nineteenth century. Many children were working long hours in dangerous factories for very low pay. Employing children was common in the city, especially among poor immigrant populations. It was not until 1938 that Congress passed the Fair Labor Standards Act (FLSA) restricting child labor. The act continued to be the primary federal child labor law into the twenty-first century. Most states also passed child labor laws while other relied solely on the FLSA.

The limits imposed by the Fair Labor Standards Act are complex and dependent on the nature of the work and age of the youth. Children must be at least fourteen years of age to work in non-manufacturing jobs outside of school hours. They must be at least sixteen for general employment during school hours, and they must be eighteen to work in occupations considered hazardous by the Department of Labor, such as manufacturing of explosives, coal mining, logging, and driving a motor vehicle.

In some states, children must also have parental permission to work at certain jobs. Under some state laws, employers in certain businesses must obtain employment certificates from

Before child labor laws, children often worked in dangerous conditions for long hours with little pay. *(The Library of Congress)*

the state to legally employ a youth under a certain age. On the other hand, parents cannot force minors to work in hazardous jobs. Criminal prosecution can result from violations of child labor laws, both involving employers and the parents depending on the specific case. Those convicted of child labor violations can be fined. An employer cannot use the defense of being ignorant of a youth's age if caught illegally employing a minor, even if the youth lied on his or her job application.

Kidnapping and abduction

Kidnapping is the aggravated (for ransom or injury) false imprisonment of a person. In colonial days kidnapping was just a misdemeanor punishable by fine or some other public punishment. There was no special category when the victim

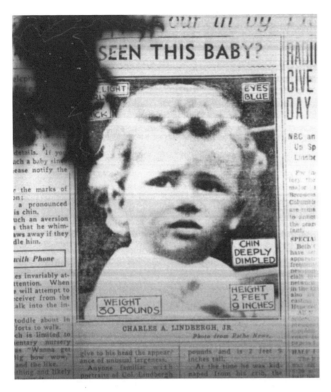

The kidnapping and murder of the Lindbergh baby in 1932 brought a public outcry for stiffer kidnapping penalties. *(AP/Wide World Photos)*

was a child. In addition kidnapping was not considered a crime unless the abduction was violent or involved international travel. The newly formed states passed kidnapping laws following founding of the United States, but most states continued to consider it a misdemeanor crime. As a result children of the wealthy were frequently targeted by kidnappers seeking high ransoms. Often the children were murdered even when the ransom was paid. Kidnappers would commonly take their victims to another state to be outside the jurisdictional territory of the state in which the abductions occurred.

The kidnapping and murder of the infant son of famous American aviator Charles Lindbergh (1902–1974) in 1932 brought a public outcry for stiffer kidnapping penalties. Congress passed the Lindbergh Law making kidnapping a federal criminal offense when the kidnapper takes his victim across the state borders.

The kidnapping of children for ransom declined through the latter half of the twentieth century, replaced by kidnapping cases involving bitter child custody cases and by sex offenders. To address parental kidnappings in violation of custody rights, Congress passed first the Uniform Child Custody Jurisdiction Act followed by the federal Parental Kidnapping Prevention Act of 1994. Most states also include parental kidnapping in their general kidnapping laws.

Abductions by sex offenders drew considerable attention in the 1990s and afterwards. Because sex offenders have a very high risk of repeating crimes, the State of Washington passed the first law in the nation in 1990 that authorized criminal justice officials to notify communities when a dangerous sex offender is released in their area.

The following years witnessed several highly publicized cases of children being abducted and murdered. As a result a series of laws were passed to stiffen the penalties for these crimes against children. The brutal rape and murder of seven year-old Megan Kanka in 1994 led to a public outcry for a national community notification system like the one Washington had established four years earlier. On May 17, 1996, President Bill Clinton (1946–; served 1993–2001) signed Megan's Law. The law required states to register offenders convicted of sex crimes against children and make personal information on registered sex offenders available to the public.

After nine-year-old Amber Hagerman of Arlington, Texas, was abducted and brutally murdered in January 1996, more legislative remedies were pursued to prosecute criminals victimizing children and to attempt to prevent such crimes. The most significant came in 2003 when Congress passed the Prosecutorial Remedies and Other Tools to End the Exploitation of Children Today Act, known as the PROTECT Act. The act made child abuse killings first-degree murders subject to the death penalty. It also strengthened penalties for kidnapping and eliminated the statute of limitations for child abduction and sex crimes. Previously once the child victim reached the age of twenty-five, the offender could no longer be criminally prosecuted. The minimum penalty for kidnapping by a non-family member rose to twenty years. In addition a person convicted in a first offense of child sexual exploitation and child pornography faced penalties from fifteen to thirty years in prison. A "two strikes" rule in the act requires life imprisonment for offenders who commit two serious sexual abuse offenses against a child. The act also prohibits any obscene materials depicting children and provides harsher penalties than those penalties provided in general obscenity laws.

A key feature of the PROTECT Act was creation of the AMBER Alert program. The program established a national communications network for alerting the public immediately after an abduction of a youth under eighteen years of age has been reported. The child must be considered in danger of harm or death. The alerts bring in the assistance of local public in spotting the missing child, their abductor, or the vehicle reportedly used in the abduction.

During the late 1990s concern also arose over the abduction of children for the purposes of selling them into international sex trade networks. To give law enforcement more tools to address this growing issue of human trafficking, Congress passed the Victims of Trafficking and Violence Protection Act of 2000.

Forms of child abuse

Child abuse is a major social problem; every child has the right to be free of physical and emotional harm. Child abuse is causing or failing to prevent actions against children that can result in serious physical or emotional harm, including sexual abuse and even death. This also includes neglect or placing a child at risk of serious harm, even if no injury results. Some forms of physical abuse include locking kids in closets, tying them to a bed, making them stand for long periods of time, or leaving them home alone. A child's right to freedom from abuse is balanced with the right of parents to discipline their children without government interference.

Child sexual abuse not only includes rape and improper touching, but also other actions such as a person exposing his or her private parts to a child or giving a child sexually explicit or pornographic material. Even if the child is not physically touched or harmed, these are still crimes of sexual abuse.

While sexual abuse is the least common form of child abuse, the most common is neglect. Neglect can lead to both physical and emotional harm. It is difficult to define neglect, because parents in poverty situations cannot provide as much care as those with higher incomes. Improper healthcare or not providing an education can also qualify as criminal neglect. Emotional abuse comes from exposure to domestic violence, drug use, dirty homes, and inadequate clothing.

Criminalizing child abuse

Real concern over child abuse did not surface until after the Civil War (1861–65) in the 1870s. At that time, the American Society for the Prevention of Cruelty to Animals went to court over an eight-year-old New York girl who was whipped and beaten regularly by her foster parents. The society argued in court that children deserved at least the same protections as animals from abuse.

The society's argument worked. The foster mother was convicted of assault and sentenced to one year of hard labor. This court victory led to the establishment of the New York Society for the Prevention of Cruelty to Children in 1874. The following year the New York legislature passed a law prohibiting child abuse.

Child abuse did not catch national attention, however, for another ninety years. In 1962 Dr. Henry Kempe published an article called "The Battered Child Syndrome" in the *Journal of the American Medical Association*. The article described various signs of child abuse to help doctors detect abuse among their patients. The signs or symptoms mentioned included skin, bone, and abdominal injuries. Behavioral clues included anxiety or depression, or self-destructive actions.

The article had a far wider affect than simply alerting physicians. Media attention about the article greatly increased public awareness of child abuse. By 1970 every state had passed child abuse laws. These laws required teachers, doctors, childcare staff, and social workers to report suspected child abuse to authorities. Failing to report suspected abuse could lead to criminal charges; eighteen states legally required anyone who suspected abuse to report it, even friends of the child's family.

Eleven-year-old Joe Roach was found chained to the bed in his home by a Houston deputy sheriff in 1954. The boy said that he'd spent the night before sleeping in the doghouse in his backyard rather than going into the house to be mistreated. *(© Bettmann/Corbis)*

Every state also has laws limiting the criminal liability of those who report suspicious symptoms. They cannot be sued or criminally charged for making reports that prove inaccurate as long as they acted in good faith or with the best interests of the child in mind. To support the growing caseload, Congress passed the federal Child Abuse Prevention and Treatment Act (CAPTA) in 1974. The act required states to create mandatory requirements for people to report suspected cases of child abuse. It was now a crime in all fifty states to not report suspected child abuse. It also created the National Center on Child Abuse and Neglect with the Department of Health and Human Services and provided federal funding for child abuse investigations and the protective services provided for abused children.

State and federal child abuse programs offered other information about how to detect abuse. For example, doctors and teachers may look for suspicious statements by parents or the child, public humiliation of a child by the parents, unexplained absences, or a sudden drop in school grades.

Child abuse as a defense in the courtroom

Individual histories of child abuse were increasingly used in criminal trials as a defense against serious allegations. One of the earliest and most publicized cases involving a defense involving child abuse was the murder trial of the Menendez brothers in Southern California. In August 1989 Erik and Lyle Menendez murdered their parents in their Beverly Hills mansion. The two brothers stood to inherit $14 million. The following March they were arrested and charged with murder. During their trial they claimed the murders were in self-defense after years of sexual abuse by their father and neglect by their mother. After an initial mistrial for one of the two brothers, a jury found them guilty in 1996 and sentenced them to life in prison.

Similarly in October 1994 Susan Smith in Union County, South Carolina, drove her car into a lake drowning her three-year-old and sixteen-month-old sons. She murdered her children in order to keep a love affair alive with a boyfriend. In her defense, Smith claimed she suffered several emotional problems including depression following years of sexual abuse from a stepfather. The jury found Smith guilty of murder but gave her a life in prison sentence rather than death, perhaps because of the defense.

Child protective services

State service agencies to protect children enforce laws prohibiting child abuse. These laws vary from state to state but some common procedures exist. Usually, reports of suspected child abuse went to local police departments, but in the 1970s child protective service agencies took over this responsibility in about half the states. Some provided free telephone hotlines to report suspected abuse.

After receiving notification of possible abuse, the agency must investigate, intervene if necessary to protect the child from further abuse, and keep written records. The investigation, sometimes performed by the police, includes interviews with the child, parents, doctors, and teachers. Agency intervention or involvement can include placing a child temporarily in a detention home or in foster care.

In the late 1990s over 560,000 youths were in foster care at any specified time. Intervention can also include monitoring of a home situation and providing counseling if needed for the parents. The number of cases each child protective worker handles can be astounding. Investigations in 1998 found some 903,000 children were abused or neglected in that year or about 13 for every 1,000 children in the general U.S. population. This was only for cases that were actually reported; many incidents of child abuse are never reported at all. About 1,087 children died from child abuse in 1998.

In severe cases, an abused child is permanently removed from a home and put up for adoption. The protective agency is required to write a report of its findings, which may lead to criminal charges against the abusing person. Abuse findings go into computer databases that include information on both known child abusers and those suspected of abuse.

Having an easily available database of abuse reports has led to concern and opposition. Opponents claim such a system could include information on innocent persons whose reputations could be greatly harmed if they are labeled as child abusers. In 1984 the Victims of Child Abuse Laws group formed to assist people falsely accused of child abuse.

Child sexual abuse and the Catholic Church

Though various cases of child sexual abuse caught the public's eye in the United States through the 1990s and early 2000s, the nation was stunned by allegations that involved the Catholic Church. The first awareness of what would later

Children's Defense Fund

The Children's Defense Fund (CDF) is a national organization that promotes the social welfare of children. The CDF lobbies Congress for funding to support various children's programs and conducts national awareness campaigns. It regularly publishes reports on the health and social well-being of children. Much of CDF's efforts have focused on saving federal programs from budget cuts.

Marian Wright Edelman, the first black woman to pass the state bar exam in Mississippi, founded the CDF in 1973. Edelman first gained national attention in the 1960s when she successfully stopped the state of Mississippi from withholding federal Head Start program funds from black American children. By the late 1960s Edelman had established the Washington Research Project, a group dedicated to fighting racial discrimination. A staff attorney for the group was Hillary Rodham Clinton, who later became first lady.

In 1973 Edelman turned the Washington Research Project into the Children's Defense Fund to focus on the needs of children. After fighting year after year to prevent budget cuts, the CDF got a boost

Founder of the CDF Marian Wright Edelman (far right) poses with a group of children on "Children's Day." *(AP/Wide World Photos)*

when Bill Clinton became president in 1993. Clinton signed two pieces of legislation promoted by CDF during his terms. The Family and Medical Leave Act of 1993 provided the right for workers to take unpaid leave to care for children or family members in medical need, while the Full Faith and Credit for Child Support Orders Act of 1994 increased enforcement of child support payments.

unfold into a huge child abuse scandal came in the early 1990s when Father James Porter was convicted of abusing some one hundred boys and girls in various Catholic parishes around the Boston area stretching back into the 1960s.

Porter was found guilty and the court sentenced him to up to twenty years in prison in December 1993. The case shocked Catholics and others around Boston, and the city's cardinal (a high ranking Catholic Church official), Bernard Law, consoled the public by stating that Porter's abuse was an isolated or single case. Law condemned the news media for its coverage of the scandal, but introduced a new sexual abuse policy for his region anyway to calm his church members.

The Boston scandal quieted down for the next several years until another area Catholic priest, John Geoghan, was investigated for 130 cases of child sexual abuse in 1998. Geoghan was forced out of the priesthood and convicted in January 2002 of child sexual abuse. The court sentenced him to up to ten years in prison. Again Cardinal Law insisted this was simply another unusual case regarding Catholic priests.

After Geoghan's case and conviction, however, many more alleged victims came forward about sexual abuse involving priests. Newspaper inquiries and criminal investigations revealed many more. Secret church documents became public in 2002 and proved the Catholic Church not only had knowledge of sexual abuse by priests but had covered it up.

The documents mentioned numerous priests, hundreds of victims, and how claims were repeatedly ignored by church officials. Some alleged victims, however, had been paid off to keep them quiet while certain priests were transferred to new churches and given brief counseling. The documents showed that even Geoghan had been transferred two times for molesting children before finally being caught by authorities. Another priest, Paul Shanley, had also been transferred to new parishes despite a history of child sexual abuse known to the church.

Massachusetts had no law that required suspected child abuse to be reported to authorities. Some cases of child rape, however, were clearly criminal acts and they too went unreported by church authorities. Documents showed church leaders made no attempt to ever inform law enforcement of these criminal activities. As public disgust grew from one revelation after another, Cardinal Law repeatedly refused to resign from his post. In a rare move in April 2002, the pope summoned all U.S. cardinals to the Vatican in Rome to discuss the sex abuse issue.

By late 2002 some 1,200 Catholic priests in the United States were accused of child sex abuse. Four U.S. bishops

Cardinal Bernard Law

Bernard Law was born on November 4, 1931, to a U.S. Air Force colonel and his wife in Torreon, Mexico. The family moved from one military base to another; as a result Law was educated in North and South America and the Virgin Islands. He then attended Harvard University and received a degree in medieval history in 1953. Following Harvard, Law entered the seminary and became an ordained Catholic priest in 1961.

During his years in the Catholic Church, Law was known for his work with immigrants and minorities. In the 1960s he was very active in the Civil Rights movement in Mississippi, and in 1968 Law took a job in the office of the U.S. Conference of Catholic Bishops. He became known among church leaders across the country and was appointed bishop in a Missouri diocese in 1973. Law became bishop in Boston in 1984, one of the most powerful Catholic Church regions in the nation. The following year he was ordained as a cardinal.

Law was immensely popular in the Boston area. He rose in international prominence as well within the church. Law also met with President George W. Bush (1946–; served 2001–) and other religious leaders shortly after the September 11, 2001, terrorist attacks in New York City and Washington, D.C.

Law's leadership began to crumble in 2002 as the child sexual abuse scandal

Cardinal Bernard Law walking away from a podium after reading another apology for his role in the clergy sex abuse scandal.
(AP/Wide World Photos)

spread in Boston, involving hundreds of victims and numerous priests over a period of decades. In December 2002 when secret church documents revealed that Law not only knew about the abuse but actually tried to cover it up, Law was forced to resign as cardinal before the pope.

In May 2004 Law received a new assignment in Rome, Italy. Much anger resulted in Boston that Law should remain in a church leadership position after being directly involved in covering up so much child sexual abuse.

resigned as the scandal went worldwide; other bishops resigned in Argentina, Germany, Ireland, Canada, Switzerland, Poland, and elsewhere. Then in December 2002 even more revealing church documents were discovered. These new documents described widespread child sex abuse in the Catholic Church and an equally large cover-up. Not only was Cardinal Law aware of all the abuse, but he actively tried to hide incident after incident of child rape from the public and law enforcement.

The second set of documents finally led to Cardinal Law's resignation on December 13, 2002. The Boston archdiocese was near bankruptcy under the weight of some four hundred claims of sexual abuse. By October 2003 Law's successor, Archbishop Sean P. O'Malley, helped negotiate an $85 million settlement with more than 550 sexual abuse victims. In May 2004 the Boston archdiocese announced the closure of about sixty-five parishes as it continued to deal with the consequences of the abuse scandal.

Child support

Protecting a child's right to a healthy, loving upbringing is a key responsibility of family courts. Family courts often address children's rights by attempting to resolve family problems, not by handing out criminal sentences. They hear cases of child abuse and neglect and enforce payment of child support (money used to raise the child).

Parents are granted freedom to raise their children as they see fit in the Fourteenth Amendment. When biological parents disagree over how to raise a child—usually occurring in divorce proceedings—family courts step in to determine child custody and support matters. In situations other than divorce, courts may still determine parents are not acting in the best interests of their child. Parents can be considered unfit if they abuse their children in any way, including the denial of medical care or financial support. A judge can appoint a guardian in such situations as the court considers other remedies.

A crucial part of divorce proceedings is child support, the payments made by one parent to the other parent who has custody rights. Both parents have a legal responsibility to provide support to a child for basic needs. Most children in single parent homes have the right to support payments, which are usually provided in divorce rulings. Other forms of support, such as paying for a child's insurance coverage, can also be ordered by the court.

States are responsible for making sure parents satisfy their child support responsibilities, which are often complicated by jurisdictional (the area within which a government agency or court has legal authority) issues. Parents often move to other areas or states for jobs or to establish a new life. To help states keep track of families, Congress passed the Uniform Interstate Family Support Act of 1992, followed by the Full Faith and Credit for Child Support Orders Act of 1994. These acts created rules about handling custody cases that span state lines, such as allowing states to pursue parents who owe support payments, even if they have moved to another state.

States set guidelines for what is considered adequate support, which usually ends when children reach age twenty-one, marry, or are able to support themselves. Civil and criminal penalties can be assessed against parents who do not make their child support payments. Criminal penalties can include jail sentences and fines and are applied to repeat offenders. Those who cross a state line to avoid paying support may also face federal prosecution.

By the early 1990s concern over the nonpayment of court ordered support grew. A report in 1992 found that $27 billion in support had not been paid. The U.S. Department of Justice established the Office of Child Support Enforcement to help states recover support dollars. The number of cases was enormous and forced states to find ways to collect support payments, such as claiming part of a parent's paycheck, charging fines, seizing owned property, even taking away a nonpaying parent's driver's license.

Lesser rights

While children have greater rights than adults concerning their basic needs, children have less rights than adults in certain other circumstances like school classrooms and at school events. Free speech and expression are limited if they are at odds with a school's educational mission, which includes courtesy, tolerance, and respect for others.

Former Massachusetts governor Paul Cellucci displays one of the state's "Ten Most Wanted" posters of individuals wanted for nonpayment of child support. *(AP/Wide World Photos)*

The courtroom is another place where juveniles have fewer rights. In juvenile court systems, unlike adults in regular courts, youths do not have the right to bail nor a jury trial. In addition, courts usually side with parents or guardians rather than children in determining what is in a child's best interest.

Children also do not have the right to file a lawsuit in court. There was some pressure in the 1990s to increase the legal standing of minors. On one occasion, a twelve-year-old boy took action in the state courts of Florida to cut legal ties with his parents. He stated that they were financially unable to provide for his basic needs, and though he won the case, an appeals court reversed the ruling saying he had no legal right to file the suit in the first place. Once adults joined him in the suit, his court victory was assured.

Children's rights advocates claim minors should be allowed to file lawsuits if they show a suitable level of knowledge. Society continues to wrestle with how much say a youth should legally have in his or her future.

Another difference in the rights of children and adults involves obscene materials. States protect the young from certain kinds of books, videos, and movies. For example, some sexually explicit materials may be considered obscene for children but not for adults. The same concept is applied to television programming. Television networks established family viewing times in the evening when children are most likely to be watching.

Creating family viewing guidelines were designed to protect children from sexually explicit or violent programs. Television networks steadily drifted from these standards in the twenty-first century. Similarly, the government has made efforts to regulate explicit sites on the Internet to protect children. Congress passed the Communications Decency Act of 1996 and the Child Online Protection Act of 1998. Several courts, however, ruled the acts unconstitutional.

For More Information

Books

Besharov, Douglas J. *Recognizing Child Abuse: A Guide for the Concerned.* New York: Free Press, 1990.

Bianchi, Anne. *Understanding the Law: A Teen Guide to Family Court and Minors' Rights.* New York: Rosen, 2000.

Fabricant, Michael. *Juveniles in the Family Courts.* Lexington, MA: Lexington Books, 1983.

Helfer, Mary E., Ruth S. Kempe, and Richard D. Krugman, eds. *The Battered Child.* 5th ed. Chicago, IL: University of Chicago Press, 1997.

Mnookan, Robert H., and D. Kelly Weisberg. *Child, Family, and State: Problems and Materials on Children and the Law.* Gaithersburg, MD: Aspen Law and Business, 2000.

Ramsey, Sarah H., and Douglas E. Adams. *Children and the Law in a Nutshell.* 2nd ed. St. Paul, MN: Thomson/West, 2003.

Sagaturn, Inger, and Leonard Edwards. *Child Abuse and the Legal System.* Chicago, IL: Nelson-Hall Publishers, 1995.

Web Sites

"National Clearinghouse on Child Abuse and Neglect Information." *U.S. Department of Health and Human Services Administration for Children and Families.* http://nccanch.acf.hhs.gov/ (accessed on August 20, 2004).

"What is Abuse?" *ChildhelpUSA®.* http://www.childhelpusa.org/abuseinfo_definitions.htm (accessed on September 2, 2004).

21

School Violence

A dramatic series of school shootings between 1995 and 1999 startled the nation. Deadly violence within schools struck fear in the public and particularly school-age youth across the nation. Beginning in 1989, there had been an increase in school violence, ranging from verbal harassment, threats of harm, and violent crime.

Overall national violent crime rates dropped after 1993 and continued at lower levels into the twenty-first century. Similarly, following a period of increased violence by juveniles (youth less than eighteen years of age) between 1989 and 1993, youth violence had begun to level off or decline as well. Crimes reported by schools dropped 10 percent between 1995 and 1999. The decrease in youth violence, however, was less than the overall trend.

Public concern about school violence rose significantly as school shootings dominated the media's attention from 1997 to 1999. This was despite the fact that these high-profile crimes occurred during a period in which violent deaths related to schools and school activities had decreased by 40 percent.

A school security camera shows Eric Harris and Dylan Klebold on a
shooting spree at Columbine High School in 1999, killing thirteen
people and injuring twenty-six others. *(AP/Wide World Photos)*

Suddenly in the late 1990s, some middle- and upper-class white youths were lashing out with planned acts of cold-blooded violence against their schoolmates and teachers. School violence was no longer considered an inner-city problem. In reaction to the rise in the number of multiple homicides, governments and school districts adopted new measures to identify and respond to possible problems before they erupted.

Though difficult, teachers and administrators turned to students for help; asking them to report threatening comments or dangerous activities. They also sought to reduce negative behavior such as bullying, which was generally ignored in the past or noticed but dismissed as typical adolescent behavior. As the United States entered the twenty-first century, the public considered schools to be dangerous places. Statistics actually indicated the opposite and showed that schools were the safest public places in the nation.

The history of school discipline

School discipline problems have substantially changed through time. Disciplinary action usually concerned talking without permission, being disruptive in class, running in the hallways, or smoking behind the gymnasium. By the 1970s dress codes became a key discipline issue; in the 1980s it was fighting among students. By the end of the 1980s and into the 1990s, gang activity entered schools. Along with it came the problems of weapons, substance abuse, and violent assaults against other students and school staff. Some students even carried firearms for protection.

Crime victim surveys in the early 1990s showed significant rates of robbery or theft and assaults in schools. Victims tended to be in inner-city schools, male, and of a racial minority. While theft was the most common crime in schools in general, assault was the most frequent violent crime. Multiple homicides in schools during this period were uncommon, though there were two in 1992. This yearly figure would more than double by the late 1990s when 3 percent of teachers became victims of violent school crime.

Until the late 1990s school violence was largely a problem of inner-city schools where there were high poverty and crime rates, drug trafficking and prostitution, and poorly funded school districts. The growth of gang activity in schools after 1989 only reinforced these perceptions. The gang presence more than doubled in just four years by 1993.

In a dramatic shift, the highly publicized school shootings beginning in 1995 took the issue of school violence to the suburbs and rural communities of predominately white America. Accordingly the focus on causes of school violence expanded to include such issues as student peer pressure, or how some students were ignored and became outcasts. These behaviors appeared to trigger violent retaliation.

School shootings

In the early twenty-first century, the top school violence concern among students, parents, and school officials was shootings, though theft and other crimes were the most common. Before 1995 school shootings were infrequent and usually did not lead to multiple deaths. One early school shooting occurred in San Diego, California, in January 1979. Seventeen-year-old Brenda Spencer used a rifle she had just received for Christmas to shoot at an elementary school across the street from her house.

During a six-hour standoff, Brenda killed two men trying to protect the schoolchildren and wounded eight children and a police officer. Spencer showed no emotion when finally captured. In March 1987 in Missouri twelve-year-old Nathan Ferris, an honor student, grew tired of being teased. He took a gun to school and when teased shot and killed the student and then himself.

The rash of school shootings of the 1990s began in Giles County, Tennessee, on November 15, 1995. Seventeen-year-old Jamie Rouse, dressed in black, took a firearm to school and shot two teachers in the head, killing one, and killed another student while attempting to shoot the school's football coach. Rouse had told several of his classmates beforehand about his intentions, but none reported the conversations to authorities.

Less than two months later on February 2, 1996, in Moses Lake, Washington, fourteen-year-old Barry Loukaitis walked into a mathematics class wearing a long western coat. Under the coat he concealed two pistols, a high-powered rifle, and

Bullying

The April 1999 Columbine shooting spree and other occurrences of school violence triggered greater efforts to curb bullying in schools. Bullying, which includes a range of behavior including teasing and threats, exclusion from social activities, and more physical intimidation, has been widespread in American schools. It was often considered a normal part of growing up. When bullying repeatedly surfaced as a cause of deadly school violence through the 1990s, parents and schools took a renewed interest in the consequences of bullying and how to restrict it.

Studies in the 1990s showed that bullying was far from harmless and actually posed serious lasting effects. Victims of bullying suffered significant negative social and emotional development. In the short term victims suffered from low self-esteem, poor grades, few friends, and had school attendance problems. Such emotional problems as de-

pression and anxiety could also develop and last a lifetime. In addition, those doing the bullying often progressed to more serious aggressive behavior when not confronted about their actions.

Schools responded with aggressive antibullying programs and instituted stricter rules and discipline. Discipline was enforced through monitoring student behavior in all parts of the school grounds by school staff. Some new school programs taught anger control, ways for a victim to cope with bullying, and overall greater appreciation of student diversity in a school. Police also became more interested in threatening behavior at schools. Many school districts that adopted these measures reported significant declines in aggressive behavior. Web sites about bullying and its effects were also created to help students as well as provide support to school staffs.

ammunition. Loukaitis killed two classmates and the teacher while wounding another student. He took the rest of the class hostage. Another teacher rushed Loukaitis, ending the standoff. Loukaitis, like Rouse, had shared thoughts of going on a shooting spree with another student. The same day Loukaitis attacked his fellow schoolmates, a sixteen-year-old in Atlanta, Georgia, shot and killed a teacher.

Shootings become more frequent

On February 19, 1997, a year after the Washington and Georgia shootings, sixteen-year-old Evan Ramsey in Bethel, Alaska, who was tired of being teased, took a shotgun to school. He killed a student and the principal and wounded two other students. He had previously told two fourteen-year-olds about his plan for retribution against those bullying him and the authority figures who had not protected him.

Later in 1997, on October 1, sixteen-year-old Luke Woodham in Pearl, Mississippi, stabbed his mother to death then went to school carrying a rifle and a pistol. There he killed a girlfriend who had just broken up with him, a second girl, and wounded seven others. When returning to his car for more ammunition he was charged and captured by the assistant principal. Again, other students knew of his plan but told no one.

Two months later on December 1, fourteen-year-old Michael Carneal of Paducah, Kentucky, carried a gun to school and fired on a small prayer group killing three girls and wounding five others. Carneal was intrigued with Satan worshiping and frequently dressed in black. Other students had heard him talk about wanting to shoot up the school. Police found a pistol, two rifles, two shotguns, and seven hundred rounds of ammunition.

The spring of 1998

The spring of 1998 turned out to be a very bloody time in U.S. school history. On March 24, eleven-year-old Andrew Golden and thirteen-year-old Mitchell Johnson set off a fire alarm at Westside Middle School in Jonesboro, Arkansas. They then fired on school staff and students as they evacuated the building. The two boys killed one adult and four children and wounded ten others on the school's playground.

One month later on April 24, fourteen-year-old Andrew Wurst carried a handgun to an eighth grade school graduation dance in Edinboro, Pennsylvania. He killed a teacher and wounded three others before being captured while fleeing.

On May 21, barely a month later, fifteen-year-old Kipland Kinkel opened fire on a crowded school cafeteria in the morning before classes began at Thurston High School in Springfield, Oregon. He killed two and wounded seven others. When police went to his home, they found his murdered parents, whom he had killed the previous day. The house was booby-trapped with several bombs including one placed under his mother's body.

On May 21, 1998, Kipland Kinkel killed his parents and then went to school and opened fire on a crowded cafeteria at Thurston High School in Springfield, Oregon, killing two and wounding seven. *(AP/Wide World Photos)*

The day he murdered his parents Kinkel had been expelled for bringing a firearm to school, but he had been released by police to his father's custody. Kinkel was small in stature and had dyslexia (a learning disability). He felt inferior to his academic parents and athletic older sister. Kinkel was routinely teased at school and felt detached from his schoolmates.

Columbine and beyond

On April 20, 1999, two students of Columbine High School in Littleton, Colorado, entered the school and killed thirteen, including a teacher, while wounding twenty-six. Seventeen-year-old Eric Harris and eighteen-year-old Dylan Klebold had planned their shooting rampage long in advance. The sixteen-minute shooting spree ended with the two shooters committing suicide. This was the bloodiest episode in school violence in U.S. history.

Harris and Klebold had an illegally modified semiautomatic handgun, two sawed-off shotguns, and ninety-seven explosive devices. The two had also planted bombs around the school, which police recovered without exploding. The two had even planned on escaping and hijacking an airplane and crashing it into New York City.

The two had also been members of a club called the "Trenchcoat Mafia." Its members wore long, heavy black trench coats. Two other persons were convicted and sent to prison for illegally supplying the modified handgun to Harris and Klebold. The shooting later inspired a controversial documentary in 2001 titled *Bowling at Columbine*. Written and directed by Michael Moore, the film explored the culture of violence, especially firearms, in the United States.

The Columbine tragedy triggered other school violence. The number of school bomb threats by students increased for a brief time, more youth began wearing long black trench coats, and Internet sites popped up praising the shooters at Columbine. School closures increased in response to threats through the brief remainder of the school year.

The Columbine shootings, in addition to previous events of school violence, finally led students to begin reporting potentially threatening situations. No longer were threats of violence by fellow students ignored or not taken seriously. On May 13, 1999, only a few weeks after the Columbine shootings, students at a middle school reported that four classmates were planning a massacre at their school and trying to recruit others to help. The four were arrested and tried as adults, charged with conspiracy to commit murder.

The violence, however, was not over yet. On May 20, Anthony Solomon, a sophomore at Heritage High School in Conyers, Georgia, opened fire on the last day of school, wounding six.

Memorial crosses on a hill near Columbine High School in Littleton, Colorado, where two students killed twelve students and one teacher. *(AP/Wide World Photos)*

After a short lull in violence, school violence struck again. On February 5, 2001, three students who admired the Columbine shooters planned an attack on their school in Hoyt, Kansas. Others discovered the plans and turned them in. Police discovered bomb-making materials, a modified assault rifle, and a black trench coat. Police charged the students with conspiracy to commit aggravated arson.

One of the worst incidents to occur after Columbine came at Santana High School in Santee, California, on March 5, 2001. Tired of being teased for his short height, fifteen-year-old Charles Williams entered a crowded boys' bathroom in school and opened fire, killing two students and wounding thirteen. In addition to the handgun he took to school, police found seven rifles at his home.

Causes of school violence

The causes of school violence are complex and varied. Forensic psychologists who study criminal behavior believe school killers are very different from other violent youth, such as gang members or drug dealers. For whatever reason, they feel powerless and begin obsessing over killing or injuring others. They may make direct threats concerning those they feel are taunting or intimidating them. They often express these thoughts and plans to fellow students. In general, other students tend to ignore the comments or simply look the other way.

The decision to kill for these youth is not a sudden occurrence, but coldly planned. Use of guns gives them the power they felt deprived of, and makes those offending them powerless. In addition, the shooters become famous with their faces splashed across televisions screens nationwide. The violent outbreak turns the tables and gives them both the power and attention they seek. This type of offender is almost always male; females approach retribution in less direct ways, such as hiring classmates or others to kill those they wish to strike out against.

Students from Columbine High School mourn the loss of their friends and classmates after a tragic shooting at their school in 1999. *(AP/Wide World Photos)*

Each case may represent a unique combination of factors. Some are physical, some behavioral, and others are learned. Physical factors can include birth complications. For example, being deprived of oxygen during the birth process can lead to brain dysfunction and learning disabilities. Violent behavior has been linked to certain forms of these abnormalities. Similarly, head injuries have been shown to increase the potential for violent behavior in certain individuals.

Behavioral problems can be linked to a difficult personality, which leads to problems of interacting with others, impulsiveness, and being unable to conform. These children may not blend into school activities and become ignored and rebellious. Some become depressed and take medication that can produce serious behavioral side effects. Broken family relationships can also be a major factor. Harshly treated children are more likely to behave violently later in life.

Being bullied or teased by others can often lead a troubled youth to violent revenge or retribution. This factor showed up repeatedly in the school shootings of the 1990s and beyond. It received the most attention from school administrators and others in the early twenty-first century.

Learning violent behavior can come from a dysfunctional or abnormal home life, perhaps involving domestic abuse or parents who do not respond well to authority figures such as the police. From this type of home environment, youth learn to react to authority such as teachers or school officials with aggression. Some believe learned violent behavior also comes from repeated exposure to violence in the media such as music lyrics, Hollywood movies, television programs, video games, and 24-hour news stations broadcasting violent or graphic scenes. Studies showed that youth exposed to an overwhelming amount of such material became more aggressive and no longer upset by violence and its consequences. These kids, it is believed, have trouble distinguishing between reality and fantasy.

Schools themselves have changed a great deal since the 1950s, and by the later twentieth century they brought a wide range of students together from often markedly different social environments. Differences appear in attitudes and behavior that can lead to social cliques or racial tensions. A major change was the emergence of gangs, which doubled between 1989 and 1993. Gang activity within schools included recruiting new members, which often led to school violence as part of initiation. In addition, illegal activities in the vicinity of the school increased, such as selling drugs and firearms.

Yet another major factor in the rise of deadly school violence was the easy availability of firearms and other weapons. Estimates in the 1990s on the number of weapons brought to school on a daily basis were staggering. The number of guns brought into schools on any given day ranged up to over 250,000 and the number of knives more than double that figure.

Effects of school violence

The effects of school violence have been extensive. Many students stayed at home out of fear in the late 1990s than ever before. Schools were no longer viewed as safe havens for the nation's children. The increased presence of police, metal detectors, and intervention programs have become daily reminders of school violence.

The thousands of students directly exposed to school violence, both the highly publicized multiple homicides and the less publicized episodes of threats and standoffs that did not lead to actual injury or death, can suffer from posttraumatic stress disorder. This condition can cause depression, anger, and anxiety. Overall, the ability for youth to learn and schools to effectively teach are greatly affected by school violence.

Prevention

To prevent school violence, schools have looked at not just focusing on at-risk youth, but have also attempted to change the social climate and culture of their facilities. Teachers and administrators joined with parents, students, police, and the local community to help maintain a safe atmosphere in their schools. Safety programs were remodeled to be much more responsive not just to outbreaks of violence, but also to the signs of potential problems. Early warning signs were identified, including extreme or uncontrolled anger, knowledge of a student's illegal possession or access to firearms, students suffering the effects of extreme poverty, those targeted or making racist remarks, students with a low interest in school, and violence at home.

Classes were also added to educated students on human diversity and socializing. Thirteen state legislatures passed laws to aid in reducing school violence. Mental health requirements were added to some school curricula and in others funding was provided to increase the capabilities of existing mental health services.

More physical measures were adopted as well. Some schools installed metal detectors and security cameras. Police

Students are required to pass through metal detectors before entering the John Bartram High School in Philadelphia, Pennsylvania. In the 1990s, many schools throughout the country took such security measures to prevent school violence. *(AP/Wide World Photos)*

became a common sight on school property. Many schools adopted a "zero tolerance" policy for weapons, issuing automatic suspensions and even expulsions to students who brought weapons to school.

Alternate education programs have also been established for students who are unruly or incapable of blending in to local public schools. Programs have been added to help at-risk students, which usually involve mentoring and how to peacefully resolve disputes or problems. In general, schools have made a concentrated effort to reach every student, help with their social skills, and set expectations of academic performance.

For More Information

Books

Bonilla, Denise M., ed. *School Violence*. New York: H. W. Wilson, 2000.

Coloroso, Barbara. *The Bully, the Bullied, and the Bystander: From Pre-School to High School, How Parents and Teachers Can Help Break the Cycle of Violence*. New York: HarperResource, 2003.

Flannery, Daniel, and C. Ronald Huff, eds. *Youth Violence: Prevention, Intervention, and Social Policy*. Washington, DC: American Psychiatric Press, 1999.

Garbarino, James. *Lost Boys: Why Our Sons Turn Violent and How We Can Save Them*. New York: Free Press, 1999.

Heide, Kathleen M. *Young Killers: The Challenge of Juvenile Homicide*. New York: Sage, 1998.

Kelleher, Michael D. *When Good Kids Kill*. Westport, CT: Praeger, 1998.

Smith, Helen. *The Scarred Heart: Understanding and Identifying Kids Who Kill*. Knoxville, TN: Callisto, 2000.

Web Sites

Bullying.org. http://www.bullying.org (accessed on August 20, 2004).

The National Campaign to Prevent School Violence. http://www.ribbon ofpromise.org (accessed August 20, 2004).

North Carolina Department of Juvenile Justice and Delinquency Prevention, Center for the Prevention of School Violence. http://www.ncdjjdp. org/cpsv/ (accessed on August 20, 2004).

"School Violence." *Constitutional Rights Foundation*. http://www.crf-usa. org/violence/intro.html (accessed on August 20, 2004).

22

Moral and Religious Influences

The influence of religion and morality on criminal justice has been of major importance throughout history. Morality is society's set of accepted rules and norms of behavior. Morality is commonly part of religious belief; a primary role of religion is to exert control over its followers by setting and promoting rules and customs for people to follow. In turn, these rules help establish criminal laws in a government's justice system.

The role of religion in defining crimes in America's colonial society of the seventeenth and eighteenth centuries was clear. Key crimes included blasphemy (showing a lack of reverence toward God), sexual deviance, and heresy (holding a belief that conflicts with church doctrine). Early punishments focused on shame and guilt as ways of bringing those who strayed back into the fold. This shame and guilt were supposed to make the offender apologize, ask forgiveness, and live a better life.

Earlier yet in the Old World execution was the favored means of punishing those who broke society's rules. The role of prison chaplains (reverends, priests, or rabbis) in the late

During medieval times the Roman Catholic Church introduced
incarceration, or confinement in a prison, as an alternative to death.
The idea spread as Protestants in northern Europe established
corrections facilities in the late sixteenth century. *(© Corbis)*

fifteenth century was primarily to help those condemned to death repent their sins. During medieval times the Roman Catholic Church introduced incarceration as an alternative to death.

The idea spread as Protestants in northern Europe established corrections facilities in the late sixteenth century. The Catholics under Pope Clement XI built the Michel Prison in 1703 for youthful offenders, separating them from adults and providing work for rehabilitation. With the expansion of prisons in Britain in the early eighteenth century, Britain had assigned chaplains to all prisons by 1733.

Religion and crime

Those who settled North America from Europe were predominantly from the Christian faith, which greatly influenced the development of criminal justice systems in the United States. Basic Christian faith held that God created the world, established certain moral laws, and that breaking these laws could lead to suffering and punishment. U.S. criminal laws derived from those moral standards and set punishments for breaking them.

Morality establishes certain accepted standards called ethics. One standard is the integrity and fairness of the criminal justice system. Some of the ethics of early Americans were placed in the U.S. Constitution of 1789 in reference to liberty (freedom) and the pursuit of happiness. These ethics regulate such matters as how police use their legal power over citizens, particularly in regard to the use of force, deception, or invasion of privacy.

Many police departments have established codes of ethics to regulate police activity. Ethics standards also influence the punishment strategies of prisons, including the use of solitary confinement, strip searches, and allowing visitors like church officials and family members. In courtrooms, ethics concerns serve to buffer or guard against the desire for retaliation, lying on the witness stand, and for honest, unbiased interpretation of evidence.

Following decades of immigration, the United States has become much more religiously diverse. Each religion has its

Shame Penalties

Morality influences how much shame a person feels, or should feel, when committing a crime. In colonial America, punishment was handed out in public so the offender would experience shame and repent for his or her actions. These punishments involved whipping, branding, or being placed with the person's ankles and wrists in a wooden stock. Even hangings were conducted in public with the offender expected to offer an admission of guilt and ask forgiveness before being hung.

By the early nineteenth century punishment went behind the walls of the newly growing prison system. No longer was public humiliation and shame part of punishment. In the late twentieth century, however, as prisons filled and incarceration expenses rose steadily, society once more experimented with shame penalties. For example, convicted offenders of some nonviolent crimes, such as buying services from prostitutes, had to publicly apologize. Others had to wear T-shirts identifying their crime, such as shoplifting.

Shame penalties were applied to lesser white-collar criminals, first time offenders, and juvenile offenders, all guilty of nonviolent crimes. In some cases judges gave convicted offenders a choice between a shame penalty, a fine, or jail time. Critics began to question the legality of such practices, due to uncertainty about the psychological short- and long-term effects of public shaming.

own traditions and offers many interpretations on crime and punishment. In addition, each member of a religion carries his or her own perspectives on crime and punishment.

Through the centuries religion has played an important role in criminal justice. In the fourteenth century, the Puritans of England introduced the concepts of bail, protection against self-incrimination, and jury trials. These ideas became central to English common law that the colonists brought to America. Religious organizations also sought to moderate punishment to fit the crime rather than setting harsh penalties on all crimes. They favored rehabilitation over retribution or vengeance. Some religious movements banned slavery, protected workers' rights, sought equality for women, and set standards for "indecent" behavior.

Religion in prisons

Religious organizations and their representatives have had a strong influence on how offenders are treated in prisons and jails. Churches, in fact, were one of the first institutions to build facilities to house offenders. The word "penitentiary" comes from the word penitent, meaning giving penance (confession and forgiveness of sin) or the idea that offenders would pay penance for their crimes.

The church provided offenders with an opportunity to admit their guilt and convert to religious traditions. An example in the American colonies was the Quakers of Pennsylvania who almost always favored incarceration over the harsher and permanent alternative, execution.

Many colonists immigrating to America in the seventeenth and eighteenth centuries came to escape religious persecution or oppression by their governments, in Britain and elsewhere. When the Founding Fathers wrote the first ten amendments to the U.S. Constitution in 1791, known as the Bill of Rights, they included the freedom of practicing religion in the First Amendment. How this freedom applied to prison inmates, however, would take years to fully resolve in the U.S. legal system.

The first state penitentiaries in the United States in the late eighteenth and early nineteenth centuries placed inmates in isolation, in their own separate cells. Religious officials or clergy interacted with inmates on a one-to-one basis. The Walnut Street Jail in Philadelphia provided inmates with a chance to reform by placing a copy of the Bible in their cells. It was believed that isolated inmates would have plenty of time to consider their actions and repent. Religious organizations began providing educational opportunities as a way to reform individuals as well. Prison chaplains would often be the prison's educator; they also helped keep prison records and performed other administrative duties.

Prison chaplains

As prisons began hiring administrators, teachers, and counselors through the nineteenth century, the role of the religious chaplain declined. By the early twentieth century the role and effectiveness of prison chaplains was questioned. In

San Quentin prison chaplain Earl Smith with a visiting pro football player in 2003. In addition to prison chaplains, volunteers representing various organizations visit prisons to promote religious activities. *(© Kim Kulish/Corbis)*

response to the declining influence of prison chaplains and religion in general in prisons, the Clinical Pastoral Education movement grew in the 1920s and 1930s.

The pastoral movement helped bring about professional training programs for prison chaplains. Chaplains were able to advise inmates in terms of religious service, counseling, and education. For example, chaplains could provide mental health counseling to help inmates deal with the psychological stress of prison life. Chaplains and other faith representatives could also help inmates find work once they were released and helped improve damaged family relationships.

In the early twenty-first century religious programs had become a regular feature of prisons, with nearly a third of inmates participating. In addition to prison chaplains, volunteers representing various religious organizations also visit prisons to promote religious activities. Maude Ballington Booth, daughter-in-law of the founders of the Salvation Army (a religion-based service organization), was one of the first people to encourage the use of volunteers in prisons. Prison chaplains usually coordinate volunteer activities. Among the religious organizations operating in several states is the Prison Fellowship Ministries.

Practicing religion in prison

Since a series of court decisions in the 1960s and 1970s, the constitutional right of prisoners to practice religion has been widely recognized. Congress passed a federal law based on the rulings, recognizing prisoner religious rights known as the Religious Land Use and Institutionalized Persons Act of 2000. The most common right exercised is the right to attend religious services in various denominations. Not only are Christian religions represented, but prisoners have the right to worship Islam, Buddhism, and other recognized religions.

Some practices not considered part of an established organized religion are not allowed. Inmates can also observe special diets and possess religious items, such as prayer beads, feathers, medicine pouches, and prayer rugs, as long as they do not interfere with prison operations.

Which faith groups are active in a prison depend on the specific needs of its inmate population. Larger prisons often offer services in many different denominations on a daily basis. Smaller facilities may offer only nondenominational (not belonging to a particular religion) services held on Sundays, with smaller activities available a couple times a week.

The four major faith groups are Catholic, Protestant, Muslim, and Jewish. Other recognized faith groups include Hinduism, Mormonism, Native American religions, Jehovah's Witnesses, Christian Scientists, and more recently witchcraft and Satan worshiping. Besides regular services, some prisons host special programs to inspire inmates to become religious. In the supermax (the highest security) prisons where inmates are isolated from other prisoners, the ministry is individualized like in earlier times.

In 2003 Lawtey Correctional Institution in Lawtey, Florida, was transformed from a regular prison to one welcoming inmates who seek a religious life. *(AP/Wide World Photos)*

Inmates seek religion in prison for various reasons. Some hope to gain a sense of direction and purpose in their lives, peace of mind, a safe haven from the rest of the prison population, to meet other inmates with similar interests, have access to prison resources or special privileges, or to influence parole considerations. Because of the last reason, prisoners involved in religious activities are frequently met with skepticism or distrust from prison staff and other inmates.

Indeed some inmates have used the religious activities as an opportunity to pass contraband (forbidden items) in prison, such as weapons, foods, or drugs. Many skeptics believe some inmates are simply looking for an early parole. Instances where former inmates who were active in religious activities while in prison commit further offenses after release add further support to these feelings. However studies have shown that the more active an inmate is in religion in prison, the less likely he will be a repeat offender after release.

Capital punishment

Undoubtedly the most controversial moral issue affecting criminal justice is the centuries old debate over the death penalty. It has been estimated that between 19,000 and 23,000 people were executed in the colonies and the United States since the first known execution in 1608 in the Virginia colony. Over 7,000 of those executions occurred after 1900. In more recent times, almost 600 occurred after 1977 in thirty-one states. Over 80 percent of the executions after 1977 took place in southern prisons with 35 percent in Texas alone. Another 3,700 inmates were awaiting execution at the beginning of the twenty-first century.

Crimes punishable by death are called capital crimes, which is derived from the Latin word *capitalis* meaning "of the head." By the late twentieth century, however, most nations in the world had abolished capital punishment. England abolished capital punishment in 1965, and it is not allowed in many of the nations that joined the European Union. Other countries that abolished capital punishment include Canada, Australia, New Zealand, and a number of countries in Central and South America.

Deciding on capital crimes

The number and type of capital offenses have varied greatly among different societies as well as the manner of executions. Some cultures, such as ancient Greece, assigned the death penalty to almost every crime, even simple thefts of food. Ancient England also had harsh death penalty laws. It applied the death penalty to over forty crimes at the time of North America's initial colonization. This number more than doubled during the eighteenth century and jumped up to 220 capital crimes by the early nineteenth century in Great Britain alone.

Though each of the thirteen colonies made use of the death penalty, they chose to use it much less than Britain. Manpower

Can Killing Be Morally Right?

Although the trend worldwide in the last decades of the twentieth century was to abolish the death penalty in numerous countries, the debate still raged in the United States. Every execution commonly drew protestors opposing capital punishment outside the prison walls. Those in favor of the death penalty believe in retribution, claiming a person who has taken another person's life or performed some other terrible crime does not deserve to have a life. They also claim the death penalty poses a much greater deterrence to violent crime than life sentences without the possibility of parole. Additionally, even if incarcerated, some inmates kill again within the prison facility.

Opponents of the death penalty most frequently cite moral and religious reasons for not taking a person's life. For example, the Catholic Church constantly promotes the protection of life, not only in opposing the death penalty, but on other issues such as abortion. The church and some other religions state that the death penalty is contrary to the sacredness of life. Society, they say, should focus on forgiveness, redemption, and reconciliation of the victim and society. Ultimate justice, they say, is with God.

Opponents of the death penalty also believe mistakes are made in the criminal justice system. The prospect of executing an innocent person, no matter how infrequent, is too much of a risk. Death cannot be reversed like other penalties. They believe life in prison keeps the person from committing other crimes. It is obvious debate over the death penalty will continue well into the twenty-first century.

was in short supply and every hand was needed to help the small, isolated settlements survive in their early years. Punishment for most crimes was fines and mutilation, such as branding or cutting off an ear. Most colonies listed about twelve capital offenses. The twelve included witchcraft, blasphemy, murder, adultery, kidnapping, conspiracy, manslaughter, sexual deviance, rebellion, and poisoning.

Pennsylvania had the fewest capital crimes with only murder and treason. By the American Revolution all but Rhode Island had at least ten capital crimes. These capital crimes were carried directly over into the new state laws. In 1790 the most common capital crimes were treason, murder, sexual deviance, rape, arson, burglary, robbery, and counterfeiting.

A group of men walking to their public hangings in Pennsylvania. In 1794 the Pennsylvania legislature abolished the death penalty for all crimes except first-degree murder. *(AP/Wide World Photos)*

A reform movement in the late eighteenth century following the American Revolution began pressing for elimination of the death penalty. In 1794 the Pennsylvania legislature abolished the death penalty for all crimes except first-degree murder. This was the first time a government distinguished between different categories of murder. First-degree murder was the willful, premeditated (thought out or planned in advance) act of murder, or murder committed with another serious crime such as arson, rape, or burglary.

Though other states soon adopted the new distinction of first- and second-degree (an unplanned or accidental killing) murder, none sharply reduced the number of capital crimes like Pennsylvania. However, Pennsylvania slowly added more crimes back to its list of capital punishment crimes through the first decades of the nineteenth century.

Once again beginning in the 1830s a movement grew to abolish the death penalty. Some religious organizations supported the death penalty while others did not. In 1847 Michigan abolished all capital punishment except for treason, and other northern states followed. Yet in the South, capital punishment increased and black slaves were the most frequent victims.

In the 1830s only five capital crimes applied to whites in Virginia but seventy applied to slaves. The movement to completely abolish the death penalty lost momentum during the Civil War and was not revived until the end of the nineteenth century. Under renewed pressure, Congress reduced the number of federal capital crimes in 1897 from sixty to three—treason, murder, and rape. The movement to eliminate the death penalty was led by Quakers and liberal Christians seeking reform in the justice system. Between 1897 and 1917 a number of states abolished the death penalty altogether. Social upheaval in the first few decades of the twentieth century, however, brought a reversal as public support for capital punishment increased again.

Violent labor conflicts had become more frequent, political radicals had fierce confrontations with authorities, and street crime increased as the population grew. After the kidnapping and murder of the infant son of American pilot Charles Lindbergh (1902–1974), federal and state governments added kidnapping to their death penalty lists.

The number of executions rose steadily, reaching very high numbers in the 1930s and 1940s. The movements to reduce the number of executions began taking effect again and states once more reduced the number of capital crimes. By the 1960s murder was the most common capital crime in the United States, followed by rape, armed robbery, kidnapping, sabotage, espionage, and burglary. In 1965 nine states had no capital crimes and four others had very few.

Deciding who dies

The death penalty was automatic upon conviction of a capital crime in England and the colonies. To avoid always handing down such harsh punishment, exclusion rules were adopted by colonial courts. First clergy were excluded, then those who could read or write, and then women. Such rules were soon restricted during the 1700s and were abolished in England by 1827.

Other kinds of exclusions were created. States such as Pennsylvania distinguished between different kinds of murder

A 1998 protest in Austin, Texas, to stop the planned execution of convicted murderer Karla Faye Tucker. *(AP/Wide World Photos)*

to avoid mandatory death sentences. In 1938 Tennessee was the first state to do away with automatic death sentences and give juries the power to decide between death and prison for a convicted offender. Other states followed this change, with New York being the last to adopt flexible sentencing for premeditated murder in 1963.

Flexible or "discretionary" procedures led to a 1972 U.S. Supreme Court ruling. The Court ruled in *Furman v. Georgia* that how state courts determined the death penalty in individual cases made it a cruel and unusual punishment and unconstitutional. The Court ruled that jury guidelines were often too vague, juries were not fully informed, and offenders were given the death penalty without following a comprehensive set of rules. After the ruling, states had to establish clear guidelines and require juries to consider the background and circumstances of an offender before determining a sentence.

Capital offense trials became two trials, one to determine guilt, and if found guilty to determine the sentence. Different evidence was considered in the sentencing phase than in the trial phase. The jury had to consider the offender's background as well as facts about the victim and crime. All states and the federal courts require appeals of anyone sentenced to death.

Capital punishment in modern America

The death penalty ruling of 1972 forced states to reevaluate their position on the death penalty as they created new laws to conform to the Supreme Court decision. The earliest new capital crime laws were also challenged, but this time the Court supported the states. In the 1976 case of *Gregg v. Georgia* the Court approved the new Georgia capital crime law by upholding the conviction of a person who had robbed and murdered two men. The Court said the new revised sentencing process, separate from determining guilt, did not violate the Constitution's protection from cruel and unusual punishment.

As the states reworked their sentencing procedures, fewer offenders were given the death penalty. Although murder was still a capital crime, it had to be related to another serious crime except when involving the death of a police officer or a child. Rape of an adult, armed robbery, kidnapping, and burglary were no longer considered capital offenses unless the victim died.

In the early twenty-first century thirty-eight states had the death penalty and twelve states did not. In the meantime Congress had passed the Violent Crime Control and Law Enforcement Act of 1994 to "get tough on crime," spurred by the newly Republican-controlled Congress. This increased the number of federal capital crimes to over fifty. Most involved murder during other crimes like bank robbery or kidnapping, or murdering someone on federal property. Capital crimes not involving murder included treason, espionage, major drug trafficking, and the attempted murder of a police officer.

Execution methods

Convicted offenders have been executed in many different ways. The Romans of 2,500 years ago burned, drowned, beheaded, and crucified offenders for a wide range of crimes from theft to murder. After the United States was founded and the Constitution was drawn up, torture was no longer practiced because of the Eighth Amendment, which prohibits cruel and unusual punishment. Offenders could no longer be burned alive at the stake (like the "witches" of Salem) or killed with burning oil as in early colonial times.

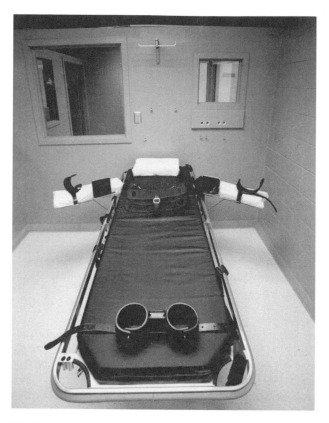

The lethal injection execution chamber at Oregon State Penitentiary. By the early twenty-first century, lethal injection became the preferred method of execution in the United States. *(AP/Wide World Photos)*

The most common method of execution in early U.S. history was hanging. At first the hangings were performed in public view, and drew large and rowdy crowds. Beginning in 1830, Connecticut hangings were moved to within prison walls away from the public. Public hangings still took place, however, into the 1930s in some states.

In 1888 New York adopted use of the electric chair. The first use of the electric chair came two years later when William Kemmler was executed in New York. Yet because of problems with the equipment, Kemmler's execution led to a prolonged and gruesome death that horrified the witnesses. Despite this troubled beginning, the electric chair became the execution method of choice for more states.

Other forms of execution included firing squads, lethal gas, and hanging through much of the twentieth century. In 1977 Oklahoma adopted lethal injection. The first lethal injection execution in the United States came in 1982 in Texas. Lethal injection became the preferred method everywhere in the United States by the early twenty-first century.

Religion and criminal justice in the twenty-first century

Morality and religious order continued to greatly influence public perception of crime and punishment in the early twenty-first century. The media, through newspapers, 24-hour cable news networks, investigative reports on major networks, Internet Web sites, movies, and political radio programs, filled the public with images of violent or socially deviant behavior. Unusual local crimes get national attention and despite a decline in crime rates, public fear continues to grow. This fear directly influences criminal justice. The results are zero tolerance policies, broader police power, and tougher laws and sentencing.

Religious organizations have often led the charge for crime prevention. The result has been less tolerance of criminal behavior and demanding people take more responsibility for their actions. As new patterns in crime arise, such moralistic reactions influence the response of the criminal justice system. Critics, however, claim these solutions are too simple and do not address the causes of crime.

In the early 2000s the state of Florida under Governor Jeb Bush, brother of U.S. president George W. Bush (1946–; served 2001–), established a series of state faith-based prisons. These were created by converting existing prisons. Inmates were then allowed to choose one of these prisons over a standard prison.

The faith-based prisons offered regular prayer sessions, religious studies, choir practice, and religious counseling. They were open to inmates of all faiths including Christian, Muslim, and Jew. To qualify for participation, inmates must be within three years of their release date and have a clean prison record. The religious goal was character development, the prison goal was to reduce crime by keeping inmates from returning to a life of crime after their release. Of the 73,000 inmates in Florida in 2002, about 44 percent were repeat offenders with the state spending $1.3 billion on prisons.

For More Information

Books

Acker, James R., Robert M. Bohm, and Charles S. Lanier, eds. *America's Experiment with Capital Punishment: Reflections on the Past, Present, and Future of the Ultimate Penal Sanction.* Durham, NC: Carolina Academic Press, 1998.

Baird, Robert M., and Stuart E. Rosenbaum. *Punishment and the Death Penalty: The Current Debate.* Amherst, NY: Prometheus Books, 1995.

Bedau, Hugo A., ed. *Death Penalty in America: Current Controversies.* New York: Oxford University Press, 1997.

Dummer, Harry R. *Religion in Corrections.* Lanham, MD: American Correctional Associates, 2000.

Levy, Leonard W. *Blasphemy: Verbal Offenses Against the Sacred from Moses to Salman Rushdie.* New York: Knopf, 1993.

Nathanson, Stephen. *An Eye for an Eye? The Immorality of Punishing by Death.* Lanham, MD: Rowman & Littlefield, 1987.

Shaw, Richard D. *Chaplains to the Imprisoned: Sharing Life with the Incarcerated.* Binghamton, NY: Haworth Press, 1995.

Speller, Adrian. *Breaking Out: A Christian Critique of Criminal Justice.* London: Hodder & Stoughton, 1986.

Stark, Rodney, and Williams Sims Bainbridge. *Religion, Deviance, and Social Control.* New York: Routledge, 1997.

Stoyanov, Yuri. *The Hidden Tradition: The Secret History of Medieval Christian Heresy.* New York: Penguin Putnam, 1995.

Web Sites

"Death Penalty." *American Civil Liberties Union.* http://www.aclu.org/DeathPenalty/DeathPenaltyMain.cfm (accessed on August 20, 2004).

Death Penalty Information Center. http://www.deathpenaltyinfo.org (accessed on August 20, 2004).

International Prison Chaplains' Association. http://www.ipcaworldwide.org (accessed on August 20, 2004).

23

Economic and Social Effects of Crime

Crime is a major part of every society. Its costs and effects touch just about everyone to some degree. The types of costs and effects are widely varied. In addition, some costs are short-term while others last a lifetime. Of course the ultimate cost is loss of life. Other costs to victims can include medical costs, property losses, and loss of income.

Losses to both victims and nonvictims can also come in the form of increased security expenses including stronger locks, extra lighting, parking in more expensive secure lots, security alarms for homes and cars, and maintaining guard dogs. Considerable money is spent to avoid being victimized. Other types of expenses can include a victim or person fearful of crime moving to a new neighborhood, funeral expenses, legal fees, and loss of school days.

Some costs of crime are less tangible (not easily or precisely identified). These kinds of costs can include pain and suffering, and a lower quality of life. There are also the traumatic impacts on friends and the disruption of family. Behavior can be forever changed and shaped by crime, whether it be weighing the risks of going to certain places or even the fear of making new friends.

Inmates led by a drill instructor at an Oregon correctional institution boot camp. About thirty states operate similar facilities, combining military-style workouts, strict discipline, and intensive substance abuse counseling. *(AP/Wide World Photos)*

Crime not only affects economic productivity when victims miss work, but communities also are affected through loss of tourism and retail sales. Even the so-called victimless crimes of prostitution, drug abuse, and gambling have major social consequences. Drug abuse affects worker productivity, uses public funds for drug treatment programs and medical attention, and leads to criminal activity to support the expenses of a drug habit.

Communities and governments spend public funds for police departments, prisons and jails, courts, and treatment programs, including the salaries of prosecutors, judges, public defenders, social workers, security guards, and probation officers. The amount of time spent by victims, offenders, their families, and juries during court trials also take away from community productivity. By the beginning of the twenty-first century it was estimated that the annual cost of crime in the United States was reaching upward toward $1.7 trillion.

Growing interest in the costs of crime

Though crime has always posed economic and social effects on U.S. society throughout history, the actual costs of crime did not become a major political issue until the late 1920s. Because of the rise of organized crime during the 1920s, chiefly from selling illegal liquor during Prohibition (1919–33), newly elected President Herbert Hoover (1874–1964; served 1929–33) created the Wickersham Commission in 1929 to assess crime and punishment in the nation. The commission released fourteen volumes of its findings in 1931, reporting on the major influence of crime on American society.

Further studies focused on victim expenses, costs for security, and the cost of the criminal justice system. Crime and its costs and effects soon became a dominant issue in American politics, often influencing voters after World War II (1939–45).

Determining costs

Estimating the costs and effects of crime is important to authorities in the criminal justice system. Policymakers weigh the various costs posed by different crimes to determine which crime prevention measures have the highest priority. Researchers have tried different approaches in assessing the costs of crime. One approach has been to look at jury awards in

The High Cost of Crime

The following annual figures estimating the various costs of crime in the mid-1990s come from the National Institute of Justice and a study by David A. Anderson called "The Aggregate Burden of Crime." The study was published in the October 1999 issue of the *Journal of Law and Economics*. Crime costs are based on approximately 49 million annual crimes and attempted crimes in the United States.

$105 billion each year in medical bills and lost earnings; $450 billion when including pain and suffering and lost quality of life

$400 billion to operate corrections facilities

$130 billion for crime prevention and loss of potential productivity of criminals and inmates

$1 trillion when including the cost of the criminal justice systems, as well as private individuals and companies taking security measures

$426 billion of the $450 billion is related to violent crime, the remaining $24 billion to property crime

$4,118 is the annual cost of crime to each U.S. citizen

civil suits. Juries in civil trials are often asked to determine the amount of money to be awarded to victims of crime. They consider medical expenses and property loss as well as compensation for pain and suffering.

Another source is insurance and government claims. When a victim suffers losses from crime, he may receive compensation from insurance companies or government relief agencies. These figures can also be used in determining the costs of crime. A third source in measuring the cost of crime is to study how much a person is willing to pay to avoid crime through such actions as purchasing expensive security devices.

Using these various sources, studies have estimated the cost associated with various types of crime. For example, the cost of larceny (theft) in 1993 was around $370 for each victim while murder was $2.9 million. One study estimated the savings to society by diverting a high-risk youth from potential crime was as much as $1.5 million per youth.

As opposed to street crime, white-collar crime is considered far more costly to society. It was estimated in the mid-

$603 billion lost to the economy from fraud and unpaid taxes

$500 million of money or valuables taken in robberies

$15 billion in property stolen

$127 billion from rape offenses; assault $93 billion, murder $61 billion, and child abuse $56 billion

$45 billion paid by insurance programs to crime victims

$8 billion paid to victims by U.S. government annually for restorative and emergency services

3 percent of all medical expenses in the nation is related to violent crimes

1 percent of annual U.S. earnings is equal to wage losses from violent crime

10 to 20 percent of mental healthcare costs are attributed to crime

$54,000 is the average cost of each arson incident; $31,000 for each assault

$25,000 to $30,000 is the annual cost of an inmate in prison

4 out of 5 gunshot victims end up on public assistance and uninsured, costing the government $4.5 billion annually

(From the National Center For Policy Analysis Web site at http://www.ncpa.org/pi/crime.html)

1990s that white-collar crime cost U.S. businesses as much as $400 billion a year, or about 6 percent of total revenue in the nation. Consumer fraud alone cost Americans about $45 billion each year.

Various agencies and organizations maintain statistics on the cost of crime in the United States though none cover the entire range of costs. They mainly focus on different aspects of criminal justice. The Bureau of Justice Statistics keeps track of expenses required to maintain effective criminal justice systems around the nation including employment costs. Other data addressing the costs to victims is available through the National Crime Victimization Survey (NCVS). No data gathering group, however, can accurately assess all of the long-term costs of crime.

Community efforts to avoid crime costs

Crime can cause property values to decline in certain areas of a town and even increase the cost of housing in other areas not suffering from crime. Studies have shown certain

Areas of urban decay, characterized by abandoned buildings and cars, unkempt vacant lots, and broken windows tend to attract the homeless and increasing criminal activity. *(The Library of Congress)*

neighborhoods with high crime rates will maintain these rates unless there is a community-wide effort to stop it. In the early 1990s studies concluded that certain neighborhoods become crime ridden as the number of abandoned buildings and cars increase, if there are unkempt vacant lots, and broken windows. Such areas tend to attract criminal activity. Crime can grow from minor offenses to major ones.

Fear of crime in these areas steadily increases and the resulting economic and social effects can span out into the surrounding city. Residents become more withdrawn and defensive and less committed to their communities. The very social fiber of the community is weakened. Some communities adopt neighborhood watch programs to revitalize the community or avoid its decay.

The rising cost of crime prevention and criminal justice systems reflects the rising cost of crime to society. Studies in the early 1990s suggested that for every one dollar spent on crime prevention programs, seven dollars were saved in crime victimization costs. Not only is the cost of crime reduced, but community tax revenues increase due to higher earnings and greater economic productivity, costs of social service programs are reduced, and healthcare expenses fall.

Such cost savings have led more communities to focus on crime prevention programs. These programs, both outside prison walls and within, concentrate on attacking the causes of crime and juvenile delinquency including poverty, inadequate housing, broken families, and limited educational opportunities. These programs can include increased vocational training, healthcare facilities, family counseling, and family planning.

Prison programs designed to prevent released offenders from becoming repeat offenders include education programs, employment training, and substance abuse treatment.

Making personal adjustments

Though violent attacks account for only about 10 percent of crime, they affect people's lives the most. Fear is a major factor influencing how people lead their lives. Violent crimes are not only the most costly crimes but also the most reported in the media. The high costs and publicity further raise the fear of crime. The costs are both monetary and emotional.

Most people fear attacks by strangers despite the fact that most assaults are by someone familiar to the victim. As a result people will seek daily routines that provide a feeling of security. These routines, however, can have the opposite effect. If a person follows the exact same routine every day, a criminal can easily predict where that person will be at a certain time. In such cases, the most important factor in crime prevention is to be aware of one's surroundings and avoid high risk areas.

A crime victim or someone especially fearful of crime may alter his or her normal routine, take self-defense classes, avoid certain areas, and even carry weapons. The hazards in every part of life are constantly being determined in a person's mind to estimate the possible danger. In crime prevention, law enforcement uses a similar calculation of risks in deciding where

Royal Canadian mounted police cadets participate in a self-defense training class. *(© Paul A. Souders/Corbis)*

to assign patrols or to alter an area to reduce potential of crime. Such measures might include adding more lighting or reducing the amount of cover in a park where a criminal might hide in wait of a victim.

Who crime affects most

The social effects of crime vary among the various segments of the general population. Statistics show that men are far more likely to be victims of crime than women. Studies show that women, however, fear crime far more than men. Other patterns reveal that the elderly fear crime more than younger adults, and children fear crime more than adults.

While women have less chance of being a victim, the crimes they suffer are more violent including rape and domestic abuse. Another factor is that women, the elderly, and the very young are physically weaker than the common offender making them feel more susceptible to crime.

Regarding factors of race and ethnicity (people who share a common culture), minorities, particularly black Americans, fear crime far more than whites. Studies show blacks are much more likely to be a victim or witness a crime. An exception to this rule is that whites commonly fear young black males.

Based on these two patterns, it is evident that a strong racial distrust is another social consequence of crime in the United States. Race and ethnicity also strongly influence people's perception of crime in particular areas, which in turn influences their daily behavior patterns.

Crime and politics

Given the extensive economic and social costs of crime, it often has a major impact in politics. Since the 1970s calls for law and order have led to tough stances by politicians on crime. Public safety is a major issue, and the fear of crime is frequently used by politicians to influence voters. Even with the decrease in crime rates through the 1990s, fear of crime remained a political issue since building more prisons, making sentences longer, and expanding police forces require taxpayer dollars.

Costs Affecting the Offender

Victims and their families are not the only individuals to directly suffer from crime. The offender and his family also suffer costs. There are lost wages of the offender while in jail or prison, lost future earnings because of the criminal record, loss of productivity to industry, and loss of a family member to others including children.

Offenders are often forced to pay a fine for their crime, the oldest form of criminal penalty in history. They may also face civil penalties to compensate the losses of their victims. Fines and civil penalties may be paid not only to the crime victim but also to local communities to reimburse the costs of prosecuting cases.

In the early 2000s the cost of crime increased dramatically after the terrorist attacks in New York City and Washington, D.C., in September 2001. The attacks killed three thousand people and presented staggering costs in terms of destruction. Congress created the Department of Homeland Security, which became operational in March 2003. The department's budget in 2004 was almost $37 billion, which was used to increase security in airports and at our nation's borders, and to develop counterterrorism and bioterrorism (the use of biological weapons such as poisons or gases) measures. Fear of further crime or terrorism drove up the costs of crime and in many cases drastically altered people's daily habits as the War on Terror unfolded.

For More Information

Books

Anderson, Elijah. *Streetwise: Race, Class and Change in an Urban Community*. Chicago, IL: University of Chicago Press, 1990.

Beckett, Katherine. *Making Crime Pay: Law and Order in Contemporary American Politics.* New York: Oxford University Press, 1997.

Cook, Philip J., and Jens Ludwig. *Gun Violence: The Real Costs.* New York: Oxford University Press, 2000.

Felson, Marcus. *Crime and Everyday Life.* 2nd ed. Thousand Oaks, CA: Pine Forge Press, 1998.

Gray, Charles M., ed. *The Costs of Crime.* Beverly Hills, CA: Sage, 1979.

Madriz, Esther. *Nothing Bad Happens to Good Girls: Fear of Crime in Women's Lives.* Berkeley, CA: University of California Press, 1997.

Skogan, Wesley G. *Disorder and Decline: Crime and the Spiral of Decay in American Neighborhoods.* New York: Free Press, 1990.

Welsh, Brandon C., David P. Farrington, and Lawrence W. Sherman, eds. *Costs and Benefits of Preventing Crime.* Boulder, CO: Westview Press, 2001.

Periodical

Anderson, David A. "The Aggregate Burden of Crime," *Journal of Law and Economics,* October 1999, pp. 611–642.

Web Site

National Center For Policy Analysis. http://www.ncpa.org/newdpd/index.php (accessed on August 20, 2004).

24

Race and Ethnicity

The United States of the twenty-first century is a result of five hundred years of immigration combined with the surviving Native American populations. The first European settlements along the Atlantic coastline in the early seventeenth century began a three-century forced relocation of hundreds of established Native American societies.

Waves of immigrants came to the United States after the early European settlers and continued into the twenty-first century. Some came by choice, others by force. Most early immigration was from Great Britain and northern Europe. Before long, black slaves were brought in from western Africa. By the late nineteenth century, east European, Asian, and Hispanic populations had arrived.

White Anglo-Saxons dominated the settlements at the time of the American Revolution (1775–83), though this steadily gave way to a greater mix of people. By the 2000 census, about one-third of all Americans considered themselves minorities. This increasing diversity of the U.S. population raised difficult issues in the criminal justice system.

Protesters outside of the statehouse annex in Trenton, New Jersey, before state supreme court justice Peter Verniero testified to the State Judiciary Committee hearing on racial profiling in 2001. *(AP/Wide World Photos)*

The terms race and ethnicity are most commonly used to describe the diversity of the American population. Ethnicity refers to a group of people who share a common culture often through language, custom, and religion. Race is based on physical appearances, such as skin color, hair texture, and eye shape. Historically in the United States, people considered "white" dominated the justice system; there were white judges, white lawyers, and white prosecutors. It was not until the twentieth century that more minorities were represented in the legal process.

Regardless of how many decades or centuries different populations have resided in the United States, ethnic background and countries of origin have remained an important aspect of a person's identity. Though race is not a scientific term, it remains a powerful social influence regarding education, income, politics, and criminal investigations. A person's race is listed on various government documents such as birth certificates, driver's licenses, school enrollments, and crime statistics. Though this information can be useful it is not accurate since many Americans are a mix of nationalities.

Race in U.S. legal history

In the United States as in other countries, recent immigrants are always suspected of the latest crime waves. In the early twentieth century white ethnic immigrants from Italy and Ireland were the focus of concern including Irish, Italian, and Polish youth gangs. As more Hispanics migrated from Mexico, the emphasis shifted to people of color in the 1930s and 1940s. Then with the rise of the Civil Rights movement, fears shifted toward black Americans in the 1950s and beyond. Throughout this time white Anglo-Saxon Protestants, often referred to as WASPs, dominated the criminal justice system and determined targets for crime fighting.

Race has also always been central to American laws. Prior to the Civil War most blacks were slaves. In legal terms they were considered property, not humans. Slaves could not bring lawsuits, marry, vote, enter into business contracts, or testify in court except against another slave. Immediately following the Civil War, between 1865 and 1866, Southern states quickly adopted Black Codes to limit the rights of the newly freed slaves.

Native Americans

Though a relatively small portion of U.S. society, Native Americans are a fast rising population increasing from two million in 1990 to around four million in 2000. American Indian communities on reservations are establishing their own tribal criminal justice systems. Some 135 tribal law enforcement agencies and Bureau of Indian Affairs (BIA) agents police Native American lands. For this reason, statistics involving Native Americans and crime are split between the different systems. Depending on the crime, where it occurred, and against whom, American Indians may be prosecuted in tribal, state, or federal courts.

Crime is a major issue in Indian Country as tribal communities face poverty, high unemployment, isolation in remote areas, suicide, and alcoholism. Some 5 percent of Native Americans eighteens year old and older is involved in the U.S. criminal justice system, twice the rate of white Americans but half the rate of black Americans. American Indians, however, experience violent crime at over twice the rate of blacks and whites. Some 124 Indians per 1,000 residents over twelve years of age experienced violent crimes including sexual assault, rape, robbery, and aggravated assault. The homicide rates in particular are triple the general population. By the late 1990s, youth gangs were reportedly forming in the remote reservations.

The Black Codes were followed by Jim Crow laws in the early twentieth century strictly enforcing public racial segregation (keeping the races separate in public places). By the late twentieth century numerous laws and court rulings had guaranteed the rights of minorities to equal access of opportunities, equal protection under the law, and due process (given fair treatment) in criminal justice systems.

Black Americans and crime

Throughout much of American history, black Americans were the most populated minority in the United States. In 2000, however, Hispanics slightly outnumbered blacks. The 2000 census counted thirty-five million black Americans or about 12 percent of the U.S. population, an increase from thirty million in 1990. Black Americans have played a particularly central role in the issue of race and criminal justice.

Los Angeles police officers search seven people arrested for selling narcotics. Violence in the black community escalated in the mid-1980s as drug trafficking and the occurrence of armed gangs increased.
(AP/Wide World Photos)

Black Americans and other advocates of civil rights claim the black segment of U.S. society is the most policed and least protected group. Black Americans were much more likely than whites to be arrested, prosecuted, convicted, sent to prison, sentenced to death, and executed. Though blacks comprised just 12 percent of the population in 2002, over 34 percent of those arrested for aggravated assault, 34 percent for forcible rape, 50 percent for homicide, and over 54 percent for robbery were black. In addition, almost 48 percent of murder victims in the nation were black in 2002.

Black Americans were not only more likely to be a crime suspect, but the victim as well. Street criminals tend to victimize those in their own neighborhoods. Since the United

States still had mostly segregated communities, blacks suffered at the hands of other blacks. Violent crime is a major public health concern among black Americans. Blacks in poor areas are seven times more likely than whites to be murdered.

Already a major problem, violence in the black community escalated in the mid-1980s as drug trafficking in crack cocaine and the occurrence of armed gangs increased. Law authorities estimated that twenty-six thousand gangs existed in the United States by the late twentieth century. One-third of their membership was black, though less than the 47 percent Hispanic composition. Only 13 percent of members were white.

Policing and minorities

Relations between minorities and police organizations have always been controversial in U.S. history. Accusations of police brutality and harassment were recurrent. Many consider slave patrols prior to the American Civil War as the first form of organized policing in the United States. Following the war local police were charged with enforcing the Black Codes followed by Jim Crow laws instituting racial segregation in public places. Police often failed to respond to the lynchings of black Americans through the early decades of the twentieth century. In these cases, there were rarely arrests or prosecutions by the white-dominated criminal justice systems of the South.

Similarly, race riots of the early twentieth century were usually assaults by crowds of whites on blacks with little reaction from police. The Civil Rights movement of the 1950s and 1960s brought open violent conflict between police and black Americans using civil disobedience tactics to protest racial discrimination. Once again police stood by on numerous occasions while blacks were assaulted by angry whites. The FBI even monitored the activities of black leaders, including Martin Luther King Jr. (1929–1968).

By 1978 police departments began hiring black Americans, and by the 1990s some of the larger cities had black police chiefs. Overall, police treatment of minorities improved as accusations of racial harassment declined. Nonetheless, major incidents continued. The beating of Rodney King by Los Angeles police officers during a routine traffic stop, captured on videotape, shocked the nation. Acquittal of the police officers who assaulted King led to rioting in Los Angeles and an outpouring of anger against the criminal justice system by blacks.

Other incidents followed with the torture of Abner Louima in a New York City police station and the shooting of Amadou Diallo in the Bronx in 1999. The acquittal of O.J. Simpson of murder in 1995 revealed great differences in perceptions of the criminal justice system between blacks and whites.

Racial profiling

Racial profiling occurs when police stop a motorist or pedestrian based on his or her race or ethnicity. At one time, profiling was a policing practice focusing on certain suspicious behavior or circumstances likely to have criminal connections or fit into past crime patterns. Statistics found that males, especially youths, were more commonly associated with crime and

Police chief of Los Angeles, Bernard Parks. By the 1990s, some of the larger cities in the United States had hired black police chiefs. *(AP/Wide World Photos)*

this led police to focus more on this particular segment of society. While profiling is said to increase the efficiency of the police as well as the safety of the officers, it has clearly been abused.

A tendency to patrol high crime areas, many of which are in or near minority residential areas, led some to believe the police were "profiling" people of color. Additionally, a disproportionate or unusually large number of young black males were pulled over by police, leading to accusations of "driving while black" or racial profiling. Black Americans believed a majority of these young men were pulled over simply because of the color of their skin, not for any violation of the law. Such cases of racial profiling and harassment escalated throughout the 1990s.

A 1999 press conference on a New York state investigation into racial profiling among the state police. The four African American men pictured were stopped on the New Jersey turnpike and shot by state troopers. *(AP/Wide World Photos)*

Racial profiling became a greater public concern following the beginning of the War on Drugs. New drug laws introduced sweeping forfeiture laws allowing police to seize and keep cash or valuable property related to drug convictions. This was a major new opportunity for revenue and led to more aggressive policing in drug enforcement, particularly aimed at drug trafficking on the streets.

A focus on black youth developed as well. Police adopted new practices such as following a vehicle whose driver or passengers seemed suspicious until a driving violation was observed. The officers then searched the vehicle during the traffic stop, but only if given the driver's permission. If a driver did not give consent, he or she could be arrested. In 1996 the U.S. Supreme Court ruled this type of profiling and policing was illegal.

Studies affirmed that minorities, particularly black Americans, were more likely to be stopped out of suspicion and searched than whites during routine traffic stops. Though race made a significant difference in making stops and searching vehicles, additional data indicated that race had little impact in arrests or citations.

Sentencing and minorities

Judges often have considerable flexibility in sentencing convicted offenders. People who commit the same crimes do not necessarily receive the same sentences upon conviction. Sentencing decisions are often based on the seriousness of the crime, the offender's past criminal record, and information provided by prosecutors, defense attorneys, victims, and probation officers. Other factors outside the immediate nature of the case sometimes influence sentencing as well, such as employment record and family stability.

Like criminal laws, sentencing practices were racially discriminatory in the nineteenth century. Just prior to the Civil War, an 1861 Georgia law specified a mandatory death sentence for rape of a white woman by a black man. A white man raping a white woman could receive a sentence of two to twenty years. Rape of a black woman had no mandatory sentence.

Black rape offenders were executed at a much higher rate than white offenders, and this trend continued well into the twentieth century. Execution rates far exceeded arrest rates. Various efforts were made to take the racial factor out of sentencing decisions. For example, in 1987 U.S. Federal Sentencing Guidelines were issued prohibiting the reference or consideration of race or ethnicity during sentencing.

Sentencing rates for black Americans, however, still exceeded their 12 percent proportion of the general U.S. population. Studies in the 1980s and 1990s showed distinct patterns in sentencing regarding racial categories. For most felonies minorities had a higher incarceration rate, especially those with prior arrest records. They also received harsher sentences for lesser crimes. Whites would often receive probation and blacks incarceration. In 1998 black Americans represented 35 percent of the adults on probation, 49 percent of the adults in prison, and 44 percent of the adults on parole.

A minority youth had a six times greater chance as a white youth for being arrested, convicted, and sentenced to jail or prison. A study in California showed that whites charged with a felony were more likely than blacks or Hispanics to have charges reduced or dismissed. Of the first-time offenders in San Francisco, the courts sentenced 4 percent of the white offenders to state prisons, 7 percent of black offenders, and 11 percent of Hispanic offenders.

Efforts to make sentencing more consistent through stricter sentencing guidelines produced little change. Black offenders who murder a white victim are still more likely to be given the death penalty than for murdering a black victim. Prosecutors can still greatly influence sentencing outcomes by deciding what charges to bring against an offender. In the mid-1990s blacks were still eight times more likely to be incarcerated than whites. In 1994 there were 1,432 blacks incarcerated per every 100,000 black residents compared to 203 whites per 100,000 white residents.

The death penalty

The segment of the criminal justice system that has drawn the most attention in regard to minorities is the death penalty. Nationwide over half, 55 percent, of those executed between 1930 and 1991 were black. Executions of black Americans occurred at such a high rate compared to other racial categories that in 1972 the U.S. Supreme Court temporarily prohibited death penalty sentences when a black defendant successfully argued the death penalty was applied to black offenders at a much greater rate than others for the same kind of offenses.

The disparity between white and black executions was found predominately in the South. Later studies showed blacks had a 22 percent chance of receiving the death penalty for murdering a white, compared to a white offender having only an 8 percent chance. The death penalty was applied in only 1 percent of cases involving a black murdering a black, and in 3 percent of cases involving a white murdering a black. A death sentence was four times more likely to be imposed if the victim was white. Between 1976 and 1995 only two whites were executed for murdering a black.

Further differences were discovered in the rate of offenders having their death sentences commuted (reduced) to life sentences. Some 20 percent of white death row offenders had their sentences commuted, compared to only 11 percent of blacks between 1914 and 1958 in Pennsylvania. At the end of the twentieth century some 40 percent of death row inmates were black.

Incarceration and minorities

The first inmate of Philadelphia's Eastern State Penitentiary in 1829 was an eighteen-year-old black American. So began a long legacy of higher rates of incarceration for black Americans. In 1989 the number of black prisoners surpassed the number of whites; by 2003 some 832,400 black Americans were in the nation's prison and jail system compared to 665,100 whites and 363,900 Hispanics.

Hispanic Americans

Hispanic Americans come from many national origins that are culturally and economically diverse. Most Hispanics in the United States come from Mexico. Overall, Hispanics are poorer and less educated than the U.S. population. The language barrier between Hispanics and police contribute to rougher treatment during arrests. Illegal immigration has caused much fear in the U.S. population. In 1990 just over 10 percent of Hispanic men were either in prison or on parole or probation. Just over 3.7 percent of Hispanic men between ages of twenty and twenty-nine were in prison in 2003 compared to 1.6 percent of whites.

As with blacks, drug offenses were a major element of prison terms. Youth gangs have been an ongoing and violent problem involving drugs and guns. Organized crime has established strong ties with Hispanics involving drug trafficking of heroin, cocaine, and marijuana from Latin America. In the late 1990s it was estimated that some three thousand Colombian drug trafficking groups were operating in the United States.

In 2003 4,834 out of every 100,000 black males were sentenced to prison compared to 681 per every 100,000 white males and 1,778 per 100,000 Hispanic males. Though the rate of black males going to prison was high, the fastest rising segment of prison population by the late twentieth century was minority females.

As in the United States, proportionately large numbers of people considered minorities in other countries are incarcerated as well including in France and England. U.S. studies showed that blacks were commonly sent to prison at higher rates and for longer prison terms than whites for the same crimes. Though blacks were always overrepresented in prisons, the differences from white population rates increased dramatically in the 1990s. The incarceration rate for blacks rose 63 percent during the decade; in contrast, the white rate rose 36 percent and the Hispanic rate 35 percent. Increases for the period were due in large part to the War on Drugs proclaimed in the mid-1980s.

Over half of those sentenced for drug offenses were black in 1998. In the late 1990s about 9 percent of the total black adult population in the United States was under correctional supervision compared to 2 percent of the white adult population. The percentage of younger adults was much higher. Some 33 percent of the black American male population between twenty and twenty-nine years of age were either in prison or jail, or on probation or parole.

Blacks were much more likely to be sent to prison than placed on probation. As a result, black men were locked up at a rate of nine times that of whites. Blacks comprised over 40 percent of the prison population, almost 44 percent in 2003, on any given day. In addition, almost as many blacks were on death row (1,514) in 1999 as whites (1,948).

The experience of black Americans in the U.S. prison system is considered by some as a modern-day version of the slavery plantations in the South. Following the Civil War, the newly developing Southern prison systems held predominately black populations. Inmates worked in cotton fields, much as slaves had before the Civil War. Southern prisoners were worked in the fields for profit, often for private companies, and occasionally for the federal government's Federal Prison Industries program.

The War on Drugs and imprisonment

Overall crime statistics suggest a key reason minorities experience a higher rate of incarceration is because they commit more crimes. The one clear exception, however, has been drug cases. The War on Drugs began with passage of the Omnibus Anti-Drug Abuse Act in 1986, which had a major impact on arrests, court cases, and prison population. Minorities, especially blacks, had higher rates for both arrests and incar-

Asian Americans

As with Hispanics, the term Asian American refers to a broad range of national and cultural identities. Asians were subjected to considerable racial prejudice in the late nineteenth and early twentieth centuries. Congress passed immigration laws as late as the 1920s prohibiting further entry of Asians into the country and blocking requests for U.S. citizenship. During World War II some 120,000 Japanese Americans were imprisoned for up to three years out of suspicion of potential wartime criminal activity based solely on their ethnicity.

The Asian American population rose from over seven million in 1990 to about twelve million in 2000. Despite a strong history of discrimination, some Asian American groups such as the Japanese have been very successful in U.S. society while others such as the Chinese have not. The Asian American population is concentrated in California, Washington, New York, and Nevada.

Many Chinese Americans live in urban Chinatowns located within large cities. Chinatowns often have very high poverty rates,

FBI Director Louis Freeh claimed that Asian street gangs are becoming more organized and are growing threats. *(AP/Wide World Photos)*

and youth gangs have been an outcome of this poverty and isolation. More recently, young immigrants from Hong Kong have formed gangs. Asian organized crime has also penetrated the United States, becoming a major force in drug trafficking.

cerations. In a 1999 report the ACLU argued that even though blacks comprised just 13 percent of drug users, blacks comprised 37 percent of drug-related arrests, 55 percent of drug convictions, and 74 percent of drug offenders sentenced to prison. These statistics indicated a strong difference within the criminal justice system regarding the treatment of minorities.

A major factor in this disparity was the appearance of crack cocaine as a major drug of choice in the 1980s. Its low cost and high potency compared to regular powder cocaine made it very attractive in impoverished inner-city areas. The new federal drug laws set penalties for the sale or possession of five grams of crack cocaine, the same as five hundred grams of powder cocaine—a felony with a mandatory minimum sentence of five years of prison.

In contrast, possession of five grams of powder cocaine remained a misdemeanor with a maximum sentence of one year in prison. One study estimated that 75 percent of cocaine users were white, were middle class, and held white-collar jobs. Several states passed laws targeting crack cocaine with stiffer penalties similar to the federal law. With police targeting inner-city areas for crack rather than the suburbs where cocaine was the drug of choice, the resulting drug arrest rates were five times higher for minorities than whites.

The overall prison population increased 84 percent in the ten-year period from 1985 to 1995 with drug offenders comprising half of the increase. Some 80 percent of drug offenders convicted and sentenced under the stiffer laws were black. Incarceration of blacks for drug offenses increased 465 percent in contrast to 111 percent for whites. The number of black women incarcerated in state prisons increased 828 percent. Over 85 percent of those convicted of crack cocaine sales or possession were black. A number of federal court districts prosecuted only crack cocaine cases involving minorities. In addition to those convicted, blacks were six times more likely to be sentenced to mandatory prison terms than white offenders.

In Minnesota, a state court ruled the state antidrug law was racially discriminatory after statistics showed the incarceration rate for blacks between 1988 and 1994 was 100 percent compared to 75 percent for whites.

Violence in minority communities

Minorities are involved in more violent crimes than whites, both as offenders and victims. Young black American males are eight times more likely to commit homicides than young white males and eleven times more likely to be arrested for robbery. Homicide was the leading cause of death for black males between fifteen and twenty-four years of age. For Hispanics of the same age range, it is the second leading cause of death.

The impact of crime on minority communities is major, both economically and psychologically. Researchers believe high crime rates come from anger and aggression, with residents often feeling trapped in poverty with no way out. Unemployment rates are generally higher, as are crime rates. These factors contribute to what has been labeled the "subculture of violence" in poor communities.

Hate Crimes

Hate crime is a crime committed against a person simply because he or she represents a certain group or lifestyle different from the offender. Most commonly hate crimes focus on race and ethnicity, but also can include religion, sexual orientation, gender, and age. In 2002 almost 49 percent of hate crimes were based on race and another 15 percent based on ethnicity or national origin. Some 67 percent of victims attacked based on race were black Americans.

The term "hate crime" came into use in the mid-1980s in the media and by politicians. The term quickly caught on in the criminal justice systems. In 1990 the FBI began gathering hate crime data, which is probably much lower than the actual number of hate crimes that have occurred. Many jurisdictions, however, did not provide statistics to the FBI until the 1990s progressed. Other factors affecting statistics include under reportage of crimes due to victims who fear retaliation and distrust law enforcement.

Hate crimes involve criminal behavior already prohibited by law, such as assault, murder, and vandalism. Hate crimes can also be against property, such as destruction or vandalism. By the early twenty-first century, over forty states had

"Three Strikes" Laws

Following a rise in crime rates through the 1980s and early 1990s twenty-four states and the federal government passed legislation known as "three-strikes" laws between 1993 and 1995. The purpose was to get tough on repeat or habitual offenders. Lengthy prison sentences were required on the third felony conviction of an offender. One major effect of the laws was a substantial increase in the incarceration of minorities.

California was one of the first states to pass a three-strikes law. Some 26,000 offenders were incarcerated under the law in its first three years. Black Americans comprised 43 percent of those incarcerated even though they represented only 20 percent of felony arrests and only 7 percent of the state's population. The incarceration rate was thirteen times higher than for whites. In Georgia 98 percent of offenders serving life sentences under their law were black. National studies showed that prosecutors were 50 percent more likely to file charges under the three-strikes laws for black offenders than for white.

Cross-burning ceremony involving the organized hate group Ku Klux Klan. *(AP/Wide World Photos)*

passed some form of hate crime legislation. Some states make hate crimes separate from other crimes, while other states passed hate crime bills that influence only the penalty phase of cases.

Hate crimes can be vicious and brutal since the crime comes from intense anger or rage. Victims of hate crimes are three times more likely to need hospital treatment. Many consider hate crimes as a form of domestic terrorism since they are commonly intended to send a message to a larger social group for whom the offender has deep hostilities. They are usually unprovoked by the victim and often appear random.

Hate crime victims are usually selected because of who they are, not something they have done. Attacks are generally based on personal characteristics of which victims have no control, such as skin color or gender. Studies show such crimes lead to tremendous emotional distress for the victims, as well as their communities and society as a whole.

The causes of hate crime can vary. Sometimes the offender suffers from severe mental illness. Other times, hate crimes are "thrill" crimes for youthful offenders, perhaps to gain acceptance among peers or as a gang initiation, or for revenge or retaliation. Organized hate groups such as the Ku Klux Klan or the Aryan Nation engaged in hate crimes for years. In the 1990s white supremacist groups had an estimated membership of 50,000, and had developed a strong presence in prisons.

Reasons for high minority crime rates

In 2002 black Americans accounted for 27 percent of all arrests, including both person and property crimes. Various factors have been cited for the relatively large presence of blacks in America's criminal justice system. Part is certainly due to the racial discrimination that permeates all aspects of American society. Studies showed police officers were more likely to shoot and use excessive force against black suspects, though this tendency had declined by the early twenty-first century.

It is also true policing occurs at higher levels in minority communities, and that black Americans are targeted much more frequently in racial profiling. Judges and parole officers are also influenced by the race of offenders. Many believe these patterns have declined through the late twentieth century as more minorities have become employed in the criminal justice system, from policing to sitting on the bench in judge positions.

For More Information

Books

Benjamin, William P. *African Americans in the Criminal Justice System.* New York: Vantage Press, 1996.

Collins, Catherine F. *The Imprisonment of African American Women: Causes, Conditions, and Future Implications.* Jefferson, NC: McFarland, 1997.

Jones-Brown, Delores. *Race, Crime, and Punishment.* Philadelphia, PA: Chelsea House, 2000.

Kennedy, Randall. *Race, Crime, and the Law.* New York: Vintage Books, 1998.

Levin, Jack. *The Violence of Hate: Confronting Racism, Anti-Semitism, and Other Forms of Bigotry.* Boston, MA: Allyn and Bacon, 2002.

Mauer, Marc. *Race to Incarcerate.* New York: Free Press, 1999.

Russell, Katheryn. *The Color of Crime.* New York: New York University Press, 1998.

Web Site

"Arrest the Racism: Racial Profiling in America." *American Civil Liberties Union (ACLU).* http://www.aclu.org/profiling (accessed on August 20, 2004).

Media

Criminal trials, by their very nature, are public events. Prosecuting attorneys are public officers of the court, judges are often elected officials, and juries who decide the fate of the accused consist of members of the community. As with all public events of importance, the news media play a major role in relaying information to the public and providing access to events the public otherwise would not have. Despite this vital public service, the rights of the media have sometimes clashed with the rights of those on trial.

Technological advances and the easing of rules regarding televised proceedings have allowed the public to enter the courtroom on a wider scale. This increased access can serve the public interest or create a circus-like atmosphere. Since people have been able to learn more about the benefits and flaws of the criminal justice process, movies, television series, and books that document trials, lawyers, judges, and criminals have soared in popularity.

History of the media and the courts

Balanced against the media's role to report news of a criminal trial is the right of an accused citizen to a fair trial with

Members of the media gather outside, awaiting the verdict in the O.J. Simpson civil trial in 1997. Media coverage of court proceedings can bring concerns about what jurors or potential jurors see or hear outside the courtroom. *(AP/Wide World Photos)*

an impartial (open to all evidence presented) jury, as guaranteed by the Sixth Amendment of the United States Constitution. The amendment reads, in part, "In all criminal prosecutions, the accused shall enjoy the right to a speedy and public trial, by an impartial jury of the State and district wherein the crime shall have been committed."

With media coverage of court proceedings comes natural and well-founded concerns among defense attorneys and civil rights advocates about what jurors or potential jurors see or hear outside the courtroom. Irresponsible reporting can prejudice (change people's perception or opinions before all the facts are presented) a jury and deny a defendant one of the most basic rights accorded to all U.S. citizens.

Perhaps the first high-profile case in U.S. history involved the trial of Vice President Aaron Burr (1756–1836). Burr shot Alexander Hamilton (1755–1804), a former secretary of the treasury, to death in an 1804 duel in Weehawken, New Jersey. Although Burr was indicted for murder in New York, he was never prosecuted and fled the country. During the indictment proceedings, however, Justice John Marshall (1755–1835) commented on the considerable media attention the case had received.

Justice Marshall issued a ruling regarding the potential problems so much publicity could cause a jury, declaring that jurors were impartial only if they were free from the influence of the media outside the courtroom. Marshall stated that the decision of a jury must be rendered solely on the facts and evidence presented inside the court of law. This principle, of course, is easier stated than practiced.

Tried in the media

The first clash of Hollywood celebrity, the media, and the law came in the case of Roscoe "Fatty" Arbuckle (1887–1933). Arbuckle was one of the highest paid and most popular actors in the growing motion picture industry. Arbuckle threw a party at a San Francisco hotel on September 5, 1921. During the party, a woman named Virginia Rappe ran screaming from a bedroom, became ill, and died mysteriously four days later. Arbuckle was charged with the rape and murder of Rappe.

The accusation caused a sensation in the national press and rumors spread wildly regarding Arbuckle's involvement in the death of Rappe. Perhaps more interested in selling his papers than in justice, newspaper publisher William Randolph Hearst (1863–1951) printed numerous articles about the story. Hearst papers published stories smearing the reputation of Arbuckle and his friends, many of whom were urged not to testify on Arbuckle's behalf for fear of losing their careers.

Hearst raised so much contempt against Arbuckle that his wife, who maintained her husband's innocence, was shot at as she entered the courthouse during one of the three resulting trials. Hearst, for his part, was delighted, boasting that the Arbuckle case sold more newspapers than the German sinking of the passenger ship *Lusitania*, which brought the United States into World War I (1914–18).

Arbuckle's first two trials resulted in mistrials (where juries are unable to agree on a verdict). Arbuckle was acquitted (found innocent) in his third trial, and many believed him the victim of a setup. The jury from the third trial even wrote Arbuckle an apology letter, a very rare event in American justice. The media frenzy and accusations were too much to overcome, however, and Arbuckle never worked in the movie industry again.

The crime of the century

The media have always covered significant trials, but the beginning of motion pictures and television presented a new set of challenges. The Lindbergh baby kidnapping, known as the "crime of the century," illustrated the increasing noise of the media and its influence upon juries.

On March 1, 1932, the infant son of world famous aviator and American hero Charles Lindbergh (1902–1974), and his wife, Anne Morrow, was abducted from their home. Despite ransom notes and other communications from the kidnapper, the baby was found dead of a skull fracture nearby. News of the kidnapping attracted the attention of the world press. Journalists and sightseers soon gathered around the Lindbergh home, destroying evidence and clues. Photographers disguised as rescue workers even set up a darkroom in an ambulance.

Members of the press trying to get a shot of Charles Lindbergh leaving the courtroom. *(AP/Wide World Photos)*

Two years later, police arrested Bruno Richard Hauptmann (1899–1936) and charged him with kidnapping and murder. The Hearst newspaper chain was once again involved, and even paid the legal fees of Hauptmann's attorney in exchange for the exclusive right to interview Hauptmann's wife during the trial. The trial itself was held in Flemington, New Jersey, near the Lindbergh home.

Journalists from across the globe traveled to Flemington and used the latest technological equipment to bring news of the trial to consumers. Over one hundred Western Union telegraph wires were strung in the courthouse attic. The Associated Press set up four teletype machines to transmit trial transcripts to New York and Philadelphia newspapers.

At this time, newsreels had become a popular medium among moviegoers. News, sports, and entertainment were shown before the main feature in theaters across the nation. During the Lindbergh trial, five newsreel companies covered the testimony. They pooled their resources and operated a remote control camera to bring the trial to thousands throughout the country. When the judge learned that court proceedings were being played in movie houses during the trial, he shut down all filming of testimony.

The jury had a difficult time staying away from the extensive coverage. Despite orders from the judge not to read newspapers, listen to the radio, or talk to anyone regarding the trial, jurors were affected by the spectacle. Each day the court was in session, the jurors made their way from a hotel to the courthouse through hundreds of newsboys who shouted the latest headlines. Observers hollered for the jury to convict Hauptmann and send him to his death.

When the jury was ready to give its verdict, the media stood ready to relay the news with speed. Reporters smuggled portable radio transmitters into the courthouse so they could signal the verdict to the outside world. The newsreel cameras recorded a crowd of ten thousand people waiting outside the courthouse. The jury found Hauptmann guilty and recommended the death penalty. The mob outside roared its approval and Charles Lindbergh, listening to the radio, disapproved such a display.

Cameras in the courtroom

Because of the Lindbergh baby murder trial, photographers and movie cameras were banned in all federal and state courts. The American Bar Association enacted Canon 35 of the Code of Judicial Conduct as it related to the media. In part it read, "The taking of photographs . . . and the broadcasting of court proceedings are calculated to detract from the essential dignity of the proceedings . . . and create misconceptions in the mind of the public and should not be permitted."

The legal community had concluded that cameras were entirely too disruptive to trials. Yet as technology improved over time and cameras became smaller, easier to handle, and less disruptive, the media once again tried to enlarge its scope of trial coverage. As with other major issues of the day, the U.S. Supreme Court had a say in the controversy between the

Lawyers and family members often make impassioned pleas to the media, which some worry may taint the jury pool. *(AP/Wide World Photos)*

rights of the media and the rights of the accused. The case of *Estes v. Texas* (1965) involved a trial that originally received great publicity because of the defendant's relationship to U.S. president Lyndon B. Johnson (1908–1973; served 1963–69).

Estes was found guilty of business fraud and sentenced to prison. In the Court's ruling, Justice John Marshall Harlan (1899–1971) declared that televised proceedings in criminal trials of great note created considerable prejudice against the defendants. Harlan believed televised proceedings lacked due process. The following year, in overturning the murder conviction of Ohio physician Sam Sheppard, the Court stated that it was the duty of the presiding judge to prevent press coverage from interfering with court proceedings.

During the 1980s the Supreme Court began allowing more access after media advocates claimed that televising trials would make media representatives strive to be more accurate in their reporting. Other changes in the media brought new issues as well. Cable news stations and the 24-hour news cycle became commonplace and included legal commentators, who were not always accurate and could create false impressions of a trial's proceedings.

The legal community and the media attempted to work together in many respects to bridge the gap between fair trials and the public's right to information regarding trials. Judges are primarily in charge of regulating cameras inside their courts and usually ask jurors to avoid television coverage of their case. No cameras are allowed in federal courts, though oral arguments in front of the U.S. Supreme Court can be watched on the C-SPAN cable network.

Detectives and the courtroom as entertainment

As shown by the popular interest in the Lindbergh case, Americans have long been fascinated by the criminal justice process and the punishment of its criminals and outlaws. The rise of television in American popular culture in the 1950s and 1960s gave the viewing public the chance to enjoy shows about crime and the law. Writers have also taken advantage of the public's fascination, and fictional murder mysteries have been popular for decades.

The first novel published in the newly formed United States was a murder mystery by William H. Brown (1765–1793) called *The Power of Sympathy*. Books profiling criminals and their trials made "true crime" (crime that has actually happened) books one of the best selling categories in the publishing world by the late twentieth century.

Edgar Allan Poe (1809–1849) is generally recognized as the father of the modern mystery story. Poe, who was born in Virginia and worked as an editor and writer, published his first mystery story "The Murders in the Rue Morgue" in 1841. Poe followed with other classic tales like "The Tell-Tale Heart" and "The Pit and the Pendulum." These stories, combined with Poe's famous poem "The Raven," popularized horror and mystery stories in the United States and Great Britain.

Poe's work paved the way for writers such as Sir Arthur Conan Doyle (1859–1930) and Agatha Christie (1890–1976). Doyle and Christie wrote about the adventures of fictional detectives. Doyle, a Scottish physician, created the most popular character in the murder mystery genre, Detective Sherlock Holmes. His great powers of observation and use of reasoning and logic to solve crimes made Holmes an enduring figure in popular fiction.

With his distinctive hat, pipe, and magnifying glass, Holmes caught the public's imagination in such novels as *The Hound of the Baskervilles* (1902) and *The Case-Book of Sherlock Holmes* (1927). Doyle's fictional detective had become so popular that when he killed him off in "The Final Problem" (published in *Strand* magazine's December 1893 issue), the public was so outraged Doyle was forced to bring him back to life—but not until ten years later.

Agatha Christie, born in England, created stories featuring the exploits of Hercule Poirot. Poirot was a retired Belgian police officer who solved mysteries by meticulously (carefully) examining the facts and clues. Christie wrote more than thirty novels featuring the fictional Poirot, the most famous among them *Murder on the Orient Express* (1934) and *Death on the Nile* (1937).

Movies, radio, and television

In addition to reading detective and mystery stories with great fervor, the public also went to theaters to watch Hollywood films of such stories. Murder mysteries also made their way onto radio and television. Perhaps the most popular radio program involving a crime fighter was "The Shadow," which debuted on NBC radio in 1930. The Shadow was never seen, only heard, and could use his extraordinary intelligence and strength to overcome his adversaries (the bad guys). The popular series ran until 1954 when television shows became a more popular way for Americans to be entertained.

American author Erle Stanley Gardner (1889–1970) created one of television's most popular heroes, trial attorney Perry Mason. Along with the help of private detective Paul Drake and trusty secretary Della Street, Mason solved crimes for more than a decade. The Perry Mason character had been featured in dozens of novels by Gardner and a radio program

American author Erle Stanley Gardner, who created one of television's most popular heroes, trial attorney Perry Mason. *(AP/Wide World Photos)*

before the series first aired in 1957. Perry Mason was played by actor Raymond Burr, and viewers tuned in to his courtroom dramas for ten years. The series is still popular in reruns.

True crime

Along with murder mysteries and legal thrillers, particularly the works of John Grisham and Scott Turow—whose books sell millions and are often turned into profitable movies—true crime literature has soared in popularity. True crime was first made popular by Truman Capote's (1924–1984) nonfiction novel *In Cold Blood*. The book chillingly retold the story of a Kansas family's brutal murder and the men who killed them. Capote's work was the beginning of what has been called the "New Journalism," in which scenes are developed dramatically, and dialogue is recreated from reports. True crime books steadily gained popularity and by 1983 *Fatal Vision* by Joe McGinniss sold 2.3 million copies. True crime author Ann Rule, who knew serial killer Ted Bundy (1946–1989) and wrote books about him, has found immense success in the industry.

True crime books usually have bold-colored paperback covers and crime scene photographs inside. Some of the most popular true crime books involve organized crime. Americans have always been fascinated with organized crime, especially the Mafia. Movies such as *The Godfather* trilogy based on the novels of Mario Puzo (1920–1999) and books like *Way of the Wiseguy* were extraordinarily popular, as was the 1950s television series "The Untouchables," based on the cases of FBI investigator Elliot Ness (1903–1957) and his pursuit of 1920s gangsters.

As televised action, legal dramas continued to be popular in the 1980s and 1990s. "L.A. Law" glamorized a corporate law firm and was reportedly responsible for a sharp increase in law school applications. In 1989 NBC introduced the first "Law & Order" series, which portrayed crime investigation from the point of view of both law enforcement and prosecutors. The series was so successful it has produced several spin-offs. Other networks produced similar programs, such as the popular CBS series "CSI" (Crime Scene Investigation).

Legal dramas like the "The Practice" on ABC and even comedies like "Ally McBeal" on Fox succeeded as the American viewing public continued to relish the action of the courtroom and the lives of lawyers and prosecutors.

The modern media and sensational trials

Cable and satellite television increasingly offers channels that appeal to specific audiences. In the 1990s and 2000s the popularity of the O.J. Simpson (1947–) murder case revealed a new interest among viewers—following the proceedings of high-profile trials. On cable, Court TV became the top channel for live trial coverage. In addition to trial coverage, Court TV also features original movies and documentaries about the justice system. Cases are presented and then analyzed by Court TV's legal experts and hosts, most of whom are attorneys themselves.

There was been no shortage of sensational trials to cover following the Simpson case. The Laci Peterson murder case in California, in which Scott Peterson, husband of the victim, was charged with killing his wife and unborn child, attracted a great deal of media coverage. Music superstar Michael Jackson (1958–) faced trial on child molestation charges, and professional basketball player Jayson Williams (1968–) was acquitted in the 2004 death of his limousine driver.

Much attention was given to another professional basketball player, Kobe Bryant (1978–) of the Los Angeles Lakers, who was charged with rape and often flew to court hearings in Denver, Colorado, by way of a private jet during the basketball season. Over four hundred television and print journalists were at the scene when Bryant made his first court appearance. With the case getting so much attention, the judge decided not to allow television cameras inside for the

The O.J. Simpson Case

On June 17, 1994, over one-third of the American public watched their televisions in astonishment. They watched as O.J. Simpson, whom many had come to know during his Hall of Fame football career and popular rental car commercials, was driven along a Los Angeles, California, freeway in a white Ford Bronco, slowly fleeing from the numerous police cars that followed him.

Five days earlier, Simpson's ex-wife, Nicole, and her friend, Ronald Goldman, were found stabbed to death outside Nicole's house in Brentwood, California. Los Angeles police had gathered enough evidence to suspect Simpson of the crime and he had agreed to turn himself in to authorities. On June 17, however, Simpson appeared to be fleeing and had threatened to commit suicide during the slow chase. The drama was shown live as network and cable stations interrupted their regular programming. Drivers along the freeway abandoned their cars to watch (some cheering) as Simpson's vehicle, driven by a friend, passed. Simpson's journey ended at his mother's home about two hours later. The event was the first in what would become a media frenzy over a trial that became a national obsession.

Media coverage of the Simpson trial, which began in January 1995, was unlike any other. Over two thousand reporters covered the trial, and 80 miles of cable was required to allow nineteen television stations to cover the trial live to 91 percent of the American viewing audience. When the verdict was finally read on October 3, 1995, some 142 million people listened or watched. It seemed the nation stood still, divided along racial lines as to the defendant's guilt or innocence. During and after the trial, over eighty books were published about the event by most everyone involved in the Simpson case.

Simpson hired a group of lawyers the media called the "Dream Team," because of their high fees and notoriety. This group

trial. Despite criticism about the amount of coverage given to these events, television programs about such trials continue to receive high ratings while newspapers and magazines sell in the millions when they report these stories.

Mixing popular culture with the legal process continues. In May 2004, an Ohio murder trial began with television cameras in place to record the entire process—including jury deliberations (discussions about the case in order to reach a verdict). The Ohio state court system approved the cameras, but only after the judge, jury, and prosecuting and defense attorneys all

O.J. Simpson, smiling after a jury announced its not guilty verdict. *(AP/Wide World Photos)*

included Johnnie Cochran, who had defended other celebrities such as Michael Jackson, forensics expert Barry Scheck, and noted law professor Alan Dershowitz. Despite "a mountain of evidence" directly implicating Simpson in the murders, Simpson's lawyers argued that their client was framed by a racist police detective, Mark Furhman.

Furhman had previously been recorded on tape making racist statements about black Americans. The defense lawyers accused Furhman of planting a leather glove with the blood of the victims at the scene of the crime. Scheck managed to discredit police tactics in examining the blood and fingerprinting evidence.

During his closing argument, Cochran sharply criticized Furhman and the police. Throughout the nation, citizens divided according to race; many blacks thought Simpson was framed, most whites believed nobody but Simpson could have committed the crimes. The jury found Simpson not guilty on both counts of murder; he was, however, found guilty in a civil suit for the wrongful deaths of Nicole Brown Simpson and Ronald Goldman.

Ten years after the murders, O.J. Simpson remains a free man and no one has been charged in the deaths.

agreed to certain rules. The film footage will become part of a documentary for ABC television entitled *State v.*

Unanswered questions

While the public certainly enjoys legal dramas, both fictional and real, and technology has been able to cover almost all aspects of a story at rapid speed, many are concerned about the media's role in crime and punishment. Having cameras and reporters involved in trials has raised questions about the rights of the accused. Do the media threaten the constitutional rights guaranteed to the accused? How does media coverage impact a potential jury, especially in sensational trials? Do cameras in the courtroom change the way lawyers or prosecutors act or try their cases?

These questions are not easy to answer and continue to be discussed on a case-by-case basis. Television cameras are still banned from federal and state courts, but they are allowed in criminal and civil courts if approved by a judge. Cable news shows and Court TV continue to provide extensive coverage of celebrity and sensational criminal trials, while police and legal dramas remain popular on major networks like ABC, CBS, NBC, and Fox. True crime books also continue to flourish, as do fictional mysteries and thrillers.

While the media and the justice system may clash over the coverage of certain trials, both groups continue to work together in an attempt to make sure that justice and the public's right to know are equally satisfied.

For More Information

Books

Cohn, Marjorie, and David Dow. *Cameras in the Courtroom: Television and the Pursuit of Justice.* New York: McFarland & Company, 1998.

The Constitution of the United States as Amended. Washington, DC: United States Government Printing Office.

Cowdery, Nicholas. *Getting Justice Wrong: Myths, Media, and Crime.* New York: Independent Publishers Group, 2001.

Dunne, Dominick. *Justice: Crimes, Trials, and Punishment.* New York: Three Rivers Press, 2002.

Fox, Richard L. *Tabloid Justice: Criminal Justice in an Age of Media Frenzy.* New York: Lynne Rienner Publishers, 2000.

Sloctnick, Elliot E., and Jennifer A. Segal. *Television News and the Supreme Court: All the News That's Fit to Air?* Cambridge, UK: Cambridge University Press, 1998.

Yalof, David A., and Kenneth Dautrich. *The First Amendment and the Media in the Court of Public Opinion.* Cambridge, UK: Cambridge University Press, 2002.

Web Sites

Court TV.com—The Investigation Channel. http://www.courttv.com/ (accessed on August 20, 2004).

Court TV's Crime Library: Criminal Minds and Methods. http://www.crime
library.com (accessed on August 20, 2004).

Famous Trials Theater. http://www.famoustrials.com/ (accessed on August
20, 2004).

Where to Learn More

Books

Abadinsky, Howard. *Drug Abuse: An Introduction.* Chicago, IL: Nelson-Hall Publishers, 1997.

Acker, James R., Robert M. Bohm, and Charles S. Lanier, eds. *America's Experiment with Capital Punishment: Reflections on the Past, Present, and Future of the Ultimate Penal Sanction.* Durham, NC: Carolina Academic Press, 1998.

Anderson, Elijah. *Streetwise: Race, Class and Change in an Urban Community.* Chicago, IL: University of Chicago Press, 1990.

Arrigo, Bruce A., ed. *Social Justice, Criminal Justice.* Belmont, CA: Wadsworth, 1999.

Austern, David. *The Crime Victims Handbook: Your Rights and Role in the Criminal Justice System.* New York: Viking, 1987.

Bachman-Prehn, Ronet D. *Death and Violence on the Reservation: Homicide, Violence, and Suicide in American Indian Populations.* New York: Auburn House, 1992.

Baum, Lawrence. *American Courts.* 5th ed. Boston: Houghton Mifflin, 2001.

Belknap, Joanne. *The Invisible Woman: Gender, Crime, and Justice.* Toronto: Wadsworth Thomson Learning, 2001.

Benjamin, William P. *African Americans in the Criminal Justice System*. New York: Vantage Press, 1996.

Besharov, Douglas J. *Recognizing Child Abuse: A Guide for the Concerned*. New York: Free Press, 1990.

Burns, Ronald G., and Michael J. Lynch. *Environmental Crime: A Source Book*. New York: LFB Scholarly Publishing, 2004.

Burrough, Bryan. *Public Enemies: America's Greatest Crime Wave and the Birth of the FBI, 1933–34*. New York: Penguin Press, 2004.

Buzawa, Eve, and Carl Buzawa. *Domestic Violence: The Criminal Justice Response*. Thousand Oaks, CA: Sage, 1996.

Carp, Robert A., and Ronald Stidham. *Judicial Process in America*. 5th ed. Washington, DC: CQ Press, 2001.

Chase, Anthony. *Law and History: The Evolution of the American Legal System*. New York: The New Press, 1997.

Clement, Mary. *The Juvenile Justice System*. 3rd ed. Woburn, MA: Butterworth Heinemann, 2002.

Clifford, Mary. *Environmental Crime: Enforcement, Policy, and Social Responsibility*. Gaithersburg, MD: Aspen Publishers, Inc., 1998.

Clifford, Ralph D., ed. *Cybercrime: The Investigation, Prosecution, and Defense of a Computer-Related Crime*. Durham, NC: Carolina Academic Press, 2001.

Cohn, Marjorie, and David Dow. *Cameras in the Courtroom: Television and the Pursuit of Justice*. New York: McFarland & Company, 1998.

Coloroso, Barbara. *The Bully, the Bullied, and the Bystander: From Pre-School to High School, How Parents and Teachers Can Help Break the Cycle of Violence*. New York: HarperResource, 2003.

Conser, James A., and Gregory D. Russell. *Law Enforcement in the United States*. Gaithersburg, MD: Aspen, 2000.

Cromwell, Paul, Lee Parker, and Shawna Mobley. "The Five-Finger Discount." In *In Their Own Words: Criminals on Crime*, edited by Paul Cromwell. Los Angeles, CA: Roxbury, pp. 57–70.

Curran, Daniel J., and Claire M. Renzetti. *Theories of Crime*. Boston: Allyn & Bacon, 2001.

Davidson, Michael J. *A Guide to Military Criminal Law*. Annapolis, MD: Naval Institute Press, 1999.

Dummer, Harry R. *Religion in Corrections*. Lanham, MD: American Correctional Associates, 2000.

Dunne, Dominick. *Justice: Crimes, Trials, and Punishment*. New York: Three Rivers Press, 2002.

Federal Bureau of Investigation. *Crime in the United States, 2002: Uniform Crime Reports*. Washington, DC: U.S. Department of Justice, 2003.

Felson, Marcus. *Crime and Everyday Life*. 2nd ed. Thousand Oaks, CA: Pine Forge Press, 1998.

Frank, Nancy, and Michael Lynch. *Corporate Crime, Corporate Violence*. Albany, NY: Harrow and Heston, 1992.

Friedman, Lawrence M. *Crime and Punishment in American History*. New York: Basic Books, 1993.

Garbarino, James. *Lost Boys: Why Our Sons Turn Violent and How We Can Save Them*. New York: Free Press, 1999.

Gordon, Margaret, and Stephanie Riger. *The Female Fear*. New York: Free Press, 1989.

Hirsch, Adam Jay. *The Rise of the Penitentiary: Prisons and Punishment in Early America*. New Haven, CT: Yale University Press, 1992.

Hoffer, Peter C. *Law and People in Colonial America*. Baltimore: Johns Hopkins University Press, 1998.

Jones-Brown, Delores. *Race, Crime, and Punishment*. Philadelphia: Chelsea House, 2000.

Karmen, Andrew. *Crime Victims: An Introduction to Victimology*. 4th ed. Belmont, CA: Wadsworth, 2001.

Lane, Brian. *Crime and Detection*. New York: Alfred A. Knopf, 1998.

Levin, Jack. *The Violence of Hate: Confronting Racism, Anti-Semitism, and Other Forms of Bigotry*. Boston: Allyn and Bacon, 2002.

Lunde, Paul. *Organized Crime: An Inside Guide to the World's Most Successful Industry*. New York: DK Publishing, Inc., 2004.

Lyman, Michael D., and Gary W. Potter. *Organized Crime*. Upper Saddle River, NJ: Pearson Prentice Hall, 2004.

Moncs, Paul. *When a Child Kills*. New York: Simon & Schuster, 1991.

Oliver, Willard M. *Community-Oriented Policing: A Systematic Approach to Policing*. Upper Saddle River, NJ: Prentice Hall, 2001.

Patrick, John J. *The Young Oxford Companion to the Supreme Court of the United States*. New York: Oxford University Press, 1998.

Ramsey, Sarah H., and Douglas E. Adams. *Children and the Law in a Nutshell*. 2nd ed. St. Paul, MN: Thomson/West, 2003.

Renzetti, Claire M., and Lynne Goodstein, eds. *Women, Crime, and Criminal Justice*. Los Angeles: Roxbury, 2001.

Russell, Katheryn. *The Color of Crime*. New York: New York University Press, 1998.

Sherman, Mark. *Introduction to Cyber Crime*. Washington, DC: Federal Judicial Center, 2000.

Siegel, Larry J. *Criminology: The Core*. Belmont, CA: Wadsworth/Thomson Learning, 2002.

Silverman, Ira. *Corrections: A Comprehensive View.* 2nd ed. Belmont, CA: Wadsworth, 2001.

Situ, Yingyi, and David Emmons. *Environmental Crime: The Criminal Justice System's Role in Protecting the Environment.* Thousand Oaks, CA: Sage Publications, 2000.

Smith, Helen. *The Scarred Heart: Understanding and Identifying Kids Who Kill.* Knoxville, TN: Callisto, 2000.

Stark, Rodney, and Williams Sims Bainbridge. *Religion, Deviance, and Social Control.* New York: Routledge, 1997.

Sullivan, Robert, ed. *Mobsters and Gangsters: Organized Crime in America, from Al Capone to Tony Soprano.* New York: Life Books, 2002.

Sutherland, Edwin H. *White-Collar Crime: The Uncut Version.* New Haven, CT: Yale University Press, 1983.

Walker, Samuel. *The Police in America: An Introduction.* New York: McGraw-Hill, 1992.

Wilkinson, Charles F. *American Indians, Time, and the Law: Native Societies in a Modern Constitutional Democracy.* New Haven, CN: Yale University Press, 1987.

Wright, Richard, and Scott Decker. *Armed Robbers in Action: Stickups and Street Culture.* Boston: Northeastern University Press, 1997.

Yalof, David A., and Kenneth Dautrich. *The First Amendment and the Media in the Court of Public Opinion.* Cambridge: Cambridge University Press, 2002.

Web Sites

"Arrest the Racism: Racial Profiling in America." *American Civil Liberties Union (ACLU).* http://www.aclu.org/profiling (accessed on September 20, 2004).

Center for the Prevention of School Violence. http://www.ncdjjdp.org/cpsv/ (accessed on September 20, 2004).

"Computer Crime and Intellectual Property Section (CCIPS) of the Criminal Division." *U.S. Department of Justice.* http://www.cybercrime.gov (accessed on September 20, 2004).

"Counterfeit Division." *United States Secret Service.* http://www.secretservice.gov/counterfeit.shtml (accessed on September 20, 2004).

Court TV's Crime Library. http://www.crimelibrary.com (accessed on September 20, 2004).

"Criminal Enforcement." *U.S. Environmental Protection Agency.* http://www.epa.gov/compliance/criminal/index.html (accessed on September 20, 2004).

Death Penalty Information Center. http://www.deathpenaltyinfo.org (accessed on September 20, 2004).

Department of Homeland Security. http://www.dhs.gov (accessed on September 20, 2004).

Federal Bureau of Investigation (FBI). http://www.fbi.gov (accessed on September 20, 2004).

McGeary, Johanna. "Who's the Enemy Now?" *Time,* March 29, 2004. http://www.time.com/time/classroom/glenfall2004/pg28.html (accessed on September 20, 2004).

Mothers Against Drunk Driving (MADD). http://www.madd.org (accessed on September 20, 2004).

National Alliance of Crime Investigators Associations. http://www.nagia.org (accessed on September 20, 2004).

National Center for Juvenile Justice. http://www.ncjj.org (accessed on September 20, 2004).

National Center for Victims of Crime. http://www.ncvc.org (accessed on September 20, 2004).

National Child Abuse and Neglect Data System (NCANDS). http://nccanch.acf.hhs.gov/index.cfm (accessed on September 20, 2004).

"National Institute of Corrections (NIC)." *U.S. Department of Justice.* http://www.nicic.org (accessed on September 20, 2004).

National Institute of Military Justice. http://www.nimj.com/Home.asp (accessed on September 20, 2004).

National Organization for Victim Assistance (NOVA). http://www.try-nova.org (accessed on September 20, 2004).

Uniform Crime Reporting Program. http://www.fbi.gov/ucr/ucr.htm (accessed on September 20, 2004).

United Nations Office for Drug Control and Crime Prevention, Organized Crime. http://www.undcp.org/organized_crime.html (accessed on September 20, 2004).

U.S. Courts. http://www.uscourts.gov (accessed on September 20, 2004).

U.S. Department of Justice. http://www.usdoj.gov (accessed on September 20, 2004).

U.S. Drug Enforcement Administration. http://www.dea.gov (accessed on September 20, 2004).

U.S. Securities and Exchange Commission. http://www.sec.gov (accessed on September 20, 2004).

Index

Italic indicates volume number; illustrations are marked by (ill.)

P

Trusts, *1:* 109
TTIC (Terrorist Threat Integration Center), *1:* 186
Tubbs, David, *1:* 95 (ill.)
Tulloch, Robert, *1:* 59
"Two strikes" rule, *2:* 365
Two-way radios, *2:* 254 (ill.), 255
Tyson Foods, *1:* 165

U

UCMJ (Uniform Code of Military Justice), *2:* 328, 333
UCR (Uniform Crime Report), *1:* 43; *2:* 242
"Unabomber," *1:* 51, 179, 179 (ill.); *2:* 279
Unemployment and crime, *1:* 214–15, 217
Uniform Child Custody Jurisdiction Act, *2:* 364
Uniform Code of Military Justice (UCMJ), *2:* 328, 333
Uniform Crime Report (UCR), *1:* 43; *2:* 242
Uniform Interstate Family Support Act, *2:* 374
Uniforms, police, *1:* 34
United Nations, *2:* 297
Unlawful entry, *1:* 78
Unreasonable searches and seizures. *See* Searches and seizures
Unreformed death row prisoners, *2:* 314
The Untouchables (TV show), *2:* 446
Urban decay, *2:* 414 (ill.)
U.S. attorneys, *2:* 287, 290
U.S. Embassy bombings, *1:* 181
U.S. marshals, *1:* 35, 35 (ill.); *2:* 248, 250, 255, 287, 290
U.S. Supreme Court, *1:* 26
USA Patriot Act, *1:* 51, 187–88; *2:* 253

V

Valley State Prison for Women, *2:* 305 (ill.)
Verona, Roxana, *1:* 59
Victim Assistance Legal Organization, *2:* 241

Victim Rights Clarification Act, *2:* 238
Victim and Witness Protection Act, *2:* 238–40
Victimless crimes. *See* Public order crimes
Victims
    assistance programs, *2:* 233–34
    bill of rights, *2:* 236–38
    Black Americans, *2:* 423–24
    colonial period, *2:* 231–32
    compensation programs, *2:* 234–35
    English common law, *1:* 9
    Federal victims' rights legislation, *2:* 238
    mediation, *2:* 237
    murder, *1:* 64
    protection, *2:* 238–40
    rape, *1:* 72–73
    right to sue, *2:* 232–33
    rights of, *2:* 235–38
    robbery, *1:* 67
    role, *2:* 242–43
    statistics, *2:* 229
    studies of, *2:* 241–43
    victim advocates, *2:* 240–41
    white-collar crime, *1:* 94
Victims of Child Abuse Act, *2:* 238
Victims of Child Abuse Laws, *2:* 369
Victims of Crime Act (VOCA), *2:* 235, 236
Victims of Trafficking and Violence Protection Act, *2:* 366
Victims' Rights and Restitution Act, *2:* 238
Vietnam War, *1:* 174–75; *2:* 329
Vigilantes, *1:* 34–35; *2:* 249
Violence
    black American communities, *2:* 424
    drop in rates of, *1:* 57
    fear of, *1:* 55
    media, *2:* 388
    minority communities, *2:* 432
    motorcycle gangs, *1:* 122
    Native Americans, *2:* 336–37
    police and, *2:* 256
    rates of, *1:* 53, 61
    women victims, *2:* 232
Violence Against Women Act, *1:* 73; *2:* 232, 297